# teach yourself

## screenwriting
ray frensham

teach yourself
70
1938
2008
celebrate with us

Launched in 1938, the **teach yourself** series grew rapidly in response to the world's wartime needs. Loved and trusted by over 50 million readers, the series has continued to respond to society's changing interests and passions and now, 70 years on, includes over 500 titles, from Arabic and Beekeeping to Yoga and Zulu. What would you like to learn?

be where you want to be with **teach yourself**

For UK order enquiries: please contact Bookpoint Ltd, 130 Milton Park, Abingdon, Oxon OX14 4SB. Telephone: +44 (0) 1235 827720. Fax: +44 (0) 1235 400454. Lines are open 09.00–17.00, Monday to Saturday, with a 24-hour message answering service. Details about our titles and how to order are available at www.teachyourself.co.uk

For USA order enquiries: please contact McGraw-Hill Customer Services, PO Box 545, Blacklick, OH 43004-0545, USA. Telephone: 1-800-722-4726. Fax: 1-614-755-5645.

For Canada order enquiries: please contact McGraw-Hill Ryerson Ltd, 300 Water St, Whitby, Ontario, L1N 9B6, Canada. Telephone: 905 430 5000. Fax: 905 430 5020.

Long renowned as the authoritative source for self-guided learning – with more than 50 million copies sold worldwide – the **teach yourself** series includes over 500 titles in the fields of languages, crafts, hobbies, business, computing and education.

*British Library Cataloguing in Publication Data*: a catalogue record for this title is available from the British Library.

*Library of Congress Catalog Card Number:* on file.

First published in UK 1996 by Hodder Education, part of Hachette Livre UK, 338 Euston Road, London, NW1 3BH.

First published in US 1996 by The McGraw-Hill Companies, Inc.

This edition published 2008.

The **teach yourself** name is a registered trade mark of Hodder Headline.

Copyright © 1996, 2003, 2008 Ray Frensham

*In UK:* All rights reserved. Apart from any permitted use under UK copyright law, no part of this publication may be reproduced or transmitted in any form or by any means, electronic or mechanical, including photocopy, recording, or any information, storage and retrieval system, without permission in writing from the publisher or under licence from the Copyright Licensing Agency Limited. Further details of such licences (for reprographic reproduction) may be obtained from the Copyright Licensing Agency Limited, of Saffron House, 6–10 Kirby Street, London EC1N 8TS.

*In US:* All rights reserved. Except as permitted under the United States Copyright Act of 1976, no part of this publication may be reproduced or distributed in any form or by any means, or stored in a database or retrieval system, without the prior written permission of the publisher.

Typeset by Transet Limited, Coventry, England.
Printed in Great Britain for Hodder Education, an Hachette Livre UK Company, 338 Euston Road, London NW1 3BH, by CPI Cox & Wyman, Reading, Berkshire RG1 8EX.

The publisher has used its best endeavours to ensure that the URLs for external websites referred to in this book are correct and active at the time of going to press. However, the publisher and the author have no responsibility for the websites and can make no guarantee that a site will remain live or that the content will remain relevant, decent or appropriate.

Hachette Livre UK's policy is to use papers that are natural, renewable and recyclable products and made from wood grown in sustainable forests. The logging and manufacturing processes are expected to conform to the environmental regulations of the country of origin.

Impression number    10 9 8 7 6 5 4 3 2 1
Year                          2012 2011 2010 2009 2008

# contents

| | | |
|---|---|---:|
| **acknowledgements** | | **viii** |
| **foreword by Andrew Davies** | | **x** |
| **01** | **introduction** | **1** |
| | why read this book? | 2 |
| | original vs. adapted | 4 |
| | screenwriting: a collaborative process | 5 |
| | defining the screenplay | 6 |
| | the 'snapshot' nature of screen drama | 7 |
| | film and television: similarities and differences | 8 |
| | starting out | 10 |
| | your writing day: self-discipline and time management | 12 |
| | the role of the Script Reader | 14 |
| **02** | **screenplay layout: your visual language** | **17** |
| | pages | 19 |
| | scene headings | 22 |
| | scene direction | 23 |
| | camera angles | 25 |
| | montages | 26 |
| | paragraphing | 27 |
| | entrances and exits | 27 |
| | character cues | 27 |
| | actor direction | 28 |
| | dialogue | 28 |
| | sound | 30 |
| **03** | **originating your ideas** | **32** |
| | pre-writing | 33 |
| | your goal as a screenwriter | 35 |
| | B.P.F. – the burning passion factor | 35 |
| | thinking creatively | 37 |

generating ideas 38
how do I generate these ideas? 38
filtering and testing your ideas 40
**04 developing your ideas: from idea to
framework 42**
some definitions 43
getting it clear 43
how do I choose my main story? 44
'writing backwards' 45
there are only eight basic stories 45
genre 48
whose story is it? 54
the three-Act linear structure: an introduction 54
the one-liner 55
taglines 56
theme 58
title 60
background and setting 61
subplots 64
some final considerations 68
**05 creating your characters 71**
choosing a name 73
creating three-dimensional characters 74
character functions/categories 76
the protagonist 76
character biography –analysis/checklist 77
backstory 80
secondary characters 81
minor characters 81
cast design 83
another perspective on cast design 85
the counter-character chart 88
character flaws 89
audience identification 90
**06 character goals, growth, motivation and
conflict 94**
character growth – the transformational arc 95
character motivation 98
conflict and character 101
types of conflict 102
principles of conflict 102
obstacles 103

developing conflict 105
final comments 106
**07 structure 109**
the classic three-Act linear structure 110
what goes into each act? 113
some observations 141
**08 structural variations 144**
the Hero's Journey approach to three-Act
structure 145
multi-plotting 152
plot variations 155
the two-Act structure 156
four- and five-act structure 157
portmanteau films 157
**09 'deep structure' 158**
the sequence 159
the scene 164
creating a scene 167
dialogue 173
subtext 179
**10 enhancing emotion 182**
character motivation and structure 183
the motivational through-line 184
momentum: building tension 186
subtext 191
raising the stakes 191
pacing 192
'upping the ante' 195
information in the screenplay 196
revealing and concealing information 197
plants and pay-offs 198
image systems 200
the rule of three 201
**11 the next step 202**
the one-page synopsis 203
the step outline 204
the treatment 206
**12 the actual writing 209**
the exploratory draft 210
**13 the craft of the rewrite 212**
first rewrite: understandability 216
second rewrite: structure 218

third rewrite: characters 223
fourth rewrite: dialogue 225
fifth rewrite: style 226
sixth rewrite: polishing 229

**14** **the 'finished' item** **231**
getting feedback 232
titles 232
presentation 233

**15** **assembling your portfolio** **237**
taglines 240
the one-page synopsis (proposal) 240
the treatment as a selling document 243

**16** **copyright** **244**
a brief and painless guide to knowing
your rights 245

**17** **agents** **250**
what they do, how to get–and keep–one 251

**18** **adaptations, shorts, soaps, series,**
**sitcoms and collaboration** **255**
adapting for the screen 256
writing short films 257
soaps, series and sitcoms 259

**19** **the industry: how it works and your**
**place in it** **264**
breaking in 265
the industry: your place in it 266
targeting the market 267
producers and how to survive them 268
taking a meeting 269
the pitch and pitching 270
in development 272

**20** **your career as a writer** **274**
know yourself – market yourself 275
reputation 276
rejection – and how to deal with it 277
writing courses and seminars 278

**21** **final comments** **280**
what do Readers and producers look for in
a script? 281
ten things you must do if you want
to be a screenwriter 283

ten guaranteed ways to fail as a
scriptwriter 284
and finally … 284
**22 screenwriting and the Internet 286**
how do I manage all this 'data'? – RSS 287
search engines 288
reference databases 289
homepages 294
screenplays online 296
auctions 298
blogs and blogging 299
groups, communities, forums, newsgroups,
e-zines and newsletters 300
social networking sites 302
podcasts 306
script competitions 306
networking, openings and opportunities 307
reviews, interviews, articles 308
miscellaneous 308
software packages 309
writing collaboration software 310
DVDs and CD-ROMs 310
**taking it further 312**
further reading 312
industry organizations 317
answers 322
**index 325**

**acknowledgements**

Copyright Permission and Rights Acknowledgements to: Richard Curtis for the script extract from *Four Weddings And A Funeral*; Rob Grant and Doug Naylor for the extract from *Red Dwarf VI*; Jurgen Wolff for the flowcharts on pages 109 and 170; Tristram Miall/M&A Film Corporation Pty. Ltd. for the *Strictly Ballroom* synopsis; *The Stage* and *Writer's Monthly* for permissions to quote from my past articles. Special thanks to Andrew Davies for the Foreword.

There are many others to thank. To various former members of London's Screenwriters' Workshop who, in some measure, contributed: Mike Belbin, Colin Clements, Barbara Cox, Paul Gallagher, Lawrence Gray, Melanie Heard-White, Peter Hogan, Roddy MacLennan, Margaret Ousby and Allan Sutherland.

Industry figures who assisted: Mike Bolland, Roger Bolton, Dick Clouser, Chris Cowie, Richard Curtis, Russell T. Davies, Charles Elton, Barbara Emile, Malcolm Gerrie (WhizzKid Entertainment), Alex Graham (Wall to Wall), Michael Hauge, Anton Hume and Graham Clayworth (BDO Stoy Hayward), Lew Hunter, Paul Jackson, Duncan Kenworthy, Lynda La Plante, Barry Smith (Reed Smith), William G. Stewart, Angus Towler, Paul de Vos, and those interviewees whose quotes got cut.

To the following for their support and encouragement during this updated rewrite:

– in the UK: Sid McLean, Rinaldo Quacquarini (The Screenwriters Store), Olga Ruocco and Nicol Wistreich

(Netribution); and all those friends whose social circles I had to withdraw from during the writing of this book – no doubt their lives improved immeasurably as a consequence... and to my tailor.

– in the USA: Tadd Kelby Casner, Arthur Lizie (Bay State College, Mass.), Christopher C Brown (New Orleans), Zak Shaikh in Hollywoodland and Timothy J. Steiner; and to my Editor at McGraw-Hill, Garret Lemoi, for support above and beyond the call of professional duty.

Special mention in dispatches: Miguel-Ángel Martínez-Cabeza at the University of Granada, Spain; and all at LBC 97.3FM – thanks for the continuing gigs; and to James Cho in Seoul (for fine support with the South Korean edition).

Finally, this book is dedicated to Me – because I deserve it.

Ray Frensham:

tyscreenwriting@yahoo.com
http://profiles.yahoo.com/tyscreenwriting
myspace.com/tyscreenwriting
bebo.com/tyscreenwriting
flixster.com/user/tyscreenwriting
twitter.com/tyscreenwriting
tyscreenwriting.ubik.net
virb.com/tyscreenwriting
Facebook: http://groups.to/TeachYourselfScreenwriting
http://tyscreenwriting.blip.tv
http://www.tyscreenwriting.blogspot.com
http://www.rayfrenshamworld.blogspot.com

**foreword**

When I started writing, there were virtually no how-to books, and no creative writing courses, let alone screenwriting courses. Now there are scores of books, and hundreds of courses, some of which I have taught myself. I have even attended one of them, Robert McKee's Story Structure course, and very useful I found it: 'Never take the ending out of the hands of the protagonist – push your hero to the limit' – all that stuff we all know really, deep down, but can't be reminded of too often. But by that time I was already established and successful as a writer.

So how did I learn to write? By doing it, of course: writing every day. There's no other way, no matter how many books you read. And if that sounds too much like hard work, at the start of your career, give up now. You have to love it and <u>need</u> to do it right from the start, because it's not going to get any easier. What I did do as well as writing, was to read every script I could get my hands on, searching for ideas and techniques that I could steal and adapt for my own work. Not just film screenplays (there were very few available then) but Shakespeare and Chekhov plays (always steal from the best). You don't need to worry about plagiarizing: your own vision of the world will shine through, if you have one.

But I could have saved myself some time if books like this one had been around when I started writing – it is so useful to have the generally accepted industry wisdom laid out for you in such an accessible, clear, entertaining, and above all, INEXPENSIVE format. This is the book that I recommend to screenwriting students. Ray Frensham has read and digested all the industry gurus – go on and read them all for yourselves, if you like, but really I think you'd do better to read more scripts and see more movies. (And here his list of websites in Chapter 22 is invaluable – worth the price of the book in itself.)

A how-to book can't make you a great writer. But this one will help. Good luck.

Andrew Davies
January 2003

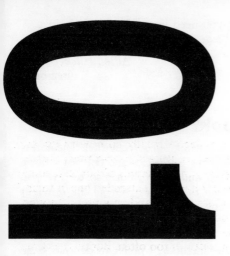

# 01

# introduction

**In this chapter you will learn:**
- what makes writing for the screen unique from other writing forms
- the different types of screenplays that exist
- how to get some discipline into your writing day
- about the gatekeeper you have to impress to get your talents and script through to the right people – the Script Reader.

To make a great movie, you need just three things: a great script, a great script, and a great script.

*Alfred Hitchcock,*
director

## Why read this book?

This book is written for the starting-out screenwriter. The aim is not just to guide you through the intricacies and craft of writing for the screen (film, television and video), but also to give you guidance on how to approach the industry. Of all the different forms of writing, screenwriting is where creativity interfaces with business the most and you need to feel comfortable and confident when dealing with both. The media like to create a mystique about themselves and their working methods; I prefer to demystify the process.

You may already have a story you want to tell but don't know how to structure it into a screenplay. Or you may only have the enthusiasm to write, but no idea what to say. However, before you write scene one, there is still a tremendous amount of work to be done.

This book covers the techniques and specialist skills used in writing for the visual medium. It covers the practical questions I and many members of The Screenwriters' Workshop have been asked over and over again through the years: how do you get your ideas? what questions should I ask about my script or characters? how do I get an agent? how can I protect my copyright? and many more.

Many books on screenwriting approach the subject by laying down rigid rules that *must* be followed, particularly in regard to screenplay structure. This one is different. Here, when any guidelines are set out, I am not declaring 'this is the way it must be done'. What I *am* saying is two-fold:

- As a starting-out writer submitting your work to a producer, director or commissioning editor (i.e. those with the power to make decisions), your script will not be read by them. It will go to one of their Readers for assessment. It is their job, at the lower end of the production hierarchy, to sort through the 'slush pile' of unsolicited manuscripts (those not submitted

by an agent). These professional readers are the people you
and your script have to get past and impress. And any 'rules'
this book outlines are the sort of points Readers have been
taught and trained to look for in script submissions. And . . .

- You, the writer, need to know the rules of the game before
  you can begin to bend and stretch them to your own design.

Writing a script is so much like writing a sonnet: you have
very specific boundaries in which to shape a story.

*Caroline Thompson,*
screenwriter: *Edward Scissorhands,*
*The Night Before Christmas, The Secret Garden*

Basically, 90 per cent of all scripts submitted are rubbish (for
reasons you will discover in this book) and rejected outright.
Approximately 10 per cent are worth reading to the end. Of those,
perhaps 2 per cent are worth following up and calling the writer
in for 'a chat', and only 1 per cent are worth further serious
consideration. (In Hollywood they claim it's one script in every
100–130, but it's nearer one in 200, and rising.) Your script needs
to get into that top 2 per cent. This book will help you get there.

It is a distillation of accumulated knowledge and *experience*
gained in the Workshop since it began in 1983, and from my
own experiences in the industry as writer, Script Reader, teacher,
Script Doctor, film finance broker and producer, and as chairman
of the SW. Most of what I teach is based on good films or
television I've seen and bad scripts I've read. You will find it
regularly illustrated with comments and experiences from writers
who have made it or are now breaking through into the world of
film and television.

There has never been a greater time for the industry. Audiences
for film and broadcast entertainment are growing, demanding
more, new and different experiences. The development of digital
technology has meant a potentially limitless expansion of
television, cable and satellite channels with the consequent air-
time that needs to be filled. There's also the Internet and the
computer games industry now. The opportunities are there to be
grasped.

Finally, this book also supplies checklists (many gained from
industry sources) and regular exercises you can use to analyse and

assess your own efforts – 'interactive' in the truest sense of the word. What it is *not* is a substitute for your actually writing something – that's up to you.

Never cross the road without a good script.

*Stephen Frears,*
director: *High Fidelity, The Grifters,*
*Dangerous Liaisons, Dirty Pretty Things,*
*My Beautiful Laundrette*

# Original vs. adapted

There are two types of screenplay: original and adapted.

An original screenplay is one written specifically for the screen and not based on any previously produced or published work (e.g. *The Sopranos, Amélie, Monsters, Inc., The Sixth Sense, Ocean's Eleven, Pleasantville, CSI, Mad Men, Anchorman, The Wire, Waking Ned, American Pie, Notting Hill, The Usual Suspects, L.A. Confidential, La Haine, American Beauty, Toy Story, Memento, Shakespeare In Love, Gosford Park*).

An adapted screenplay is one based on source material. For example:

– a book: e.g. *Angela's Ashes, The Lord Of The Rings, Babe, The Bourne Ultimatum, The Da Vinci Code, Revolutionary Road, The Talented Mr. Ripley, Cold Mountain, Harry Potter…, The Sum Of All Fears, Interview With The Vampire, Frankenstein, Schindler's List, About A Boy, Minority Report, Field Of Dreams, Get Shorty, The Notebook, Shrek, Red Dragon, Jurassic Park, The Firm, The Last of the Mohicans.*

– a play: e.g. *Plenty, Richard III, East Is East, Romeo and Juliet, La Cage Aux Folles,*; or a musical (*Chicago, Dreamgirls*).

– other media: e.g. *Spider-Man, Superman, Batman, X-Men, Fantastic Four* (comix); *Tales Of The City, Bridget Jones's Diary, Sex And The City* (newspaper columns); *Mars Attacks!* (bubblegum cards); *Road To Perdition, The Dark Knight, 300* (graphic novels); *The Avengers, The Beverly Hillbillies, The Addams Family, Mission: Impossible, Scooby-Doo, Charlie's Angels* (TV series), *Tomb Raider, Resident Evil* (computer games), etc.

Stories based on historical events or on biographies (e.g. *Saving Private Ryan, Erin Brockovich, Ali, A Beautiful Mind, The Dish, Black Hawk Down, Titanic, Flags Of Our Fathers, The Cat's*

*Meow, Wilde, The Birdman Of Alcatraz, Pearl Harbor, The Queen, World Trade Center, Hollywoodland*) are a grey area but tend to be classed as original.

Over 60 per cent of all produced screenplays are adapted, but nearly all first-produced scripts are original. Why? Because screen adaptation is a specialized skill (see Chapter 18) and because prior to starting a serious adaptation you need to obtain/buy the rights to the source material.

The rules of good screenwriting, however, apply to both forms.

Now list five other examples of each type of screenplay. Take a look at the films listed in your local paper. From what you know of them, work out what you think the screenplay credit will be for each film. Then check with the credit block on the film's poster. Were you right? You might find some posters carry only a simple 'screenplay by . . .' with no reference to whether it is original or adapted. Why do you think that is?

## Screenwriting: a collaborative process

The first thing you should realize is that *screenwriting is a collaborative process* – often painfully so, and it's simply a part of the beast you're going to have to deal with. You may be the sole author of your script, but from the moment you put that final full stop in place and send it to someone, the writer becomes part of a team. If you want total control over every word and image, write a novel or stageplay – the only way you'll achieve it in this game is to direct and produce your own work.

If your script is 'optioned' by a producer – where they buy the rights to exploit that property for a set period of time – it will go into 'development'. Here the producer will discuss the script with you and probably give you 'notes' asking you to rewrite or change certain parts to their suggestions (if amicably agreed) or demands (if not). Once a script goes into pre-production it is subject to input from the director, actors, set designers, special effects people and technicians. The script will be shaped further during actual shooting (making screen drama is the art of the possible, and budget is the bottom line) and the whole thing can change again in post-production when it is edited.

Why do you think that filmmakers do not settle for a writer's original vision? Does collaboration breed creativity or is it a case of too many cooks spoiling the broth?

If the thought of making changes simply to appease others either bewilders, upsets or angers you, congratulations: you've just taken your first step to becoming a screenwriter!

It is the writer's screenplay, but the director's film – get used to it.

*William Goldman,*
screenwriter/author: *Butch Cassidy And The*
*Sundance Kid, All The President's Men,*
*Misery, Maverick,* etc.

Writer/director Wolf Rilla called the script a blueprint, and that's exactly what it is: a diagram of possibilities, used by the production cast and crew to realize the drama. It is created many months, sometimes years before the production appears on the screen. So at the start of your journey it is important to understand some of the technical parameters and visual possibilities in the screen media.

# Defining the screenplay

They say film is the major art form of the twentieth century. Certainly other forms cannot reproduce the camera's controlled ability to enlarge and focus on what an audience sees, making it seem more real than real. This enlargement and focused intensity generates a level of *emotional realism* and *emotional identification* which is incomparable: it is to have this experience that audiences flock to watch the screen.

However, this experience takes place *in the mind of the audience* – and that is the area you must inhabit. The territory of the screenwriter is the *emotional experience of the audience*.

But to say that a screenplay is an emotional experience is not enough. A screenplay *structures* that emotional experience, giving it *direction* and *meaning* and a final climatic moment of catharsis.

The modern mainstream film screenplay may be defined thus: the story of a *character* who is *emotionally engaging* and who, at the beginning of the screenplay, is confronted with a *problem* which creates an *inescapable need* to reach a *specific goal*. The attempt to do so *inevitably* generates *almost overwhelming obstacles* which are finally overcome by the *transformation and growth* of that character.

# The 'snapshot' nature of screen drama

Every story ever told is a collection of fragments. We don't recount every scene or detail that happened along the way, we select what we choose to tell (and leave out) and structure it into a good tale – even when we tell a joke.

Screen storytelling – and the screenplay – is the most fragmentary form of storytelling there is (after comic books). A film's story may take place over several days (or, as in *Driving Miss Daisy*, several decades) but you only have two hours of screen time to tell it in. So you select those fragments which create something that maintains the illusion of being a coherent and cohesive whole story.

If a novel or stage play – with its capacity to digress, address the audience directly, examine psychological insights, etc. – may be equated to making a home video, then screen drama can be seen as a series of snapshot photographs (i.e. scenes) brought together to create a larger overall picture. It is your job to choose the right snapshots – and learn what to *omit* – and assemble them in the order that is the most dramatically effective, drawing out the maximum emotional impact.

How do you decide what to omit? You leave out anything that the audience can *deduce* for itself. If a woman in an office says she is hungry and is going out to get a sandwich, what are the possible scenes? Let's consider the obvious ones:

1 Office. Pam says she's hungry and is going to get a sandwich.
2 Office, near door. Pam puts on her coat and exits.
3 Stairs. Pam descends the stairs and reaches the street door. She exits.
4 Street. Pam emerges from the door and crosses the street to the sandwich bar.
5 Sandwich bar. Pam enters from the street and queues at the counter.
6 Queue. Pam moves slowly in the queue and finally reaches the counter.
7 Counter. Pam orders a sandwich, waits as it is being made, and is given it in a bag.
8 Shop. Pam takes the bag to a nearby table and sits down.
9 Table. Pam opens the bag, takes out the sandwich and lifts it to her mouth.
10 Mouth. Pam takes a huge bite out of the sandwich. Now she's happy.

Now *you* decide which are the most meaningful steps in the above story. Choose the smallest necessary ones to tell this story coherently (answers: Taking it further). Leave out the steps you think the audience can deduce. To leave steps in, ask yourself: is this meaningful to the story? does this move the story forward? would it damage the sense of the story if it were left out?

# Film and television: similarities and differences

Although both film and television deal in the same visual language and devices, there are a number of purely technical differences that should be initially appreciated.

| Film | Television |
|---|---|
| Mainly shot on location with interior scenes shot either in a studio or on location. | Shot exclusively in a studio. Nearly all scenes are interiors (with occasional filmed exterior inserts). |
| A one-camera shoot, with the same scene filmed a number of times: firstly a master shot (a general all-encompassing shot), then separate takes for each of the main characters speaking, followed by any specific close-ups required. | Usually a three-camera shoot (a general shot including all the main characters and the set, plus one camera each for the main speakers). |
| Script format (see page 21) fills the entire page. Dialogue central, description runs across the page. | Script format (see page 22) uses the right-hand half of the page only. The left-hand is blank, i.e. everything on the right side of the page happens in front of the camera, the left side of the page is what happens behind the camera (this space will be filled in later with camera directions – the technical shooting script). |

| | |
|---|---|
| Dialogue and (especially) visuals share the task of conveying the story and action. | Dialogue tends to carry the story and action. |
| Can carry numerous characters (possibly from ten upwards) but we focus on one of two specific people. | Can carry only a few characters (between five and seven). In series and soaps characters appear consistently. |

Also, remember the size of the screen – it matters. Film is much larger, demands a more visual kind of storytelling, and writers' and directors' ambitions are bigger. Television, although still a visual medium, is more intimate, and because it is more dialogue-driven, there is more reliance on 'talking heads' cutting and showing each character as they speak their lines. Moreover, if writing for a commercial TV channel, be aware there will be advertisement breaks and structure it into your script, building into each segment a climax or cliff-hanger that will hook your audience into returning after the break.

It is generally agreed that American films are more visual than their British and European counterparts, which are considered more literary (probably due to the tradition of that country) and more dialogue based. However, things are changing. But when an audience wants a truly moving, exciting, escapist or emotional experience, they still turn to the movies first.

Generally, the industry still considers film the highest attainment – it is 'art'; television is all that popular stuff that gets shoved into people's homes (and if you write for the theatre or novels, you are considered a 'proper writer'). But the fact remains that with cinema, people have to make a conscious decision to see it, to travel and pay money to experience it. And being in a cinema is what they call a 'total experience' – even if that experience includes rustling sweet papers and the chattering voices behind you on their cellphones.

> Unlike film, theatre is done on nothing and everybody is so nice. When the money comes in, so do the talentless pricks.
> *Jez Butterworth*,
> writer/director: *Mojo, Birthday Girl*

An old actors' maxim that might well be applied to writers is: they do theatre for the love of it, do television for the exposure and films for the money. Certainly money is in inverse proportion to the artistic fulfilment involved, but it also increases the more collaborative the process. And screenwriting is a *collaborative* craft.

I am proud to say that twenty-three people contributed to the script for *A Fish Called Wanda*.

*John Cleese*

## Starting out

It is so easy for writers to spend all their time thinking or talking about writing rather than actually doing it. When you sit down and face that blank piece of paper there are thousands of reasons for not doing it (making the tea, reading the newspaper, watching TV). Of course you should ruminate on your ideas and script, but it's easy to do this at the expense of actually getting something written down. It's a good excuse, but it's still an excuse. So:

> WRITE – Or Be Written Off

Think of it this way: writing is like a muscle that you need to keep exercising every day, even if it's for only thirty minutes.

However raw the script, the voice should be apparent and still excite. Speak in your own voice and your originality will shine through. The craft can always develop later.

*Tony Marchant,*
screenwriter: *Holding On, Goodbye Cruel World, Swallow, Crime And Punishment*

Don't expect a fully formed script to be delivered from the very start, or expect your own style to emerge directly onto the page at first effort. It really is a case of: write and write and keep on writing until you have written all the rubbish out of your system. It takes a while for you to discover your own voice. Often you will find other people telling you what your style is, which is why professional writers always recommend joining a writers' group for informed, constructive feedback. Remember:

> Writers Train By Writing

It is also very easy for the writer to keep exerting energies on the same scene or sequence, writing and rewriting over and over again attempting to get it just right. In reality all you do is plough the same furrow, digging deeper and deeper while never actually reaching the end of your story.

So give yourself permission to write rubbish: don't set out to write it, but don't get hung up on it either. Get it written down first, then move on to the next scene until you reach the end. The time to revise is *after* you've got something on paper. In Art Arthurs' famous words:

---

### Don't Get It Right – Get It Written

---

Writing a screenplay is a process of moving step by step towards your vision of how it should be. Accept those steps. Don't try to rush them. Relax and enjoy the process. And whatever you do, don't even attempt a rewrite until you have finished your first exploratory draft.

---

### Think Visual

---

The screen is primarily a visual medium, so learn to think like a camera. The standard maxim states: '**Show – Don't Tell**'. Remember this always. But never forget that *the territory of the screenwriter is the page*; it is your job to translate those images into words and the job of your script to *create the movie in the mind of the reader* – hook them, engage them, tell a great story that keeps them turning those pages until the end. Start to change the nature of your thinking processes: think visually and you will start to write visually.

> The one thing Corolco did say when they bought *Basic Instinct* off me was: it was superbly crafted and they paid that amount of money because the script conjured the movie from the page.
>
> *Joe Eszterhas,*
> screenwriter: *Jagged Edge, Music Box, Flashdance*

---

### Look And Learn

---

Finally, immersing yourself in the medium is *essential*. Screenwriters are mostly self-taught by way of reading published scripts, analysing videos and attending the occasional course. Indeed, much of it needs to be self-taught: a process of trial and error. So watch as much of it as possible. Read all the scripts you can lay your hands on. However, make sure they are original script drafts and not ones specially 'adapted' for book publication, as some are – see Chapter 22 for many useful websites and Taking it further for retail suppliers. But look and read with a critical eye. Use the points covered in this book to analyse the productions. Why does one film work and another fall flat? Look for the Acts, character development, plots and subplots, scenes and sequences, dialogue and subtext, etc. What made you keep turning one script's pages while another was a plodding read? Did the script *create the movie in your mind*? How did it achieve this? Was the style of writing particularly lively, gripping or funny? Did that translate to the screen version? What effect did it have on you – the audience? Learn from others, both those who have succeeded and those who have produced turkeys.

---

IMPORTANT NOTE: The Audience

Throughout this book, whenever the term *audience* is used, it means TWO things:

(i) the people watching the screen

and (ii) the person reading your script for the first time.

Bear this in mind at all times – not just when reading this book, but every time you sit down to write your script.

---

## Your writing day: self-discipline and time management

You need commitment to write a good screenplay. To succeed you must be willing to discipline yourself and put in the work.

*Joe Eszterhas,*
screenwriter:
*Basic Instinct, Jagged Edge*

I just treat it as a job, like any other job, except it's better paid. I get to work by 10 and, apart from lunch, work through till about 6 or 7, then I knock off.

*Paul Attanasio,*
screenwriter: *Quiz Show, Disclosure,*
*Donnie Brasco, The Sum Of All Fears,*
*Homicide: Life On The Streets*

The first step is possibly your toughest: learn self-discipline. Remember that this muscle needs daily exercise: the more you do it, the stronger it becomes. If you have limited time, set yourself a daily minimum word target (like Kingsely Amis' 500 words a day). Don't worry so much about the quality, the idea is to get into the habit. The secret is to know yourself, how and at which times of the day you function best, and under what ideal circumstances. We are all different. You need to discover that best time within yourself, and exploit that period to the fullest – *regularly*. Make an appointment with yourself – and keep it.

I try to give myself deadlines and write in my calendar 'First draft due one month from now'; I plan that out and try to meet those deadlines. I need a deadline because it is so easy to do something else.

*Tom Schulman,*
screenwriter:
*Dead Poets Society,*
*Honey, I Shrunk the Kids*

It's all down to self discipline and learning how to manage your time. There is no 'wrong' way of going about creativity. Just because nobody else has done it your way before or you know of no-one working in this way, does not make it wrong or any less valid. Your rule should be: Whatever You Feel Works Best For You – Do It.

You've got a screenplay, 120 pages, there's a lot of white spaces, and it's full of double-spacing. There's no reason why you can't write three pages a day; it's not like writing three pages a day of a novel. Not many words, not many words.

*William Goldman*

Some interesting websites worth exploring (the first two are from Jurgen Wolff, a name you will hear more of):

tameyourinnercritic.com and timetowrite.com
write-brain.com
and a book: Kenneth Atchity, *Writing: Making the Most of your Time* (Thomas & Lochar).

# The role of the Script Reader

As already mentioned, the Script Reader is the industry's first line of defence against the writer. They work alone, unseen, are poorly paid and they wield a huge amount of power over the new writer. Few writers have a good word to say about them, but Readers are considered a necessary evil by the industry. Production executives simply don't have the time to read through the vast numbers of screenplays submitted to them. Many are so badly written or poorly conceived they need to be sifted out before anything with the slightest potential is found. Script Readers are the screening process that filters out most of the rubbish. Once a screenplay has been read, the Reader will present a one or two page review (called 'coverage') to the producer or head of development. This assessment will give a brief plot summary followed by the reader's personal comments and conclude with two recommendations: one for the script and one for the writer. This recommendation will usually take the form of one word: Pass, Consider or Recommend. A sample blank Reader's report sheet is shown opposite.

It is possible that the recommendation for the writer will be different to that for the script. You may have a great hook and an interesting story (Recommend) but it may be badly written (Pass).

If a Reader does not recommend a script by an unknown writer, it will be rejected automatically. If they do recommend the script it will be passed onto the people who count. So your first task is to get past the Reader with a positive recommendation – for both you and your script.

Before reading a script, the Reader will first pick it up and feel the weight – does it *feel* like the right length? Then they will look at the last page number – shorter scripts are read first, the longer ones left till last. For feature films, a script of 90–100 pages will put a smile on the Reader's face; even up to 110 pages is acceptable. The *maximum* acceptable is *120 pages*. I know it sounds silly – ideally a script is as long as a script is – but there are good reasons, and it is important to keep the Reader on the writer's side. If a Reader is put off by a heavy script, they will approach it with a negative attitude.

Next, the Reader will run their thumb over the page edges and fan the script briefly, gauging the ratio of black print to white paper on the page (they want to see lots of white): is it written to the right layout and does it look like a proper screenplay? Layout and presentation are important (Chapter 02).

## SCRIPTS/FORMAT NOTES

| | |
|---|---|
| TITLE: | |
| AUTHOR: | |
| AGENT: | TEL: |
| READER: | DATE: |

OUTLINE:

COMMENT:

RATING:   1   2   3   4   5   6   7   8   9   10

**figure 1.1** sample coverage (Reader's Report) sheet

Then they will read the first ten (nowadays possibly just five) pages, skip to read the last five pages, followed by reading a couple of randomly chosen scenes from the middle of the script. If they are satisfied and impressed, they will then read the complete screenplay from page one to the end.

You get them to do this by making your script interesting, engaging and easy to read. It has to work on screen, in the mind of the Reader and on the page too. So many scripts, although they may be structurally perfect and may make great movies, are incredibly boring on paper. Your job is to *seduce the Reader*.

Getting past the Reader is just your first step, but as with all first steps, it could be the one that trips you up. This book will help you get through that barrier. The journey starts here.

> Why did Miramax pick up *The English Patient*? Because it was the best script I'd read all year.
>
> > *Harvey Weinstein,*
> > M.D., Miramax Films

> The script (*The Full Monty*) was so good that we gave it the green light within a few weeks of receiving it.
>
> > *Jim Wilson,*
> > Director of Production,
> > *Fox Searchlight,* L.A.

Some handy websites for you to visit:

dannystack.blogspot.com/2005/10/script-reader-uk.html

groups.yahoo.com/group/ScriptReader

moviemaker.com/directing/article/script_readers_getting_past_hollywoods_gatekeepers_3172 [Article: exactly what is says]

quickstopentertainment.com/news/jan03/156.html [Article: Day Two in the Life of a Hollywood Script Reader]

StudioReaderStan.com

# 02

## screenplay layout: your visual language

In this chapter you will learn:
- how to put your screenplay in the right format
- how to present your work, and yourself, to the industry.

Get hold of a professionally formatted script and note everything; from simple instructions like INT. and EXT. to the exact length, and *never stray from that format*. You might submit a masterpiece but if it's not properly laid out, the reader may give up after scene one.

*Lynda La Plante,*
writer: *Prime Suspect, Widows,*
*Trial And Retribution, Framed,* etc.

Before starting the creative journey it is important to establish some basic details about how scripts are laid out on the page and the technical language used.

The first thing to understand is:

---

**Correct Presentation And Layout (Format)**

**Are The First Essential Steps**

**To Selling Your Screenplay**

---

So play by the format rules – some are flexible, many are not. Their purpose is *clarity* and *communication*, to make your script an easy read for the Reader. Don't fight them – use them.

All scripts submitted must be typed, on white A4 sized paper and on one side of each sheet. Any which are not are always returned unread. If sending to the USA, remember they prefer 8½″ x 11″ paper. They should also be typed using 12 point Courier font. Why?

- it's an easy read
- it helps the Reader time a script. Film format: 1 page of script = 1 minute of screen time. TV format: (generally) 1 page = 30–40 seconds of screen time
- it allows other readers in the production process to understand quickly the content of the scripts and the intent of the writer.

Many novice screenwriters put enormous energy into perfecting their story, structure, characters and dialogue, yet forget the packaging. In this business, both content and packaging are critical. Producers and agents feel: a writer professional enough to get the packaging right is also professional enough to script a strong story. Hence, it is essential you get hold of some properly formatted scripts (both film and TV) – Chapters 22 and Taking it further. Reading them will soon show you what you can and can't change. Your aim is a *professional* and *readable* script.

# Pages

Covers and title pages will be covered in Chapter 14. Page one is your first page of text. Pages are numbered in the top right-hand corner or the centre bottom of the page. Also on page one:

- **Feature film format:**
  You do not place the title at the top of the page. The first information to appear is FADE IN: in the top left-hand corner (FADE OUT. appears in the bottom right-hand corner of the last page, at the end of your script).

- **Television format:**
  UK (taped/studio) scripts have their own specialized layout (see Figure 2.3, page 22). Commercial TV scripts have a break (for the ads) and are labelled Part One and Part Two, etc.

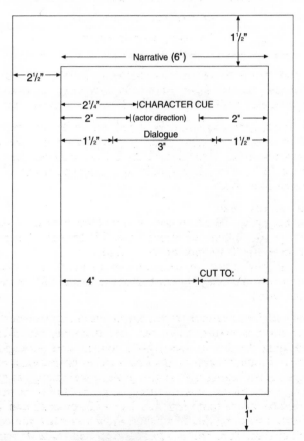

**figure 2.1** film screenplay format dimensions

INT. BEDROOM. MATTHEW & GARETH'S HOUSE  -  NIGHT

GARETH and MATTHEW, asleep, cuddled.

INT. CARRIE'S FLAT. BEDROOM  -  NIGHT

CHARLES and CARRIE are in bed.

> CARRIE
> I kind of knew this would happen.
> The moment I said 'yes' to Hamish,
> I had an awful suspicion there'd be
> one final fling.

INT. FIONA'S BEDROOM. TOM & FIONA'S HOUSE  -  NIGHT

FIONA, awake, in bed reading.

INT. TOM'S BEDROOM. TOM & FIONA'S HOUSE  -  NIGHT

TOM, asleep, flat on his back, pyjamas buttoned to his chin.

INT. KITCHEN. CHARLES AND SCARLETT'S HOUSE  -  NIGHT

SCARLETT, drunk and asleep under the kitchen table.

INT. CARRIE'S FLAT. BEDROOM  -  DAWN

> CARRIE
> I think it's time you went.

> CHARLES
> But it's 5 in the morning.

> CARRIE
> And at nine in the morning my
> sister-in-law comes round. We're
> discussing bridesmaids.

> CHARLES
> You're right. I've got very little
> to contribute on that one.

Silently CHARLES dresses.

> CHARLES (cont)
> Would  you  like  to  go  out
> sometime....

> CARRIE
> (not lifting her head
> from the pillow)
> No thanks.

> CHARLES
> Why?

**figure 2.2** sample film script layout
source: *Four Weddings And A Funeral* © Richard Curtis

| 40. EXT. (OB) | STREET OF LAREDO      DAY |
|---|---|

THE APOCALYPSE BOYS WALK SLOWLY
THROUGH THE SWIRLING MIST AND STOP.
**KRYTEN** STEPS OUT TO FACE THEM.
LISTER, RIMMER AND CAT FILE OUT
AFTER HIM, AND THEY FAN OUT ACROSS
THE STREET.

DEATH
Got yourself a little help, Sheriff?

KRYTEN
Now I remember. You're a computer virus. You
travel from machine to machine, overwriting the
core program.

DEATH
Have infection will travel, that's me. Let's see if
we can't tip the balance a little, here.

DEATH HOLDS UP HIS ARMS. A BOLT OF
BLUE ELECTRIC SHOOTS UP INTO THE SKY.
MIX TO:

| 41. INT. | OPS. ROOM |
|---|---|

A BLUE SPARK SHOOTS OUT OF **KRYTEN'S**
HEAD AND TRAVELS UP THE WIRE
CONNECTING HIM TO THE A/R CONSOLE.
THE CONSOLE FIZZLES LIKE THE
NAVICOMP DID BEFORE, AND WE SEE THE
MONITOR SCREEN.
"SPECIAL SKILLS" AND FLASHING BESIDE
IT: "ERASE".

| 42. EXT. (OB) | STREET OF LAREDO      DAY |
|---|---|

AS BEFORE.

CAT
What's he doing?

RIMMER
He's stalling. He spotted us for what we are: a
bunch of mean, macho, bad-ass desperados who are
about to kick his boney butt clean across the Pecos.
(THROWS TOOTHPICK TO THE GROUND)
Enjoy the show.

- 35 -

**figure 2.3** sample television script layout
source: *Red Dwarf VI* (Episode 3: Gunmen Of The Apocalypse)
© Rob Grant & Doug Naylor

All TV shot on film, TV films and mini-series use film format. All American teleplays (including sitcoms) use film format and are written in Acts (two acts for half-hour, four Acts for one-hour) and this is typed at the top of the page above FADE IN: Each Act begins on a new page. Note that with filmed or taped series the series name is also included. Each Act begins with FADE IN: and ends with FADE OUT.

Note: the most notable thing about the first page of most film scripts is they contain little, if any, dialogue: you are trying to set the scene and atmosphere, establish your main character, intrigue us, draw the audience in, and get the Reader to read the full screenplay, not just the dialogue (they easily do!) Think Visual.

## Scene headings

Scene headings, or slug lines, provide the basic where-and-when information for the scene that follows. Each new scene has its own slug line and they are always written in capitals. The information is set out in a very specific order, e.g.

INT. CHURCH. REGISTRY ROOM – NIGHT
EXT. MANOR HOUSE – DAY

**Where**

(a) Stated first is whether the scene takes place:

INT. (interior – e.g. in a room)
EXT. (exterior – e.g. in the street)

(b) then the general location is given, (c) followed by the specific location, e.g.

INT. CASTLE. BED CHAMBER – DAY

You may often find (b) and (c) reversed, e.g.

INT. BEDROOM. CHARLES'S HOUSE – NIGHT
EXT. SCARLETT'S CAR. MOTORWAY – DAY

This is fine, as is:

EXT. STREET. DOWNTOWN NEW YORK – DAY

The object is clarity for the Reader. You decide, but if in doubt, stick to (b) then (c).

Note: If your scene takes place inside a car or train compartment, this is still an INT. scene, even though the car or train is outdoors, e.g.

INT. CAR – EVENING
INT. MOVING CAR. LONDON STREET – DAY

You may also find INT./EXT. – this is where the camera's P.O.V. (point of view) is placed inside filming or watching an event outside (e.g. a scene happening out in the street being seen by someone inside a car), as in:

INT./EXT. CHARLES'S CAR/STREET – DAY

or EXT./INT. where the scene is happening inside (e.g. a house) being shot from outside (e.g. the garden), as in:

EXT./INT. GARDEN/HOUSE – EVENING

**When**

Usually, DAY or NIGHT is sufficient. You may find DAWN, MORNING, AFTERNOON, LATE AFTERNOON, DUSK, LATER, SAME TIME, or A FEW MOMENTS LATER, if there is sufficient reason for using these. You may sometimes need to use FOLLOWING or CONTINUOUS if the scene or (particularly) conversation continues unhindered from the previous scene but shifts location. Generally, sticking to the simple DAY or NIGHT is easiest.

The rule is: a new scene occurs whenever there is a change of either *location* or *time*.

NOTE:

- Scenes are never numbered in writers' scripts in film format. They only get numbered in later production drafts. However, UK TV scripts generally do have numbered scenes (check the series format first). American TV is as per film format.
- Scene headings are generally not underlined, though this is sometimes practised in UK television formats.
- Always double-space between the heading and the text and between scenes.

# Scene direction

Also called 'the business' and 'the blackstuff', this is the text which contains all the descriptions (i.e. non-dialogue) of the characters' actions and natural events relevant to the story.

Mostly written in lower case, clear, concise and uncluttered, not justified, it should be written in the *present tense*, e.g.

> Mr. Blonde closes the door after them. He then slowly turns his head towards the cop.

Characters names are always in lower case except for the first time they enter your script, when they are in upper case or capitals. If the weather is important to your scene, write it here in the business at the start, and in capitals.

All camera directions (if you must use them) are done in upper case throughout, although be careful and very sparing with these technical directions. Remember, you are not directing this film – and Readers can soon tell if you secretly harbour these ambitions by their overuse. Some scene directions, however, you will find commonly in scripts:

| | |
|---|---|
| v.o. | (voice-over) |
| o.s. | (off screen) |
| M.O.S. | (without sound) |
| P.O.V. | (point of view) |
| f.g. | (foreground) |
| m.g. | (mid-ground) |
| b.g. | (background) |

The last three are self-explanatory. Voice-over refers to dialogue that runs over the top of the scene, as in *Blade Runner*, *Goodfellas*, *Malcolm In The Middle*, *George Of The Jungle*, *Memento*, and the opening of *Field Of Dreams*, *Maverick*, *Road To Perdition*, *Election*, *Spider-Man* and *Out Of Africa*, etc. It is (usually) narrated by the main character and tells part of the story. It is never heard by the other characters and may reveal the thoughts of the character speaking. It should be minimized. If used, it is placed where the dialogue goes and written out in full. For example:

> KAREN (v.o.)
> I had a farm in Africa.

o.s. refers to dialogue actually heard by the other characters (and the audience) but spoken by a character who cannot presently be seen on screen.

M.O.S. is used when you have people talking on camera but the audience does not hear the dialogue. For example:

In the b.g. Charles and David talk together M.O.S. They both use sign language. Charles is very deft and comfortable with it.

Try to minimize your use of M.O.S.

P.O.V. (i.e. the camera is seeing things through one particular character's eyes) is used a little more often.

## Camera angles

Leave them out! A sure sign of an amateur is an abundance of camera angles (pans, dollies, zooms, close ups, etc.) in a script. Many scripts available to buy are shooting scripts, which will include these directions. But writers, in their drafts, should not do so. Some directions you may occasionally come across are:

| | |
|---|---|
| LS | (LONG SHOT) |
| MS | (MEDIUM SHOT) |
| CS | (CLOSE SHOT) |
| C/U | (CLOSE UP e.g. of the face) |
| Tight C/U | (e.g. on the eyes alone) |
| Two-shot | MS of two characters |
| Three-shot | MS of three characters... etc. |

But it should *not* be necessary to use any of these terms in your own script; they only clutter. If you really have to use them, be very sparing. If it is absolutely essential to your screenplay, there are ways of getting round them. Instead of 'LS of a mountain chalet' try 'In the distance...' or 'Smoke rises from the chimney of a distant chalet...'.

Use of 'We see' or 'We hear' are valid ways of describing what the audience should focus on, for example:

We see two pairs of hands fumbling for the key in the door lock.

We hear a CRACK of thunder, then a scream.

but they should be used infrequently, as substitutes almost always exist. When in doubt, leave them out.

Remember, your script should focus on the storyline and characters, not the specifics of production. Create the movie in the mind of the reader and leave the job of directing to the director.

# Montages

This is where you are creating a series of shots to build up a collective picture or feel (they tend not to include your main characters and there is usually no dialogue in a montage). They can be written in a number of ways. For example:

MONTAGE:

A – The volcano ERUPTS ash and fire into the sky.

B – People run wildly through the streets. PANIC.

C – Looting of stores. People running with armfuls
      of clothing and food.

D – Military police trying to restore order.

E – Planes flying overhead.

Note the double spacing between the lines. Remember, one script page = one screen minute. If a fight lasts for three minutes on the screen, call the shots so that, on the page, it will run for three pages. Rather than write this:

INT. BAR – DAY

Jake storms into the saloon. He grabs a bottle and
breaks it on the bar rail. He advances across the floor.
It is a stand-off with Clint.

write it like this:

INT. BAR – DAY

Jake storms into the saloon.

He grabs a bottle and breaks it on the bar rail.

He advances across the floor.

It is a stand-off with Clint.

This way, not only are you using up your minute but you are highlighting the important action. It is also an easier form to read. Lastly, never write something like 'A montage to bring tears to your eyes'. Call up the images, create the picture and atmosphere – think visual.

Try to obtain a copy of the scripts for *Raging Bull* and *Fight Club* – see how they depicted the conflicts on the page.

# Paragraphing

Long unbroken paragraphs of 'business' are ugly to look at and difficult to read (a Script Reader scans the page downwards). So try to break up your paragraphs into units of action or ideas. My advice is never have a paragraph longer than four or five lines. Numerous one, two and three-line paragraphs are acceptable and probably to your advantage. Breaks in sentences within paragraphs are done with dots (...) or two dashes (- -). If breaking from one page to the next always try to end your sentence before going on to the next page.

# Entrances and exits

How do you move from one scene to another? The convention is you will CUT TO: (written in the bottom right hand corner at the end of your scene). However, even when it is not written, the Reader knows there is no other way to do it. So best not clutter up the text with CUT TO: each time. You will save space and probably add another three or four pages to your script.

Other terms you will find are:

FADE IN          (always at the start of a script)
FADE OUT         (at the very end)
DISSOLVE TO:
FADE TO BLACK
FREEZE FRAME

Remember, if you FADE OUT or FADE TO BLACK on one scene, you must always FADE IN on the next. But unless you can absolutely justify them, stick to CUT TO: or better still, leave them out.

# Character cues

The name of the character speaking that piece of dialogue, in capitals, is situated approximately 1½″ in from the edge of the dialogue; it is never centred (see pages 20–21). Normally all your characters will have names, but characters whose functions in the story are minimal and/or brief may simply be given roles, e.g. FARMHAND, SECRETARY and so on.

# Actor direction

This is where you, the writer, issue direct instructions to the actor on how to deliver the dialogue you've written. Best advice is: don't, *unless* the tone of delivery is in direct contrast to the meaning of the words:

> JOHN
> (sarcastically)
> This is gonna be a great party.

They are always in brackets, in a line to themselves and set half-way between the CHARACTER CUE and the Dialogue. Generally, don't intrude on the actor's (and director's) territory.

Actor direction is, however, useful if your character is specifically speaking to someone and there are several people within earshot, for example:

> JOHN
> (to Sandra)
> Where's my shirt?

or like this:

> The phone rings.
> JAN
> Griffin Mill's office... one
> moment.
> (to Griffin)
> Bonnie Sherow.
> Griffin nods, he'll take it.

You do *not* put action descriptions here:

(Incorrect)
> JOHN
> (hitting Sandra)
> Where's my shirt?

(Correct)
> JOHN
> Where's my shirt?
> He hits Sandra.

# Dialogue

After the business comes the dialogue. It runs immediately below the name of the character speaking, and fits into a column approximately 3″ wide down the centre of the page (see pages 20–21).

All dialogue is single-spaced and there are no large blank spaces in between words unless they are filled with something, either (beat) or (double beat), meaning pause and longer pause. This can be written either of two ways:

(i)

> THE ANGEL
> (not even breathing hard)
> I'll let you fall down for free

He looks down at the stunned quartet.

> Maverick was mine anyway…
> (beat)
> …' cept now it's personal.

(ii)

> THE ANGEL
> (not even breathing hard)
> I'll let you fall down for free

He looks down at the stunned quartet.

> Maverick was mine anyway…
> (beat)…' cept now it's personal.

Do not use hyphenation to break words from one line to the next (although those that are naturally hyphenated may be broken onto the next line):

(*Incorrect*):

> JOHN
> I never said that. No, I dis-
> tinctly remember.

Likewise, do not use hyphenation to break dialogue from one page to the next. End the dialogue sentence at the bottom of the page and begin the next sentence at the top of the next page.

When a character's dialogue has been interrupted by description (not by another character's dialogue) then it is shown thus:

> JOHN
> I didn't mean to do this.
> I hope you can understand.

He takes a knife and approaches Sandra. She writhes and sweats, the rope pulling tighter at her wrists.

> JOHN (Cont'd)
> You see, I really am so sorry
> about all this mess.

If only one line of description (business) intervenes, you don't have to repeat the character cue unless clarity is threatened.

## Sound

Any sounds that are crucial to your script (and are not made or caused directly by the actor) must be included in the Business in capitals, for example:

A police car siren SHRIEKS through the dark streets.

Norma turns as a floorboard CREAKS in the old tower.

Jake HEARS the noise of running water from upstairs.

Sandra's fist CRASHES through the window.

The SOUND OF ethereal music GROWS (or FADES)

A KNOCK splits the silence.

You may also find the term OVER used, which means the same as v.o. (VOICE OVER) but for sounds. So here's how it all comes together:

INT./EXT. WAREHOUSE – DAY

We follow Mr. Blonde as he walks out of the warehouse . . .

. . . to his car. He opens the trunk, pulls out a large can of gasoline.

He walks back inside the warehouse . . .

INT. WAREHOUSE – DAY

. . . carrying the can of gas.

Mr. Blonde POURS the gasoline all over the cop, who's BEGGING him not to do this.

Mr. Blonde just sings along with
Stealer's Wheel (OVER)

Mr. Blonde LIGHTS up a match and, while mouthing:

MR. BLONDE
'Clowns to the left of me
Jokers to the right. Here I am,
Stuck in the middle with you.'

He MOVES the match up to the cop

. . . when a bullet EXPLODES in Mr. Blonde's chest.

Note that specifying exact music in scripts is not normal. Tarantino can do it. A danger is that new screenwriters tend to capitalize every little sound so that every other word of their narrative is in capitals. Again: think. Use sparingly; when in doubt, leave it out. Lastly, *never – ever – write anything in italics*.

> If a script is not correctly formatted, even with the best will in the world, I'm reading it very negatively from the start because I'm thinking: this person is unprofessional, they haven't even bothered to take the time to find out how it should be laid out. It doesn't have to be glossy, just easily readable.
>
> *Paul Marcus,*
> Producer: *Prime Suspect 2, White Boyz, Kwik Stop*

A useful book on format:

Cole & Haag, *The Complete Guide to Standard Script Formats* (Vol. 1 – Film; Vol. 2 – television)

...And some (free) screenplay formatting software to download (See also Chapter 22 and Taking it further):

http://www.films.com.br/introi.htm [Article, formatting your script]

scriptologist.com/Magazine/Formatting.formatting.html [Article, as above]

generalcoffee.com/genie.html [Free download Script Genie]

indelibleink.com/swright.html [Free trial download of Screen Wright software]

oscars.org/nicholl/format.html [Download format samples, courtesy of the American Film Academy]

screen-lab.co.uk [Click on Script Format; Free MS Word script template download]

apotheosispictures.com [ScreenForge formatting – requires $45 registration fee]

everybodyswrite.com/shop.php [To buy: Screenwriters Initial Draft Pad templates to use if hand writing your script]

# 03 originating your ideas

In this chapter you will learn:

- how to generate ideas
- how to recognize the strongest ones and filter them down to the ones 'with legs'
- how to add that special voice that is unique to you.

'You can't wait for the muse to find you, you have to call it out.'

*Ethan Hawke,*
Actor and author

When I started writing full-time all I had to talk to was my word processor. I had to learn how to bounce ideas off myself.

*Andrew Davies,*
writer and adaptor: *A Very Peculiar Practise,*
*Pride and Prejudice, Bridget Jones's Diary*, etc.

# Pre-writing

Why are there so few good scripts around today? It's to do with how much work you put into it before you sit down and write it. It's a very disciplined hard job, but it pays off.

*Adrian Dunbar,*
co-writer: *Hear My Song*

Any novice writer will naturally put immense efforts into the actual writing, pouring it out in one massive creative burst and then feel it's perfect as it is. But this approach ignores any aspects of craft. In truth, the actual writing (called the *exploratory draft*) is only about 5 per cent of the process. All the preparation leading up to that – developing ideas, creating characters, structure, scenes and sequences – is called the *pre-writing*, and is covered in the next nine chapters.

Generally, the process of screenplay creation breaks down like this:

Pre-writing =  65%
Actual writing = 5%
(exploratory draft)
Re-writing =   30%

The more you work on the pre-writing, the easier your exploratory draft should become.

Writing a screenplay is a succession of breakdowns: moving from the general to the specific. Now study the flowchart on page 35. It gives an overview of the entire process from idea to delivery. Don't worry if some terms mean little at present. The chart is there to refer back to as you progress through this book.

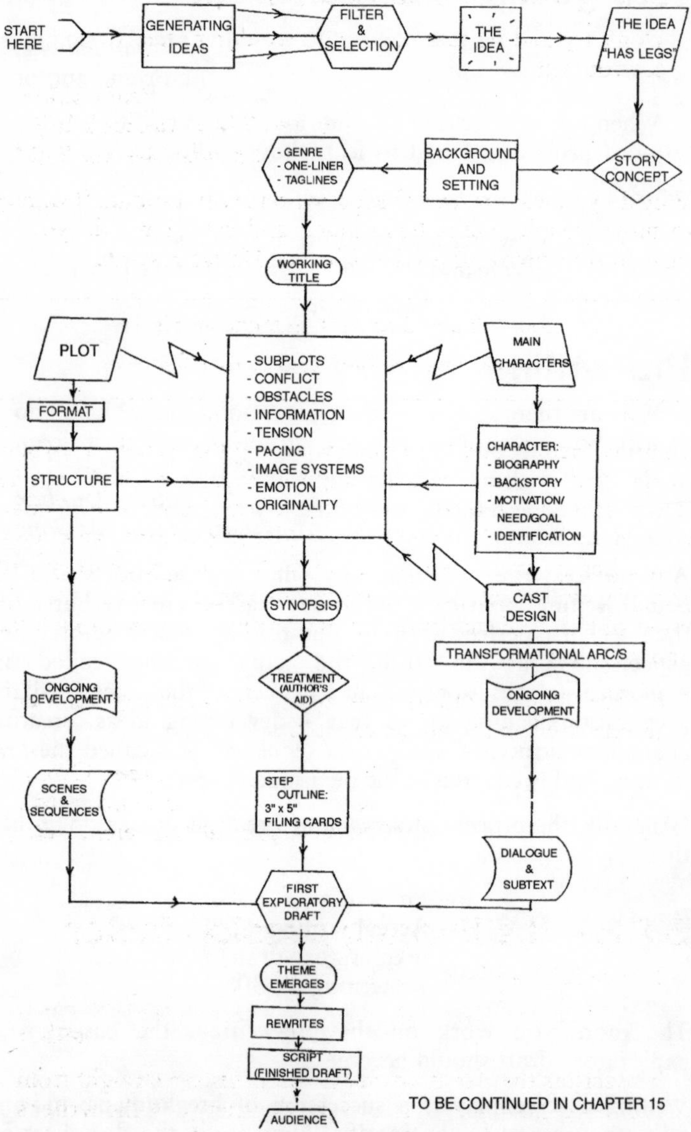


**figure 3.1** flowchart: the screenwriting process

# Your goal as a screenwriter

Don't try and write a movie you wouldn't want to go and see yourself.

*Paula Milne,*
writer: *The Politician's Wife,*
*Die Kinder, Second Sight*

Why do you want to write? Most writers will respond: 'I wanted to move people, make them laugh and cry'. How do you do this? In screenwriting teacher Michael Hauge's words:

> Your Primary Goal As A Screenwriter Is To
> Elicit An Emotional Response In Your Audience

To hook them in and keep them watching that screen or turning to the next page to see what happens next, *seduce the reader.* Every scene described, every line of dialogue, every image created must work towards your aim. Remember this at all times. Engage your audience successfully, tell a great story well, and you will elicit that emotional response. Try to enter the mind of the audience and understand the way emotions affect and work on us.

I once thought drama was when the actors cried. But drama is when the audience cries.

*Frank Capra,*
writer/director:
*It's A Wonderful Life,* etc. ... etc.

# B.P.F. – the burning passion factor

I write because I Hate. A lot. Hard.

*William Gass,*
author

The scripts that really work are those written straight from the heart, passionate pieces with the energy of the writer's voice, even though the structure may not be perfect – that can be fixed later.

*Paul de Vos,*
screenwriter/producer

Ultimately, writers need to write what they're passionate about, not what seems to be currently commercial.

> *David Friendly,*
> producer: *Courage Under Fire, Dr. Dolittle,*
> *My Girl, The Chamber*

Whenever producers or script editors are asked 'what do you look for in a script?' one word crops up every time: *passion*. Passion in the writing, your ideas and their expression. Of course they look for an original core idea, engaging characters and a sense that the writer has a knowledge of structure; it is taken as read that the manuscript will be professionally presented and laid out to the relevant format. But even if plot, characters or structure might be a little shaky, if there is a certain intensity to the writing – the voice that comes across – they may at least be gripped by that (and possibly call you in for a chat).

This is where the writer's voice comes into play. It is the difference between being asked 'what is your script about?' and 'What is your script *really* about?', those deep-down ideas and thoughts you want to put across to an audience (see Chapter 04 – Theme). Do you have them?

> What's the point of writing a beautifully structured script, with all the right technical points in it, if the writer has nothing to say?
>
> *Lynda La Plante*

So, whether you are writing your masterpiece of arthouse cinema or an episode of a soap opera, write about things *important to you*. Dig deep inside yourself, access your own experiences through life, take one aspect or incident that has been important to your own development. But don't just take this one aspect and write it down exactly as it happened for you. Take that specific idea and develop it, fictionalize and add to it, to make some universal truth that will mean something to others – your audience.

> If you're not passionate about it, why is anybody else going to be? Besides, you won't enjoy the process anyway.
>
> *Paul Marcus*

# Thinking creatively

Writers think in a number of different ways:

(i)   Inductively     – from the specific to the universal
(ii)  Deductively    – from the universal to the specific
(iii) Logically       – i.e. causality: how things happen in the world, one thing following another
(iv)  Non-Logically – i.e. coincidence: by definition meaningless, but life itself contains coincidences
(v)   Creatively      – discovering hidden links or relationships between two unrelated things (ideas/people) no-one has seen before

Thinking creatively leads to you discovering unexpected twists in a plot or character. For example: you have a man and woman violently wrestling on the floor, one has a knife. If one stabs the other, this is predictable; if the nature of the fight changes and they start to make passionate love, suddenly you have spun them off in a new direction and played with audience expectations.

As a writer, always look for the unpredictable, the unexpected twists in everything you write – it will keep the audience on their toes and eager to know what comes next. That same eagerness that makes the viewer glued to their seat until the end is the same emotion that makes your reader turn to the next page. William Goldman said you should have a surprise on every page. Do you agree? – or would these lead to a surfeit of surprises and immune your audience into submission?

One thing, however, is certain: ideas won't come by just waiting for inspiration:

> The art of writing is the art of applying the seat of the pants to the seat of the chair.
>
> *Art Arthur,*
> writer

---

Now watch any (preferably all) of these films: *The Sting, Maverick, House Of Games, The Grifters, The Others, Fight Club, The Usual Suspects*. Note down the moments in the story where you are caught by an unexpected plot twist. Repeat the process with other films, preferably those you have not seen before.

# Generating ideas

Today's writers are a weakened generation because they
grew up watching movies, so now they're just recycling
them. Be original. Real cinema is about the imagination.

*Michael Leeson,*
screenwriter: *The War Of The Roses*

At this stage of pre-writing you will be using two different types
of thinking: firstly, *inductive* – a divergent, opening-out, almost
stream-of-consciousness thinking strategy. Your aim? To come
up with as many and as diverse ideas as possible. It is non-
judgemental, because at this stage you are only interested in
quantity.

This is followed by *deductive* thinking, where you sift, filter and
test your ideas, selecting those you feel are strongest, have the
most 'legs' (to use an industry term).

Just sit there putting any thoughts you may have, however
stupid they may seem, onto your computer or the page;
you want to be as free as possible. Later, your inner critic
is your friend – that gut thing that's saying 'this is great',
'this is terrible' or 'this character isn't working'.

*Tom Schulman*

# How do I generate these ideas?

- Personal experience: you have lived a life – use it. (But please
  don't write your life story exactly as it happened.) Take a
  specific from your experience, extend it into something which
  might have meaning/resonances for others.

  I'd like to thank my parents for making me the way I
  am, and my analyst for making it marketable.

  *Ruby Wax*

- Others' personal experience: as above, but pick on something
  in the lives of your friends, family, people you've met; not the
  whole person, but elements of that person/their experience.
  Collect these aspects and make into a new composite.
- Some lines of dialogue/a character: always carry a notebook
  (and pen) for overheard conversations, characters that catch
  your eye; note their dress, speech, mannerisms, etc.
- Newspapers: keep a file of clippings/stories that stimulate you
  (a fertile source area – especially for contemporary TV
  drama).

- An advertising slogan/song title/newspaper headline: if it stimulates you, create a new story from that source.
- Visual stimuli: look at photographs or a painting. What moves/intrigues you about it? What story could this scene be telling? Take an interesting newspaper photo: create a new backstory (everything that happened up to the moment that shot was taken); what is each character's history? what happened after this photograph was taken?
- Brainstorming: pick a subject, list down a free-association of thoughts and feelings that come to you, unstructured odds and ends. A technique regularly used in advertising.
- Mind mapping: write a key idea or subject in the centre of a page. Write associated ideas in bubbles around, with a line linking each one to your core idea, then draw bubbles of associated ideas coming from those bubbles until you build up a spider's web of words and ideas.
- 'What-If' scenarios: ask yourself 'What would happen if this happened?' For example, if I woke up tomorrow and discovered I was blind/had developed ten-feet arms/turned into a cockroach/if the world were to end in 24 hours/if time stood still? . . . and so on (a good method for finding surprising twists). Most stories start this way.
- Dreams: keep a notepad beside your bed to record stories/images from your dreams (example: Mary Shelley's *Frankenstein*).
- Visualization: we all visualize in dreams, daydreams and our imagination. This is conscious creative visualization you can tap into at will and bring under control, accessing the unconscious via conscious relaxation techniques. Relax *completely* in absolute silence and mentally recall an imagined favourite location or a person in your past: draw on all your remembered senses – visual, auditory, taste, smell, movement, feelings. Use your mind as a film screen to project onto it whatever you are imagining.
- Adaptation: (novels/real-life stories, etc.) Fine as a writing exercise, but if you're serious, obtain the copyright owner's permission first.
- Intertextuality: another word for plagiarism. Steal from others – but don't make it obvious (*Reservoir Dogs* is *The Asphalt Jungle* meets *The Killing* (Kubrick, 1956) meets *City On Fire* (Ringo Lam, 1988 – Hong Kong), *Clueless* a reworking of Jane Austen's *Emma*, *10 Things I Hate about you* is a reworking of *The Taming Of The Shrew*, and *She's All That* is a modern-day *Pygmalion*). Indeed, movies like *Scream* and *I Know What You Did Last Summer* positively revel in ironically intertextualizing previous genre models.

These are just suggestions. You need an eclectic approach to ideas. At this stage, it's not the getting there that is important, but how you do it that's interesting. Keep an ideas file. Whenever one occurs to you, write it down, drop it in the file, forget about it. Writers need to generate a continual stream of scripts and proposals. (Most professionals work on more than one project at a time, all at different stages of development.)

I have a shoebox: for ideas, fragments, snatches of conversation I hear. I scrawl it down, throw the scraps in the box. Every time I start a new script I start picking through the pieces. Suddenly you get five pieces together and think: this is almost the first Act of a movie, if I flesh it out a bit.

*Shane Black,*
screenwriter: *Lethal Weapon,*
*The Long Kiss, Goodnight, AWOL*

It's fun being a sponge, soaking up these little bits of real life, mixing them all together and coming up with something new.

*Adrian Lyne,*
director and writer: *Fatal Attraction, 9¹/₂ Weeks,*
*Unfaithful, Indecent Proposal, Flashdance*

> Using any or all of the above devices, generate thirty different ideas or subjects. These may be just one word, but list them. Remember, make no critical judgements on them at this stage – you want quantity. Now put the list aside and read on.

## Filtering and testing your ideas

By now you may have realized that, for a writer, ideas for stories are everywhere and finding them isn't the problem. Figuring out the story that has the most 'legs' (potential) is more the problem. Even more difficult is trying to discover which story *you* care about, the one that generated in you the strongest gut-emotional response, and which story you feel you can tell well. How can you do this?

Apply the following to each of your story ideas:

(i) Answer all these questions about each idea: Who is it about?/What?/When?/Where?/Why?/How?

(ii) Has it got 'legs'?: Is it going somewhere? Is it dramatic? Can I dramatise it in a series of scenes with a minimum of explanation? Does it have a plot? Can I create one for it?

(iii) What is at stake? It should be something vital and specific – not just for the character/s involved, but for me as a writer.

(iv) Look for the unpredictable, the original, the uniqueness in your ideas and characters. Look for the surprises.

(v) Is it my story to tell, something I really care about? Can I draw upon my own emotions/experiences, then apply them to that idea? Is it something I only partly understand or does it need working out? Is it something I know I *should* care about (war/cancer/famine) but don't truly?

(vi) Is it too personal a story for others to become involved in or be affected by? Can the idea be worked in a caring, original and uncompromising way to make it meaningful to somebody else?

(vii) Now play Devil's Advocate: think of all the objections to that idea: weaknesses, reasons why you should not pursue it further, etc.

Tip: If your idea happens to be a TV script about people working in a TV show, or a movie script about people making a movie, my advice is: *drop it*. Producers hate industry in-jokes. Those that exist (e.g. *The Player, Swimming With Sharks, ivans xtc*, the TV comedy *Action, Bowfinger, Tropic Thunder, Live!, S1mOne, Get Shorty, Adaptation*) are made by established film-makers with track records.

---

- Now that you have your list of thirty ideas, run each one through the questions above and select those ideas which seem the most promising, have the most 'legs' (use your gut reaction/emotional response). Put the other ideas aside.
- Take two or three of these unrelated words/ideas from your chosen list and juxtapose them together. Now find or make links between them. Then write one sentence for each group of linked ideas.
- For those ideas you have selected, develop a story for each of them, with a beginning, middle and end. (Use only one or two sentences for each segment.) This may not work for all your ideas, so drop those that don't convince or work for you.
- For the ideas that remain, expand to a fuller outline, including your major scenes (a couple of sentences for each scene) and breaks for each segment: beginning, middle and end.

---

If, after all this, you still feel strongly enough about your idea, then perhaps it is strong enough to continue…

# 04

## developing your ideas: from idea to framework

**In this chapter you will learn:**
- to filter and focus your ideas and characters further
- to start working them into a manageable three-Act beginning–middle–end story ... with depth
- to create a working title for your project
- to examine the setting of your project
- how subplots work.

Movies are about story: is it well told, is it interesting? If it isn't it doesn't matter how talented the rest of it is.

*William Goldman*

## Some definitions

**Story** This is the series of events which form the screenplay *in chronological order*

**Plot** The most interesting and dramatically effective way of telling the story

And these are the ways the terms will be used throughout this book.

## Getting it clear

Having decided on your story idea, you should now start to move from the general to the specific, asking yourself all sorts of questions about it so you can analyse it and get the best from your story. Questions covered in this chapter are:

- Why do I want to write this screen story?
- Who do I think will want to watch it?
- What is it about?
- Who is it about?
- Why is it mainly about this character rather than any of the others?
- How important is the setting or background? Will the audience need any special information in order to understand the story?
- How do I want the audience to feel while they are watching it and after it's over?

You may find you have a background but need a plot. Often you will have one idea, but it is not enough until you have two ideas – one about character, one about situation – that you can make a story. You also need an end.

Now try to express your story in these terms:

**It is a story about ( CHARACTER ) who wants to ( DO SOMETHING ) and ends up ( SUCCEEDING/FAILING/ CHANGED ).**

This is your *story concept*.

And remember, being a visual medium, these 'somethings' are visible actions and desires that can be seen on the screen – they form the action of your story. Expressing your story concept will help you achieve clarity about your characters and the action of your story.

The success of the independent movie is because people like the story. The story is now the star.

> *Roger Simon,*
> screenwriter: *Bustin' Loose,*
> *Scenes From A Mall*

# How do I choose my main story?

**Your gut response**

What affects you the most emotionally?

**Look for the end**

How do you know you've got a good story? Many writers reply 'Not until I've got my ending.' Make sure you've got your end. The genre (page 49) of story you're telling might give you clues to what this might be. Remember your story concept.

Is the ending dramatic enough with a big enough final climax? Has it a climax at all? The story with the strongest ending/biggest climax will usually tell you it should be your main story.

**Ask yourself: what is original about my story?**

And keep asking yourself this throughout the writing and rewriting stages. Originality is not just one element, it is a mix of elements.

**Examine the dramatic structure**

Not just the overall three-Act structure (see Chapter 07), but the smaller three-Act dramas going on inside the overarching one (inside Acts/subplots etc.); which one is the most dramatic? The strongest one usually leaps out and tells you 'this is my main story'.

**Surprises**

What are they? Where are they? Always look for the unexpected, the twists in the story that will catch your audience off-guard asking 'what happens next?'

It's so hard to tell good stories. It's very tedious and often mind-bending work to come up with an interesting story with enough twists and turns to sustain a journey.

*Chris Carter,*
writer/creator: *The X-Files,*
*Millennium, Midnight Caller*

## 'Writing backwards'

Screenplays are written backwards. That is: the prime focus for both writer and audience is the final climax at the end of Act III. So, having decided on your end climax – where you need to get to – you work backwards to make sure that everything in the plot – other climaxes, set-backs, decisions made, etc. – works 100 per cent towards that scene and moment. However, don't get too disturbed if your end hasn't come to you yet – it will. Remember, the filmmakers didn't know the end to *Casablanca* even during filming.

> Now ask yourself this question: do I believe in this story? If you do, then carry on . . .

## There are only eight basic stories

How many stories do you think have been told on screen? Thousands? More? In fact, the answer is eight. They are listed below, together with examples. Can you list other examples?

1 **ACHILLES**
The fatal flaw that leads to the destruction of the previously flawless individual (*Samson and Delilah, Othello, Superman, Sin City, Zodiac,* TV's *Dexter, Fatal Attraction* and *film noir*). This is also the cornerstone of the crime drama – the flaw belonging not to the hero, but the villain (*Columbo, CSI – Crime Scene Investigation, Murder She Wrote, Inspector Morse*).

2 **CANDIDE**
The innocent abroad, naive optimism triumphant; the hero ('good man') who cannot be kept down (*Chariots Of Fire,*

*Forrest Gump, Indiana Jones* and *James Bond* films, *Mr. Bean, Billy Elliot, Erin Brockovich, Amélie, A Beautiful Mind, Wall.E,* Captain Jack Sparrow in *Pirates Of The Caribbean,* the *Jason Bourne* films).

### 3 CINDERELLA
The dream come true; unrecognized virtue recognized at last; goodness triumphant after being initially despised; rewards achieved through transformed circumstances (*Pretty Woman, Rocky, Strictly Ballroom, Star Wars, My Big Fat Greek Wedding, Shrek, Erin Brockovich, Kung-Fu Panda*).

### 4 CIRCE
The chase; the spider and the fly; the innocent and the victim; mostly the temptress ensnaring the love-struck male (*Godfather I, Othello, Double Indemnity, Body Heat, 9½ Weeks,* film noir, *Amélie, Insomnia, Dangerous Liaisons, The Last Seduction*).

### 5 FAUST
Selling your soul to the devil may bring rewards, but eventually there is a price to be paid; the long-term debt; the uncovered secret that catches up with us sooner or later and damns us; the inescapability of Fate (*Wall Street, Bedazzled, The Seventh Seal, The Skulls, Boiler Room, Devil's Advocate, Traffic, The Red Shoes, Kill Bill, Sin City, The Dresden Files,* horror and spaghetti western genres. Also present in some modern video games which, these days, have fully developed plots, e.g. *Grand Theft Auto IV*).

### 6 ORPHEUS
The gift taken away, the loss of something personal. Either about the tragedy of the loss itself or the search which follows the loss (*Dr. Zhivago, Rain Man, Signs, Jason And The Argonauts, The Fountain, Batman Begins, The Constant Gardener, Kill Bill*).

### 7 ROMEO AND JULIET
Boy meets girl, boy loses girl, boy finds/does not find girl – it doesn't matter which (*West Side Story, When Harry Met Sally, The Graduate, Sleepless In Seattle, Notting Hill, Titanic, Shakespeare In Love, Wall. E, The Constant Gardener, Kiss Kiss Bang Bang*).

### 8 TRISTAN
Triangles (eternal or otherwise); man loves woman and unfortunately, one or both are already spoken for (*Fatal Attraction, The Graduate, Jules et Jim, Pennies From Heaven, Remains Of The Day, Dangerous Liaisons*).

> Each of these stories has an original source. Research the original
> stories and myths and read them. What makes them so special that
> even today they are still used as blueprints for screen stories?

These eight basic stories can be presented in many different
forms – tragedy, comedy, history, whodunnit, soap opera, etc.
and can be mix'n'matched, even inverted, but they still form the
basis of all stories and plots.

And just because I've outlined eight core stories here doesn't
mean it is set in stone, some will say there are fewer.
Screenwriter Lorenzo Semple Jr. maintained there were only two
basic stories: Fish Out of Water and The Odd Couple. The
screenwriting tutor Michael Hauge observed you could even
reduce all these stories down to just one: David And Goliath –
the individual against impossible odds.

> The most popular story is Romeo and Juliet. Why do you think
> this is so? Now list five screen dramas which come under this
> heading. Then try listing five where Romeo and Juliet appear as a
> secondary story element.

> List as many films as you can which combine the following:
> Achilles + Cinderella, Faust + Orpheus, Circe + Tristan, Candice +
> Romeo and Juliet.

You will probably find your own story idea slotting into one
(hopefully more) of these categories. This is no bad thing:
audiences and commissioning executives want something new
and different but also something simultaneously familiar (called
the 'comfort zone'). The danger is in sticking exclusively to one
archetype (you risk obviousness and banality). Find new ways
of telling it: combine, reshuffle, adapt, expand on them.

> Now run your story idea past one or more of the above eight
> outlines. Can you  make it better by adding any elements from
> 1–8? Can you increase the conflict/set-backs/love/character mix,
> etc? The more elements you add, the more original you may find
> your story becoming – and the less like other things you've seen.

Remember, you are looking to get the maximum drama and emotional impact out of your script. Once you have decided on what plot area your story falls into and what appeals to you, your next step is to place it within a genre.

# Genre

In America, before they make a film, they always ask you: 'What shelf is the video going on?'

*Anthony Minghella,*
writer/director: *The English Patient,*
*The Talented Mr. Ripley, Cold Mountain*

Everything we write is in one genre or another, or is a combination of genres. Genre refers to the type of story: the tradition within which your tale is set as it relates to previously made films/dramas. Not simply tragic, comedic or historic, it is more focused than that. Here are some conventions:

## Romance

Two people fall in love, overcoming various obstacles, winning out in the end (*Romeo And Juliet, Titanic, War Of The Roses, The Mask, Wall.E*) In *When Harry Met Sally* the obstacles are themselves; they each believe friends can't be lovers. In *My Big Fat Greek Wedding* the obstacles are self-image and different cultures.

## Comedy

A funny story where nobody gets willfully hurt (*Airplane, Ruthless People, Throw Mama From The Train, Notting Hill, Shrek, School Of Rock, Wallace & Gromit*).

## Buddy movie

Two characters who are complete opposites (and thus repel each other) are compelled to stay to work together. The repulsion changes until by the end they are best buddies (*Lethal Weapon, Midnight Run, Training Day, Strictly Ballroom, Sideways, Kiss Kiss Bang Bang*).

## Film Noir

Dark and deadly. A man whose life experience has left him sanguine/bitter meets a woman to whom he's sexually and fatally attracted. Sometimes he comes to cheat, attempt to murder/actually murder a second man (*The Maltese Falcon, Double Indemnity, Fight Club, Basic Instinct, Body Heat, Devil In A Blue Dress, Seven, Sin City*).

Let's look at a few more of these genres and their conventions in a little more detail:

## Science-fiction

The sci-fi film is usually about calamity (often social calamity) and represents the dark, negative side of our dreams and aspirations. The characteristics are:

- the central character is often the innocent victim of the story's events
- they may not defeat the antagonist at the end of the film
- human relationships – the ability to feel emotion – often represents an antidote or counter-attack to the social situation
- the antagonist may not be human, it is often social or environmental; and the sheer power and size of this opposition often makes a statement about the nature of human existence: its smallness, its vulnerability, its destiny
- despite possible defeat, sci-fi movies generally provide a thematically optimistic and hopeful ending, and that is often derived from its counterbalancing human relationships
- the human characters in the story are usually ennobled by their attempt to win or their ability to survive
- they tend to be more plot-driven than character-oriented.

## Adventure

The adventure film (and action-adventure film) tends to appeal directly to the adolescent qualities in its audience (Indiana Jones, James Bond etc.). Its characteristics are:

- the central character is usually male, who must save the world, or a significant part of it; their success (or failure) in the story has dramatic implications for the world they live in
- the central character tends to be a grown-up child, often with an appealing sense of fun and/or naivety; humour and humility are two major elements of this character-type and genre
- the central character is often very competent with a variety of physical and/or intellectual tasks and with gadgets/tools they will need to save the world
- the adventure story is very plot-intensive with a great number of physical and mental challenges that the hero/ine must overcome

- the villain is supremely villainous, an antagonist of immense and formidable powers and is the ultimate challenge to the protagonist/hero (whose success will be the ultimate success)
- the story is very fast-paced, often leaving little time to dwell on relationships (which can be seen as superficial). Sex and violence are also treated in a fairly casual, less confrontational way that lessens their impact on the audience (this is deliberate!)
- ritual and mythology are more important than realism and complexity: i.e. actions may move away from the strictly realistic and may even teeter on the edge of melodramatic and/or farcical. Remember: modern technology, or aspects of it, may represent a 'modern mythology'
- characters in adventure movies tend to be stereotypes.

### Horror

Horror movies trace their origins in the nineteenth-century literature of the likes of Edgar Allen Poe, Mary Shelley and Bram Stoker. The stories tended to examine their characters' reactions to modern civilization, which they saw as a 'veneer' that could fall away at any moment to reveal the savage, the beast, the monster – the primordial 'thing' beneath. The touchstone of this genre is the human unconscious and subconscious. The characteristics are:

- the central character is rarely a hero/ine; they are nearly always a victim
- the villain may derive from a scientific mistake, a social or psychological nightmare or a religious or cosmic violation
- as in a nightmare, violence and sexuality have no limits
- the struggle may be seen by its participants as a struggle between God and the Devil. Religion may play the role of a weapon or protector, usually temporary
- children are often gifted in this genre, possessing powers not shared (or at least not understood) by the adults
- human relationships do not have that redeeming or saving quality (as in sci-fi); in fact, they may be part of the trap
- the location of the events is critical to these events (e.g. the house built on the graveyard in *Poltergeist*)
- the 'final explanation' will derive in part or fully from the supernatural or the irrational.

## Bollywood

Originating from India's film capital, Bombay/Mumbai, Bollywood films are a phenomenon that, for decades, has created its own industry which, only now, Hollywood and the rest of the world are beginning to take notice of and take seriously. Bollywood movies are all about extravagance and value for money: an audience getting its money's worth. Although more modern Indian movies are nudging towards Hollywood models, the core Bollywood conventions are:

- a big star lead/name actor (or two star leads)
- great songs (a hit song or two is essential): lots of catchy musical numbers married to spectacular dance set-pieces (about five or six per film), sometimes integral to the plot, often not; and glamorous costumes
- melodramatic plots: huge emotional arcs with mixtures of romance, tragedy, comedy, action-adventure, etc., and anything else you can throw in!
- the plots often employ formulaic ingredients: star-crossed lovers and angry parents; love triangles (handsome leading man/attractive but innocent female/dastardly heartless suitor or betrothed); family ties; sacrifice; the courtesan with the heart of gold; kidnappers; conniving villains; corrupt politicians; long-lost relatives and siblings separated by fate; dramatic reversals of fortune; convenient coincidences
- kissing is taboo (although the Bollywood genre is becoming more 'westernized' today with more modern liberal conventions)
- a happy ending (essential)
- a two-hour plus running time, even a three-hour movie (with intermission) is quite common. Value for money!

Other genres are: Western, Gangster, Melodrama, Suspense-Thriller, Mystery, Biography, Historical Romance, Melodrama, Musical, Road Movie, Martial Arts, Cult, Gross-out comedy, Generation X, Documentary. Can you think of more?

> Now list three films for each genre. Can you list their conventions in three sentences?

Now go to the website www.imdb.com/sections/Genres (genre browser with top ten lists of movies genre by genre) and see if yout list of genres and film examples matched up.

Next visit the website www.filmsite.org/genres and see if their genre conventions matched yours.

It is also possible to mix genres, for example: Coming-of-age/Action/Adventure (*Spider-Man*), Sci-fi/Noir (*Blade Runner*), Horror/Noir (*Angel Heart*), Sci-fi/Horror (*Event Horizon*), Teen/Horror (*Scream, I Know What You Did Last Summer, The Grudge, Cry Wolf*), Comedy/Western (*Blazing Saddles*), Romance/Comedy (*Four Weddings And A Funeral*), Romance/Comedy/Western (*Maverick*), Urban/Western (*Once Upon A Time In America, Gangs Of New York, The Fast And The Furious*), Crime/Noir/Comedy (*Dead Men Don't Wear Plaid*), Heist/ Comedy caper (*Ocean's Eleven, The Italian Job*), Bollywood/ Hollywood (*The Guru*), Action/Suspense/Thriller (*xXx, Speed*), Martial arts/Hollywood (*Crouching Tiger Hidden Dragon, The Matrix*), Sci-fi/Action/Comedy (*Men In Black, Mars Attacks!*), Crime/Noir/Comedy (*Kiss Kiss Bang Bang*), Sci-fi/Western (*Serenity*) and so on.

> Can you think of other mixed genres? Name three other films for each type listed here.

However, the only way to really understand this idea of genre is to watch lots of films or TV made in that particular style. Be aware of it next time you watch something, because genre 'defines' an audience's expectations.

And because genres set up these expectations in an audience, if you understand the genre you are writing in and work within those conventions, it not only helps you focus the boundaries of your story, you also stand a better chance of emotionally connecting with your audience.

If you think that writing within a genre limits your story choices, try to look at it like this: technically, it does limit your choices, but in a good way; because it keeps you focused. Your job is to be aware of genre while you are writing so that you may exploit the expectations created by genre in ways that surprise and engage your audience.

Also, please do not confuse Genre with Structure (see Chapter 07), as some novice writers seem to do. Genre determines the scope of your story, Structure is the storytelling technique: the ordering of the scenes that unfold the story action and reveal character.

If you are confused about genre in relation to the story you want to tell, examine the central action of your main character; it often indicates the genre within which you are working. For example:

- Does the main action of your story involve your main character defeating or destroying a monster? Then you are working within the Horror genre.
- Is your central character threatened or menaced by someone? Then it's probably a Thriller.
- Does the main action of your story involve some kind of technology or a machine menacing your hero/ine? You're probably writing a Techno-Thriller.
- Is your main character trying to catch a criminal or seek the truth about something? Your script would fall within the Crime genre or Detective story.

So, if you look at your idea in terms of genre it may help you decide what sort of plot, characters and themes (page 59) you are dealing with. It might give you an indication as to what your story ending might be like. Does it?

Try not to see genres as a limitation. Think creatively, beyond conventional imagination to arrive at original and unique solutions.

> When working on a project, I try and think 'what are the great films in that type and their great remembered moments', and try to aim for that. With *Misery* I always had *Psycho* in my head, with *Butch Cassidy* it was great Westerns like *Shane*.
>
> *William Goldman*

Some websites worth investigating:

breakingin.net/Genrestructure.htm [Genre and structure]
hollywoodlitsales.com/levy2.shtml [Teen genre movies]
suite101.com/article.cfm//military_movies/17948 [Writing War movies]

# Whose story is it?

If an event happens – e.g. a car crash, bank robbery, September 11th 2001 – each one of the witnesses and participants will have their own version of that event. Their own point of view (P.O.V.) is their story. So, decide on who's telling the story, whose eyes we are seeing these events through, and your main story and sub-stories (subplots – page 64) and their course will begin to clarify.

# The three-Act linear structure: an introduction

In Chapter 07 we'll be examining the screenplay's three-act structure in detail, but at this stage we should just establish the basics. People refer to this template as the Classic Hollywood Film structure, but its origins lie with Aristotle, and it actually forms the basis of nearly all good dramatic structure.

| Act I | The Set-Up | Establishes Main Character(s), Setting, Situation, a Conflict and Goal. Protagonist (or Hero) begins the journey to achieve that goal. |
|---|---|---|
| Act II | Development | Develops the main story; establishes and develops obstacles to that goal; develops the Protagonist and other characters; adds depth and meaning to the story concept. |
| Act III | Pay-Off and Denouement | Contains Climax and Resolution: the main climax occurs; the goal has been achieved/task completed; all the characters' relationships and subplots are resolved, and finally the audience are allowed to wind down, feeling satisfied at the end. |

In a film screenplay, these Act lengths generally work out thus:

with each Act ending in a climax and each one being greater than the one before, until we reach the major climax at the end of Act III. Familiarize yourself with it now. Can you begin to create your story in this way?

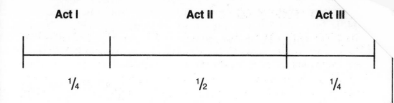

figure 4.1 divisions of a film screenplay

> Now try to express your story in one sentence using no more than 25 words. In this sentence, focus on the core idea of your story. Refer to the story concept, it may help.

## The one-liner

This one-liner will not only help you focus on your story, but can be used as a device in your *pitch* (Chapter 19) when you are selling the idea to someone. Put simply, this sentence should *make me want to watch this movie* and encapsulate that single solid concept which attracts an audience. For example:

> The story of a simple Iowa farmer who, against all odds, finds the courage to believe in his dreams. (*Field Of Dreams*)

> Three men search for a missing fortune in a big mansion while a woman hides in one of its rooms. (*Panic Room*)

> *The Odyssey* – in Space. (*Star Trek*)

> *Hamlet* in furs. (*The Lion King*)

> When a policeman helping an investigation in Alaska, accidentally kills his partner, he is blackmailed by the killer he is investigating. (*Insomnia*)

> A rock wannabe with an eye for the main shot forms his own band – with a group of schoolchildren. (*Rock School*)

> In the future, criminals are caught before they commit their crimes, but one of the officers in the Special Unit is accused of one such crime and sets out to prove his innocence. (*Minority Report*)

> *The Karate Kid* – with a panda! (*Kung-Fu Panda*)

A revenge-seeking gold digger marries a womanizing Beverly Hills lawyer with the intention of making a killing in the divorce. (*Intolerable Cruelty*)

*Romeo and Juliet* – on the Titanic. (*Titanic*)

A dislikeable man is forced to repeat the same day over and over again and cannot escape; can he find a way out – and love? (*Groundhog Day*)

This is similar to what eighties Hollywood called the High Concept – that single core concept which sells the movie and helps the producer imagine the poster, for example:

> *Alien* = *Jaws* in space
> *Top Gun* = *Rocky* with jets

High Concept means I can hold the film in the palm of my hand, so straightforward, so simple.

*Steven Spielberg*

When asked: 'What's your story about?' the one-liner is your reply. Now do it.

Making a one-liner out of it is easy. Making a great one-liner is hard.

*Julian Krainin,*
Head, Krainin Prods.

Useful websites:

www.imdb.com [Internet Movie Database: one-liners, taglines... everything]
www.rinkworks.com/movieaminute [short précis film reviews]

## Taglines

Now try creating some taglines for your project. These are the kind of short, pithy slogans you see on film posters that capture, at an emotional level, what it's about, or the kind of short descriptive billings used in weekly TV guides ('a gripping tale of family passion, intrigue and drama'). They are also increasingly used in film trailers, usually at the start – to hook you. Their sole purpose is to *attract an audience*. They are about creating the right expectations – in producers, agents, the audience. Although taglines (also called log-lines and strap-lines) won't come into play until the final stages, when packaging your script as a selling document, writing them here will help you focus on your project and clarify its 'through-line' (thrust and integrity).

Taglines consist of *two* key elements:

- The Rule of Three
- Contrasts: start with a factual description, then take the imagination on a journey

Examine how both elements are used in these examples:

'She brought a small town to its feet,
and a large corporation to its knees.'          *Erin Brockovich*
                                                            (2000)

(i) '3 Casinos. 11 Guys. 150 million bucks.
Ready to Win Big?

(ii) 'Are you In or Out?'          *Ocean's Eleven* (2002)

'He was the perfect weapon – until he became a target'
                                    *The Bourne Identity* (2002)

'The List is Life. The Man is Real. The Story is True'
                                        *Schindler's List* (1994)

'This is Benjamin... He's a little worried about his future'
                                            *The Graduate* (1967)

(i) 'The Future Can be Seen
The Guilty Punished
Before the Crime is ever Committed
... until it comes after You.'

(ii) 'What would you do if you were accused of a murder
you had not committed... yet?'     *Minorty Report* (2002)

'In search of wine. In search of women. In search of
themselves'                                    *Sideways* (2004)

'Love is a Force of Nature'

                                    *Brokeback Mountain* (2005)

'September 11, 2001.
Four planes were hijacked.
Three of them reached their target
– This is the story of the fourth (the one that fought back)'
                                            *United 93* (2006)

'What we do in Life echoes in Eternity'     *Gladiator* (2000)

'Somebody said "Get a Life" – so they did'

*Thelma and Louise* (1991)

'The true story of a real fake'

*Catch Me If You Can* (2003)

**Note:** don't expect the taglines you work out here to be the ones you create later.

---

Here are some more films (with release dates). Can you guess which ones from just the taglines? (Answers at the end of Taking it further):

1 'Five criminals. One line-up. No coincidence' (1995)
2 'On the Air, Unaware' (1998)
3 'Every family has a destiny. Every son holds the future for his family. Every father is a hero to his son' (2002)
4 'Fear can hold you prisoner. Hope can set you Free' (1994)
5 'America was Born in the Streets' (2002)
6 'How far would you go to become somebody else' (1996)

---

Now create some taglines for your project. When thinking them up, ask yourself:
• Does it go to the emotional heart of my story?
• What does it tell me (as an objective observer) about my story?

---

You will find many more taglines at these sites:

filmscape.co.uk/taglines/numbers.html
filmsite.org/taglines.html
imdb.com [Internet movie database]

… or simply put the words 'movie taglines' into a search engine and surf away.

## Theme

In my younger days I was writing but then I discovered something: I had this great urge to communicate, but I had nothing to say.

*Bruce Joel Rubin,*
screenwriter: *Ghost, My Life,*
*Stuart Little 2, Deep Impact*

I cannot stress the following enough: Theme is a *vital* ingredient in a screenplay. When discussing your script with an industry professional, two questions always crop up: 'What's it about?' (your one-liner), followed by: 'What's it *really* about?' This is where your theme enters.

Theme is that universal statement about the human condition you, the writer, want to make; those ideas or words you want your audience to take away with them at the end to help them live fuller, happier, better, more rounded lives. Theme applies to your audience, but it also answers the question: '*Why* do I want to write this script?'

Theme taps into mythic structures and your Burning Passion Factor, it gives your screenplay emotional depth. It is not a statement in dialogue. It is more related to, and embodied in, the development and growth of your main character; it derives from the successful combination of all the elements of a screenplay – and it should take the whole of the screenplay to say it properly. Indeed, theme, like plot, almost always sounds foolish and shallow when simplified into a couple of sentences.

An audience's interpretation of theme is always subjective: *Tootsie* may be about a man who dresses up as a woman in order to get a job. To its director, Sidney Pollack, it was 'an exploration of love that had friendship as its basis, and whether these two could co-exist' (compare *When Harry Met Sally*). For Michael Hauge, the theme is: 'in order for a relationship to succeed, we must be honest – to ourselves, and others' (compare *Groundhog Day*, *The Mask*).

The theme of *Shrek* goes something like: first impressions aren't everything; there is something wonderful – warts and all – about who we are, and if you project the real 'you', people will come to know us and love us and see the strengths inside of us. *Billy Elliot* is about the importance of pursuing a dream, and in your own way (Billy's letter from his mother embodies this: 'Always be yourself'). The story of the Australian film *Lantana* may revolve around a crime, but the theme is to do with the multiple crimes of the heart – the entangled nature of the lantana plant's roots.

The overt theme of *A Beautiful Mind* may be about learning to confront and deal with one's own personal demons, but for director Ron Howard it was more about 'it isn't enough to just have a beautiful mind; to be a complete, rounded person you need to have a beautiful heart too'. And, in fact, virtually all the writings of Philip K. Dick (adapted for the screen as *Blade*

*Runner, Minority Report, Total Recall, Imposter,* etc.) consistently return to two major themes: what is reality and what is/makes us human?

In *Witness,* a film we shall examine in depth in Chapter 07, the theme is the collision of two worlds with opposing values: the city values of the gun and masculine individualism vs. the earthly seasonal non-violent Amish with their high regard for community; is it possible to move from one world to the other without being tainted or affected in some way? Ideally don't we need a balance of both?

Theme is about 'writing from the heart'; you have to trawl into your inner self and emotions to discover what your personal themes are; they are about how you see the world, and what you want to say to your audience about the nature of society and living one's life.

In general, you will not know the theme of your story before you start writing it. Rather, it is something you discover while writing your exploratory draft, or after. Don't worry about it or force it; let theme come to you in its own time. The time to develop and texture it into your screenplay is during the rewriting.

> This new generation of screenwriters are completely versed in Hollywood structure, but the depth is missing. They aren't really writing about anything.
>
> *Dan Pyne,*
> screenwriter: *Pacific Heights,*
> *Doc Hollywood*

> Alan (Ball) wrote it from the heart as well as the head.
> *Sam Mendes,* director,
> on *American Beauty*

## Title

> *Paper Moon* is such a great title they don't need to make the movie, just release the title.
>
> *Orson Welles,*
> writer/director: *Citizen Kane,*
> *Touch Of Evil* etc.

Watch some or all of the following films. What do you think the theme of each one is? (Answers at the end of Taking it further):

1 *Field Of Dreams*

2 *Spider-Man*

3 *Erin Brockovich*

4 *The Legend of Bagger Vance*

5 *A.I. (Artificial Intelligence)*

Choosing the right title for your script is essential: good ones hook the audience, bad ones put them off. It has to grab their attention, be memorable, impart the essence of your script and tell us something about the setting, core idea and the characters.

What do these titles evoke for you?

| | |
|---|---|
| *Star Wars* | *Star Trek* |
| *The Fast And The Furious* | *Six Feet Under* |
| *Psycho* | *Because The Voices Are Talking* |
| *Fatal Attraction* | *To Me* |
| *Gladiator* | *Xena, Warrior Princess* |
| *Dan Dare* | *The West Wing* |
| *Catch Me If You Can* | *The Fugitive* |
| *feardotcom* | *The Sopranos* |
| *American Beauty* | *Dynasty* |
| *Hulk* | *Walking With Dinosaurs* |

Each one conjures up an automatic mental picture and a subconscious emotion about it, and stimulates our curiosity. Ask yourself this: would *you* have gone to see a story called *Romeo and Ethel the Pirate's Daughter*?

When *Oklahoma* was first released, it bombed, especially in the Provinces. Then they added the exclamation mark. *Oklahoma!* went on to be a fantastic success.

Your final title is probably the last thing you decide on after the script has been completed, so at this stage give it a working title, perhaps one word or the subject matter, to give your project an identity.

## Background and setting

You need to know completely the world your story is set in to make it believable for your audience (i.e. make them suspend their disbelief). It doesn't have to actually exist, but they must believe that it could.

Ask yourself these questions:

- What type of world is it? How do I want to affect my audience? Will they feel recognition at a world similar to theirs? Can I capture their imagination with a world they've never seen but which will appeal to them?
- Is it a *realistic* world close to the real world the audience live in? Is it one they might live in, in another country or another time in history?
- Is the world *exotic*? Maybe the world exists but the audience would never visit it (e.g. Everest, the moon).
- Is it *fantastic*? Maybe it doesn't exist in reality but it may in some fantasy. (Some things may resemble the world as we know it, but the rules may be different.)
- Is it the world of a particular fictional *genre*? The audience will know this is not reality, that cowboys were probably never like this, but still . . . The rules of conduct will generally be the same as in present-day reality.
- What is the *climate* like? How does it affect the lives of the people? Can they live outdoors or must it be mostly indoors because of the cold? Are there any illnesses/special dangers only found in this world as a consequence?
- *Landscape* – is there beauty in the natural surroundings? Are the inhabitants aware of this? Are there any animals? What are people's attitudes towards them? Are they work beasts or pets?
- *Society* – how do people live in this world? As groups, couples, singly? Are they isolated or does everyone know what everyone else is doing? Are they at war or at peace with each other? Is there enough food? Do they have houses? If not, where do they live?
- *Economy* – how do people make a living? What do they earn? Do they work to live or live to work? Do they work at all? Is there poverty? How do they travel? Is travel fast/slow/organized/chaotic?
- What is the arrangement of *power* in this world? All social situations (including love) have an uneven distribution of power; do people have power over their own lives? Can they decide what to do tomorrow? Are they governed by the need to work or by some overlord? Are they tied to their job/land or can they study/work independently? Do they have spare time? Do they have wealth and power over others? Do they wish to be free? Remember: knowledge and information are power.

- What are the *rituals* of this world? A family meal, washing your hands, washing the car, catching a bus, all are rituals.
- What are the *ethics* of this world? What are the moral constructs? Where are the boundaries of right/wrong, good/evil, legal/illegal?
- How important is the *spiritual life* in this world? Is there organized religion or cult/s? Does it enrich or limit their lives? Does the religious establishment have powers over their lives outside of the hours of worship? Is organized religion unimportant but the inner spiritual search paramount?
- Are the *emotions* important in this world? Do people talk/sing about love/hate? write/read poetry? have affairs or feuds? Is it acceptable to express emotions openly or are they suppressed through custom/for some particular reason (institutional or professional discipline etc.)? Is it a world where it is considered important to be controlled and unemotional at all times?
- Are the creative and performing *arts* important (to the society in general, to your character/s in particular)? Or is everyone glued to their home computer game? How do people amuse/entertain themselves/each other? Is there any leisure time?
- Are people in general *content* with this world? Do they wish to change it or long to leave it? If they did, would they miss it?
- If you were an intelligent, perceptive alien landing in this world for the first time, what would strike you most about it? Looking closer, would you find those first impressions misleading?

The setting of your story fixes it in time and space, that is, historically (past? present? future?) and with regard to place (specific locations, streets, rooms).

Although you may feel the setting limits you on what is possible in the story, it focuses you as a writer. A story must not only have a general world canvas as a backdrop, but it must also have a specific setting, a smaller world. That world must be small enough for you to understand all of it, like a creator God. Not knowing fully the world of your story means you will not be able to make real choices in that world. You will then tend to borrow from other recognizably similar situations. This leads to clichés and stereotypes. Be original; the depth of that originality produces better and more believable answers and solutions.

# Subplots

Although your script will have a main plot, it won't be enough to sustain your script and give our understanding of the main story and main character/s depth, colour and meaning. You need subplots – additional stories linked to and involving other characters or other incidents which have an influence on the main plot and the way your main character reacts. They are vital. You should have:

- A main plot
- A main subplot
- Other subplots

Short-form television drama will have a main plot and a subplot (possibly even a second subplot); beyond that, it could strain. Films have a main plot, a main subplot and between three and five significant other subplots (seldom more). TV serials, mini-series and soaps will have a dozen or more plot strands.

Audiences are very visually literate today. Even if a subplot is slight, or appears briefly, your audience will still receive it, however subtle.

The important thing about subplots is:

The kind of relationship a subplot has to the main plot must be one of these four:

> Whatever Your Main Plot Ends Up Being, All Your Subplots
> Should Inform And Feed Into Your Main Plot

- **Contradictory:** going against the core idea of your main plot
- **Complementary:** resonating the ideas in your main plot
- Acting as a **Set-Up:** and hooking your audience until you introduce your main plot
- **Complicating:** the life of the main plot (e.g. by introducing a love story into an action-adventure drama such as *Speed* or *xXx*).

Subplots will carry and embody the message/theme of your screenplay; usually they tell us what the story is really about (redemption, community vs. individualistic values, the search for identity, good vs. evil etc.) For example, the main plot in *Field of Dreams* is about building the baseball diamond, but the writer was more interested in exploring the father-son relationship and the role of dreams. In *Witness* the writers were more interested in the John Book–Rachel relationship (as were the audience). They explored this via the subplots, especially the main subplot.

A fast-moving, complex film such as *Tootsie* has at least five subplots:

> Now watch *Witness*. Write down what you think is the main plot and the subplots, and what relationship (of the four above) they had to the main plot. Can you chart each one's development?

1 Michael–Julie (actress in the soap)

2 Michael–Sandy (his insecure friend)

3 Michael–Les (Julie's widowed father)

4 Michael–Brewster (the soap's lecherous doctor)

5 Julie–Ron (the soap's director)

… arguably six (Michael–Jeff, his flatmate), each one further complicating the main plot of Michael's attempt to get, maintain and then quit his acting job. Each subplot has something to say about the nature of love and friendship, each has its own internal structure and each grows out of and intersects the main plotline. See pages 66–7.

So subplots have a number of dramatic uses:

> Watch *Tootsie*. Did you notice so many stories being carried out simultaneously? Probably not. The joy of a well crafted script is that not only does it manage to carry all these stories simultaneously, it integrates them, along with the theme, with consummate ease – you don't notice it and can't see or feel the joins.

- *To show parallel action.* Have two distinct stories, linked or not, so you bounce between them to illuminate your main story.
- *To reveal subtext.*
- *To reveal different aspects of your character.*
- *To surprise the audience.*
- *To delay the development of your main story.* This is useful in comedy (where it's easy to divert from the main story for some minutes and create set-pieces) or where your main story is quite thin.

| | SET-UP | 1st TURNING POINT | DEVELOPMENT T |
|---|---|---|---|
| MAIN PLOT → | Michael can't get a job. | Michael gets a job – as Dorothy. | Michael becomes very successful. |
| SUBPLOTS ↓ | | | |
| 1. MICHAEL – JULIE | Michael (as Dorothy) meets Julie on first day at work. He's attracted to her. | Julie asks him to dinner. Their friendship begins. | They become friends. They go to the country. They talk. Dorothy encourages Julie to break up with Ron. Dorothy helps Julie out by babysitting. |
| 2. MICHAEL – SANDY | Establishes the long-term friendship between Michael and Sandy by showing them in various situations (at birthday party, preparing Sandy for her audition). | Michael & Sandy make love, changing the nature of their relationship & putting their friendship in jeopardy. | Sandy's insecurities increase. She invites Michael to dinner and confronts him about his behaviour. |
| 3. MICHAEL – LES | Les meets Dorothy. | Les starts to fall in love with Dorothy. | They sing together when Dorothy visits farm with Julie. Les takes Dorothy dancing. |
| 4. MICHAEL – BREWSTER | Michael is warned that Brewster is a 'lech'. | Brewster begins to be attracted to Dorothy. | They work together. Dorothy tries to avoid Brewster, who keeps trying to kiss her in their scenes. |
| 5. JULIE – RON | Establishes that Julie and Ron are dating. | | Michael notices the condescending way Ron treats Julie. |

figure 4.2 *Tootsie* subplot structure

| 2nd TURNING POINT | CLIMAX | RESOLUTION |
|---|---|---|
| Michael tries to get out of his contract – but "she's" so good no one will let him out of it. | 'Dorothy' reveals herself to be Michael. | |
| | | |
| Dorothy tries to kiss Julie. Development: Julie won't see Dorothy. | Michael says 'The hard part is over'. They've become friends. | Now they can continue their relationship. They leave together. |
| Sandy discovers Michael is in love – with another woman – and she discontinues their friendship. | Sandy opens in a new play. | She and Michael are friends again. |
| Les proposes. | Michael gives the ring back. | Les forgives him. |
| Brewster sings outside Dorothy's window and makes a pass at her. | Michael unmasks and Brewster realizes Dorothy's not a woman. | |
| | Julie breaks up with Ron as a result of Dorothy's lessons about self-respect. | |

- *To introduce another character.* Each significant character should have their own story (see Chapter 04).
- *To reveal backstory* (see Chapter 04).
- *To provide a context or setting for your main story.* For example, *Chinatown* begins as an investigation of someone's wife, develops into a corruption scandal, and ultimately into a story of incest. The subplot can create the context for the final climax and hold the first part of the storyline together, especially when there are a number of characters involved.

In a script, the movement between plot and subplot gives movement to your story. If plot and subplot were unconnected your stories would seem free-floating, unrelated – and irrelevant. It's the skill in how you integrate your subplot into the texture of the whole that gives your script believability as well as complexity. Too many subplots not well integrated will lead to a muddy, unfocused script weighed down by too much going on (cf. Spielberg's *1941*).

# Some final considerations

## Cost

Film and TV making is expensive and producers are forever cost-conscious. A first script that is knowingly expensive is a candidate for rejection; it demonstrates lack of understanding of the industry. I am not saying write only small-scale scenarios or limit your imagination, but you should at least be aware of the things that add heavily to a budget, for example:

- special effects
- period drama with many historical settings
- lots of exotic locations
- any scenes with specific weather (for example, an outdoor snow scene in a summertime shoot)
- insisting that a major star be cast as the lead part.

The cheaper your budget, the more imaginative and inventive you are forced to be.

*Roger Corman*
writer/producer/director

Watch a selection from these films: *Reservoir Dogs, The Blair Witch Project, My Little Eye, Big Night, ivans xtc, Trees Lounge, She's Gotta Have It, The Brothers McMullen, Festen, The Idiots* and *Lock, Stock And Two Smoking Barrels* or any of director Mike Figgis's digital experiments (*Timecode, Hotel*). How did they get round the 'no-budget' problem? Did they do it well?

## Research

If you are writing about an activity or subject you have little experience of, it is essential for you to do background research, in order to give your setting credibility and believability. But beware the dangers of over-research. You may reach a point where something 'just wouldn't happen in this job'. Tough. You are looking for the dramatic truth, hence it would. So set it up and build it to make it look like it would happen in those circumstances – you're not writing documentary. As they say in journalism: Never let the facts get in the way of a good story.

> People are always telling me: 'You should hear about all the funny things that happen at my work.' I say to them: '*You* just tell me about your job. Let *me* make it funny.'
>
> *Allan Sutherland,*
> comedy writer

## Medium

When a Reader receives a script or a producer is pitched an idea, they instinctively know the ideal format for that idea. Most novice writers seem to think solely in terms of feature films. But the type and complexity of your story, plots and subplots and the number of characters should indicate to you whether there is enough to fill 90+ minutes of the big screen.

Ask yourself: to do my story justice could it be best told in a full-length feature (between 90 and 120 minutes)? Would, say, 60 minutes of TV serve it better, or even a mini-series? Is it actually a 30-minute story ambitiously stretched to feature length? Is it really a 4-hour mini-series crammed into 90 minutes?

As a basic rule of thumb, think of it like this:

**TV Drama**     60 minutes or longer. Up to six main and secondary characters; studio based with limited location shooting.

| | |
|---|---|
| **Feature Film** | Between 80 and 120 mins. Seven or fewer main and secondary characters; broad visual canvas, location shoots; fits a genre. |
| **TV Mini-Series** | Two or more feature-length episodes running on consecutive nights/weeks; very broad canvas with tendency towards family sagas and often set against major historical events. Usually book adaptations. |
| **TV Serial Drama** | Anything up to 13 or even more main and secondary characters, with perhaps 50 or more storylines running at different times and of varying length. Usually told in 30 or 60-minute chunks, transmitted regularly (weekly/nightly). |

So be objective about your idea and honest with yourself:

* Is it fit for the big screen?
* Is it the right format/length?
* Would it sit more comfortably in a different format, e.g. television or straight-to-video or computer game?

Every tale has its own ideal length. This is to do with the decisions you make: where does my story start? where does it end? Picking the right format for your story will give you confidence – in yourself and in the story.

> People have approached us regularly to make a *Simpsons* movie. But each episode we do has enough story, character, developments and one-liners to sustain an entire movie. I just don't see the point of taking a half-hour compact piece of work and stretching it out to 90 minutes.
>
> *Matt Groening,*
> creator: *The Simpsons, Futurama*

---

Examine the quote above, spoken in 2003.

Now watch *The Simpsons Movie* (made in 2007).

Do you think that the movie has enough in it – jokes, story, funny ideas, dialogue etc. – to make it stand alone as a movie; or do you think it's like an episode of *The Simpsons* spread rather thinly over 87 minutes?

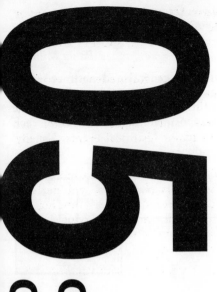

# 05

## creating your characters

**In this chapter you will learn:**

- how to create three-dimensional, well-rounded, believable characters
- how to construct a cast design of different character types and roles that function together to bring out the best in your story
- how to get your audience to relate to them.

Your characters will lead you through the story maze. You don't know where. Trust your characters and you will trust your story.

*Paula Milne*

So far we've looked at things in general and abstract terms. Now let's start to flesh things out. The two main building blocks of a script are: *character* and *structure*. They are symbiotic, the yin and yang: both feed, support, illuminate and drive each other.

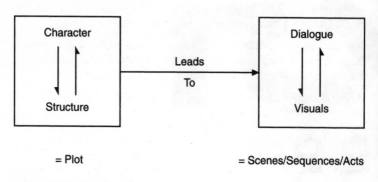

figure 5.1 the building blocks of a script

Creating credible and convincing characters is probably the most difficult and elusive thing for any writer. This chapter offers you tools and a starting point to help you come to grips with it.

'Getting' your character is the hardest part of writing a screenplay, and probably the most important. Every story is to a greater or lesser extent character driven, even *The Fast And The Furious, Robocop, Tomb Raider* and even *Johnny Mnemonic*. Think of the films you like best. Almost always there is something about the characters that won you over, that engaged you enough to care about them, to feel tense when they were in danger. So how do we do it?

This chapter will examine the two most important factors when creating characters for a script:

• the creation of the characters themselves; their biography and backstory
• the design of your cast.

But first, let's give your characters some names.

# Choosing a name

The name you give your characters is important, so choose good, strong ones: names evoke certain feelings in an audience. Think of some: Indiana Jones, Priscilla, Bruce Wayne, Forrest Gump, Malcolm X. *Field Of Dreams* has Ray as its main character: an ordinary, nondescript name for an ordinary, nondescript, unmotivated Iowa farmer. *Thelma and Louise*: an unusual name (but sounding like that of a typical Southern American housewife) and a fairly regular name – two degrees of normality for two far-from-ordinary characters. Why do you think the main character in *Witness* is called John Book?

Remember, some names are generation-specific: for example, Rose, May, Ethel, Blanche, George, Norman, Sharon, Tracey, Kevin, Jason, Kylie, Matt, Tiffany, Amber, Buffy, etc.

Also, consider the way names can be used to underscore an emotion: a character who has always been known by their last name might be annoyed by the pointed use of their first name, as would calling them, say, Mike, when they insist on being addressed as Michael; the same applies with nicknames. Watch *Scent Of A Woman* and note its use of Charles, Charlie and Chuckie; similarly, the use of Leonard and Lennie in *Memento*.

If you've seen the film *Insomnia* you might have noticed the ironic choice of giving the main character a name like Will Dormer; and calling one of the characters in *Minority Report* – a movie about sight and foresight – Dr. Iris (sic) Hineman was no accident. Likewise, in *The Truman Show*, you have a protagonist Truman Burbank (true-man/Burbank, as in Hollywood, California) opposed by the God-like presence of a character named Christof. And the naming of the main players in *Road To Perdition* Michael (Mike) and Michael Jr., while perhaps initially confusing, neatly reflects one of the movie's themes: the idea – the fear – that the son will follow in his father's footsteps as a gangland assassin. Ron Burgundy? Homer Simpson? These are all names carefully chosen.

Tip: A good source of names is one of those books that list names for babies.

Try to give each of your characters names that do not share the same initial (unless there is a vital plot reason for it) or that sound the same. Three characters in the same story called Ray, Ricky and Reg, or Jack, Jacques and Jake would only confuse your audience (especially the Script Reader).

# Creating three-dimensional characters

There is a near infinity of possibilities. You have several characters, let's say four. Anything A says or does can provoke one of four reactions from B, C and D. That's 256 permutations. B's response will multiply the options by a further 256. Before you've got two lines of dialogue you are juggling with 65,536 potential subplots. The only control you can exert is what you know about your characters.

*Norman Lebrecht,* journalist and
author: *The Song Of Names*

---

As A Writer, Your Goal Is To

Create three-dimensional Characters.

---

This means characters which are intriguing, which catch the audience's attention, and which are above all believable. The more you know about your characters the more well-rounded they will become in your writing, and the more your audience will enjoy and believe the work. When descriptions are flat, when dialogue doesn't come alive, when characters act in implausible ways, often it is because the writer has not taken the time to really get to know his or her characters fully. When you know your characters inside out, like a best friend, you'll know exactly what they would and would not say and do.

Many of what I thought were my funniest lines were cut, because they were jokes that came from me, from the page, and not from the characters themselves. The audience had to believe a character would come out with a particular line.

*Simon Beaufoy,*
screenwriter: *The Full Monty,*
*Among Giants, Blow Dry*

The thing is to get your characters talking to each other. Once you've got to that point, you understand your character even more.

*Tony Marchant*

Even though you will not actually use over 80 per cent of your character information in the script, you need to know it. Not just because it clarifies and focuses things in your mind, but also because at some point, someone – be it script editor, producer, director, or (especially) actor – will point to the script and ask you 'Why does the character say/do this?' You must have a plausible answer, and doing thorough work on your characters will give you that answer.

I approach it in terms of: I'm looking at this character Richard Goodwin, and I'm trying to understand why he makes the choices he makes: why work for this committee rather than make more money in Wall Street? Why does he choose to prosecute Charles Van Doren and champion Herb Stempel and why feel ambivalent about that championing? I try to connect the dots of those actions, understand a personality that would make those choices; understand that character in a way that makes those choices intelligible and believable.

*Paul Attanasio*
on writing *Quiz Show*

A fundamental principle to understand here is:

> We Learn About A Character
> From The Decisions They Make

This applies most especially to your main character (the protagonist). Their goals (outer motivation) drive the plot: their *decisions* expressed as *actions* dictate the path your story will take. Take a look at *Spider-Man*: it's a film all about characters making decisions and, for Peter Parker, learning to accept responsibility for those choices – good and bad.

Consider characters as having three dimensions:

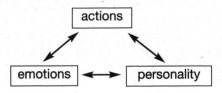

**figure 5.2** character dimensions

Use just two of these and you will have flat or stereotype characters that don't leap off the page.

## Action

- physical (visual) action
- verbal action (dialogue) covering action, emotion and personality
- emotional action (see below)
- psychological action (inside a character's mind, encompassing thoughts, feelings, dreams, states of mind, etc. and

manifested externally in *decision-action*, the formulation of a goal, a decision to act or not to act).

### Emotions

Screenplays *are* emotion, dramatized through conflict; emotional action derives from a character's *emotional make-up* meeting an obstacle, and in turn generating an *emotional reaction*.

- *Emotional make-up* is your character's capacity or tendency to feel joy/love/frustration/compassion/hate/despair/nothing. It includes their temperament and their capacity to move into an emotional state (anger/despair/etc.) quickly or not.
- *Emotional action* or *reaction* can be a kiss, a special look, a display of grief, etc.
- *Personality* is a combination of integrated interior attributes (attitudes/aspirations/beliefs/life-P.O.V./intentions/etc.).

## Character functions/categories

All characters have a specific function to fulfil in your screenplay. You can divide these into three basic categories:

- **Main character/s** Your protagonist and anyone who advances the story in conjunction with them
- **Secondary characters** Those who interact with your protagonist and have a significant effect on your plot or main character/s (antagonist, mirror and romance – see cast design, later)
- **Minor characters** Those who add colour, atmosphere or comic relief, deliver messages, open doors and generally contribute to the world of the story.

## The protagonist

This is the character

- you want your audience to focus on
- whose P.O.V. they experience the story through
- who will travel the journey in the story of your screenplay
- with whom the audience will most identify
- who, by definition, will be on screen most of the time.

Often called the hero or heroine, the protagonist is the one who should

- drive the plot (their outward motivations and goal/s are the engine of your story)
- initiate the action.

Can you name the main character for the following films? *Forrest Gump, Back To The Future, The Matrix, Spider-Man, Amélie, Unforgiven* and *Braveheart*?

Although the protagonist is usually your main character, it is not always the case. In *Rain Man*, Raymond (Dustin Hoffman) is the main character, but Charlie (Tom Cruise) is the protagonist, the one who travels the journey from being a self-seeking avaricious business type to an unselfish rounded person. In *The Third Man*, Harry Lime (Orson Welles) is the main character, but the protagonist is journalist Holly Martins (Joseph Cotton), as with Kane and the journalist in *Citizen Kane*.

Watch *Heat*: which do you think is the main character and which the protagonist – De Niro or Pacino? And what about *Fight Club* – is it Brad Pitt or Edward Norton? Now do the same for: *All The President's Men* – Redford or Hoffman?; *Don Juan De Marco* – Depp or Brando?; *Changing Lanes* – Affleck or Jackson?; *Good Will Hunting* – Matt Damon or Robin Williams? – after all, both their characters have a developmental arc. Other films you might try it with: *Analyze This, Birdy, K-Pax*. No doubt, you can think of others.

# Character biography – analysis/checklist

You should try to write complete biographies (of between two and ten pages, sometimes more) for each of your principal characters, from birth to the point where they enter your script. Why? Because you will be startled at the end of it to realize just how much you have fleshed out your original character idea. Suddenly you will understand why your character does this action or wears that particular garment. Sometimes you will find your characters changing the direction or thrust of your original story. Don't be afraid of it. Use it to your advantage and re-examine your plot in the light of what you have now discovered about your characters.

This approach can be time-consuming. So here is a handy checklist to speed things up; these are the kind of questions actors ask themselves. Remember, the audience don't need to know all this information – in fact, you probably won't use

80 per cent of what you write down – but you the writer should know and be able to answer every question.

- What is their gender and age?
- What is their weight, height, build, colour of hair, eyes and skin? Are they right or left-handed? Do they have any facial expressions, a squint or any disabilities? Do they have a limp or missing finger? Do they wear spectacles or contact lenses? How do they walk or move? Do they have any mannerisms or habits? Do they smoke? What are their attitudes towards each of these?
- How do they speak? What do they sound like? What pitch and speed is their voice? Any favourite sayings or words? Do they use slang? or swear?
- Do they live alone or with other people? Do they have any children? What is their relationship to them? What kind of children are they?
- Do they have a partner, or one or several lovers? Are they celibate? Married? Do they have dependent relatives, flatmates or pets?
- Where do they live? Do they own their home? How much does it cost? How is it furnished? Are they domesticated, tidy or messy?
- Are they successful in material terms? Do they have a good job with enough money? Are they worried about their finances? Are they financially independent? Do they like their job? If not, what would they rather do? What are the power relationships in their work with co-workers, boss, or employees?
- Are their parents living? Do they like them? Was their family rich, poor, struggling to keep up appearances? What have they inherited from them, both physically and psychologically?
- What kind of education did they have? Was it a military background? What were they expected to do with their life?
- What is their nationality? Do they live in their country of origin? If not, why not? How do they feel about this?
- What is their sexuality and their attitude towards it? How important is it? Do they have any hang-ups? What are their attitudes towards someone else's sexuality?
- When they are at home for an evening alone, are they happy with their own company? Do they read books, magazines, newspapers, the back of cornflakes packets? What music do they play to themselves? What do they eat? Can they relax? Do they knit, sew, write letters, watch television, revise their

notes from an evening class? What are their hobbies, if any? Are they quirky? Are they a collector? What do their hobbies, music and books tell us about them?

- Are they a cool or a sexy person? Are their relationships fiery and passionate or calm and carefully controlled? Do they have a nasty temper? Are they charming? Do they control their emotional life or does it control them? How do they express tension or do they internalize stress? How do they express pleasure?
- Do people like them? Do they do what they want? Do they admire or respect them? What do they most like or dislike about themselves? What aspects of themselves do they praise, deny, or want to change?
- Do they run their own life, or are they usually obeying other people, or doing things in order to please or take care of others?
- What is their favourite colour? What is their star sign and birth stone? Do they believe in astrology? Are they religious or spiritual? If so, what are their beliefs and practices? What are their moral beliefs and code of ethics? Do they have a phobia or phobias?
- What do they want from life? What are their goals in the short, medium and long term? What do they *really* want from life and why? When they die, how do they want to be buried: six foot under, cremated, at sea? Do they want their ashes scattered anywhere specific? Any particular music played at their funeral? Have they thought about death at all? Does death bother them?
- What is their relationship to the other main characters in the story? Who or what is trying to prevent them from achieving their goal(s)?
- Do you like them? Do you respect them? How do you want the audience to feel about them?
- Within the drama/film/story, what is their goal or dramatic need? What are they trying to achieve, gain or change during the course of the piece?
- At the end of the script, what is their development? How have they changed? What have they learned, about things or other people, themselves?

Another handy exercise, and again based on how actors approach their part, is to take your character through a typical day in their life. What time do they wake in the morning? How do they wake up? With vigour, or do they lie there waiting to muster the energy? Maybe with a cigarette? How do they smoke it? What do they do next?... and so on.

As I start learning (a part), the character becomes like a photographic plate. The image begins to show itself to me ... If I can hear the voice and begin to see how he moves, then all I have to do is become that image or imitate that image and bring it to the screen.

*Anthony Hopkins,* actor

Remember, the point is not to use all this information but to have it in your mind (and on paper) to draw upon if needed. Who we are effects how we talk, think, what we do, how we feel, what we say, so the more you know who your characters really are, the more you will be able to make their actions and words specific, characteristic and believable. Your characters will sound and act like real people, not cardboard cut-outs created to serve a plot.

Now write a thorough biography for your main character.

# Backstory

Besides a character's biography, you should also work out their backstory. This can be defined as the story of your character and the relevant events in their lives that happened to them immediately before they entered the script. Normally, the relevant backstory for your character/s will only be a matter of weeks long, but it can also be hours, months or years – your story will dictate the timeframe. For example, in *The Truman Show,* the drowning of Truman's father (seen in flashback) happened many years before the film started, yet we know those years have been deeply traumatic. In the comedy *George Of The Jungle,* George's complicated backstory was encapsulated very cleverly in the cartoon before the opening titles, aided by the witty voice-over. Without it, an audience would have been disorientated.

As with your character biography, write a two–ten page backstory for each of your principle and secondary characters. The key use of backstory is it can provide important information about your character/s and events you can use during the telling of your story. Another advantage of backstory is it helps you decide exactly where to open your script (as the motives your characters possess in Scene 1, Act I clearly derive from events in their immediate backstory).

In practice, writers often write a combined backstory and biography. Remember, these are tools only: you use them, they do not dictate to you. As you develop and write the script, the story will probably evolve away from these original ideas and make you return to both biography and backstory and revise accordingly. Don't worry. Your story is your guide.

## Secondary characters

When creating these (particularly with the antagonist/opposition and the romance), follow the same procedure as for your main character. Know them inside out, but beware of letting them get out of hand and becoming too memorable – they must never upstage your main character. Try to make their dialogue as individual as possible, but don't start writing it too soon or they may run away with you.

## Minor characters

Beware, it is in the creating of your minor characters that you are in the greatest danger from cliché and stereotype (it usually indicates the writer has not done enough work or thought). Thus it is essential you make as much effort on your minor characters as you do with your principal ones. Nothing is easier than to bring in a couple of stereotypes to chat, hang around for a scene or two and conveniently move the plot on a bit. You may not even notice you are doing it, as you're too focused on your protagonist's tormented soul.

When thinking about minor characters, consider the following:

- Every time you bring in a new character *think what you are doing*. If you have seriously thought through all those 'Getting It Clear' questions in Chapter 04, then you should know what story you are telling and hence the function of your minor character. If you have worked on your main and secondary characters, you should be in the habit of providing depth of characterization. If you have thought about the world and setting of your story, then you know what background your character has.
- Then consider how complex this character needs to be. There may not be time or space in your script to get too elaborate. So, how are you going to make this character original within

the parameters you can afford? Can you give them a distinctive dress style, physical presence or body language? Can you give them a speech idiosyncrasy or dialect, a surprising hobby or area of expertise? Do they have a characteristic emotion – perhaps one unexpected in view of their social role? These all may help as short cuts, but they may not make your character completely original, so don't lean on them too much. Remember, do all your thinking before you get to dialogue.

- Look around you. People are endlessly fascinating, sometimes odd. Notice, when travelling on public transport, that punk engrossed in a Jane Austen novel or the bus driver whistling an opera tune.
- Learn from other writers. Charles Dickens' bit-part players were often exaggerated but never dull.

As usual, it's down to doing enough work. Stereotype minor characters are usually produced by writers who get as far as their function in the script but no further. Even non-human characters need well thought-through biographies to make them believable (e.g. *Toy Story, Chicken Run, Stuart Little, Titan A.E., S1mOne, Babe, Star Wars, The Lion King, Monsters, Inc.,* and Gollum in *The Lord Of The Rings: The Two Towers*).

As a writer, you invent your characters, or take them from life, and modify them. You don't get them ready-made from some box of stock types. So every time you bring in any new character, think. Don't just look at their function in the script or within that scene. Ask why they are there. Should they be there at all? Could their role or function be performed by an existing character? Ask yourself these questions about each character's relation to your story:

- Is it a main or secondary character, or a bit-part?
- Are they the protagonist, antagonist, or do they switch sides?
- What is their relationship to the plot? Are they essential to the main story, the sub-plot, or simply a conveyor of information?
- What makes them different from every other character in the story? If there are similarities, you should change them.

When creating a character and their dialogue, if it helps you get a clearer mental picture during the writing stage, try imagining the best possible actor in that role. But, be aware that every actor carries with them a 'baggage' of character types they have played in the past, and this baggage may impose limitations on your imagination and creativity. Moreover, when finally submitting your script to someone in the industry *never* give them casting suggestions or include an ideal cast list. This is tantamount to telling them their job and indicates a naivety of the production process.

> In *Dead Poets Society* I started with the story and that told me what kind of characters I would need ... Start thinking objectively about your characters.
>
> *Tom Schulman*

# Cast design

It is no use having a well-rounded protagonist unless you have other characters to relate to or react against. Your choice of characters may well be the most crucial decision you make in writing your screenplay. Each character fulfils a function in your story and represents or expresses different aspects of your theme. Hence your story, its premise, the problem set-up by the inciting incident (see Chapter 07) and theme will dictate or influence the cast you design and the type of principal characters you create, each one fitting the nature of the problem in some way.

It may seem simplistic, but you have **four main primary character types** to choose from:

1 **Hero/ine**
   This is your Protagonist (page 77). It is this character's job to keep the story moving forward, hence their goal(s) and external motivation drive your plot, their decisions initiate the action. And they must want to pursue these goals to the very limit.

2 **Opposition character**
   The Antagonist (also called the Nemesis) is the character who most stands in the way of your hero/ine achieving their goal and creates obstacles in their path. They are a visible character who visibly confronts the hero – remember, good villains make good drama. Also they must push your protagonist to their utmost credible limits.

Note that occasionally, characters you would normally consider antagonists are in fact protagonists. These characters are called anti-heroes (e.g. Travis Bickle in *Taxi Driver*, Renton in *Trainspotting*, Norman Bates in *Psycho*,

Tom Ripley in *The Talented Mr. Ripley*, Patrick Bateman in *American Psycho*, D-Fens in *Falling Down*). However, even these unlikeable characters are not without some endearing qualities. Why do audiences seem to like these creations? Can you list more?

### 3 Mirror character

Also called the Reflection or Support, this is the character who is most aligned to the protagonist. They support the protagonist's goals (or are in the same basic situation), add depth to the character of the protagonist via dialogue, making your protagonist more credible, more believable. A protagonist working alone without this Sancho Panza-type figure will cause difficulties for you in letting the audience know exactly what is going on with your protagonist and your plot.

### 4 Romance character

This is the character who is the object of your protagonist's romantic/sexual desire, the active romantic pursuit – the prize, if you like, at the end of the journey (it is usually one person; in *Erin Brockovich* it's the attainment of self-worth and mutual respect). This character alternately supports and then creates obstacles to the protagonist achieving their goal. The protagonist's emotion grows out of conflict; if there is no conflict in the relationship, things will get boring.

Remember, if you are going to create a romance character, it is important to get your audience to identify or 'fall in love' with your romance  as much as your protagonist.

Here are some important principles regarding these primary character types:

- their category is established when that character is introduced
- they should all have been introduced by the end of Act I, certainly by the start of Act II (even if we don't actually see a character, by this point they should have at least been mentioned or their presence established)
- each character stays in their designated category throughout the script; changing categories will only diffuse the focus of your script
- you don't need all four, but you must have a protagonist, an opposition and either a mirror or romance; you can have two opposition figures or any two other character types but as a rule-of-thumb, stick to one protagonist or hero/ine

- you don't have to explore all these characters' inner motivation and conflict (although with your protagonist it is vital).

It's all about you, the writer, understanding the purpose and function of the characters within your story. Understand their function and it can help you determine if that character is pulling their full weight in the tale.

You may find it helpful to construct a cast design chart like the one on page 86.

> Now watch each (or some) of the films listed in the chart on page 86. Do you agree with the roles I've assigned to each character? If not, why do you disagree? How would you assign them?

## Another perspective on cast design

Probably the most influential book on screenwriting of the last ten years was *The Writer's Journey* by Christopher Vogler. Taking as his springboard Joseph Campbell's works on the power of myth in storytelling (see Taking it further), Vogler adapted and expanded the ideas to suggest new ways of looking at characters and screenplay structure (see Chapter 08).

He urged us to view characters as wearing a series of masks and outlined what he saw as seven character archetypes:

1 **Hero:** The Protagonist character who embarks on the quest (external and/or internal); who is willing to sacrifice their own needs on behalf of others. While this Hero character remains a 'constant', staying in their archetype throughout the story, the other characters in the story are more fluid and may well switch archetypes from any of the remaining six at different stages in the tale. Moreover, the other six archetypes may embody facets of the Hero's own personality at different stages in the journey, reflecting the Hero's capacity for good and evil.

2 **Mentor (Wise Old Man/Woman):** Usually a positive figure who aids or trains the Hero; they teach and protect the Hero, giving them magical gifts or support (Obi Wan Kenobi in *Star Wars*, Gandalf in *The Lord Of The Rings*).

3 **Threshold Guardian:** At each gateway to a new world along the story's development (see Chapter 08 on Vogler's

| | Hero /Protagonist | Opposition /Antagonist | Mirror /Support | Romance |
|---|---|---|---|---|
| **Witness** | John Book | Paul Schaeffer | Carter (later, The Amish Community) | Rachel |
| **Field of Dreams** | Ray Kinsella | Initially it's Mark. Ultimately, it's Ray's image and memories of his father | Annie, his wife (Also, later, Terence Mann) | A settled soul and a contented life. |
| **Shrek** | Shrek | Overtly, Lord Farquaard; Actually, Shrek's own self-doubt | Donkey | Princess Fiona |
| **Minority Report** | John Anderton | Initially, Danny Witwer. Actually, Lamar Burgess | Agatha, the precog | Lara, John's estranged wife |
| **Monsters, Inc.** | Sulley | Initially, Randall. Ultimately, Mr. Waternoose | Mike | Boo, 'the kid' |
| **Erin Brockovich** | Erin Brockovich | Overtly, the PGE Corporation (later, Kurt and Theresa), actually, the perception of Erin by others | George, the neighbour. Later, Ed Masry | The achievement of self-worth |
| **Cruel Intentions** | Sebastian Valmont | Kathryn Merteuil | Kathryn? No. Ultimately, it's Sebastian's journal | Annette Hargrove |

figure 5.3 character roles

structure) there are powerful guardians at the threshold blocking the Hero's path. They present a menacing face to the Hero but, if properly understood, can be overcome, bypassed or even turned into allies. Threshold Guardians are not usually the main villain or antagonist, more like lieutenants or emissaries of the villain, mercenaries charged with guarding the villain's lair.

4 **Herald:** The character who, in Act I, calls the Hero to adventure. As in medieval chivalry, the Herald archetype issues challenges, announces the coming of significant change (i.e. from the Hero's 'normal' life outlined in the opening scenarios) – e.g. The voice in *Field Of Dreams*: 'If you build it, he will come'.

5 **Shapeshifter:** Fellow travellers who assume disguises and tell lies to confuse and/or dazzle the Hero. An elusive concept to grasp due to the unstable, changing (and flexible) nature of the role, this mask can be worn by any of your other archetypes to suit their purpose in the story at that point. A Hero may shapeshift in order to escape a trap (*Sister Act*) or overcome a Threshold Guardian; villains or allies may wear the mask to confuse or seduce the Hero; a Mentor may prove to be an enemy (*Monsters Inc.*).

The Shapeshifter brings doubt and suspense into a story. Whenever a Hero asks themself a question (Is she friend or foe? Is he faithful to me? Where do I stand with this person? Will they betray me?) a shapeshifter is normally at work. This archetype is a catalyst for change, represents a deep-seated urge in our Hero for transformation, and dealing with a shapeshifter causes the Hero to develop, grow and progress.

6 **Shadow:** The villain/s or antagonist/s who try to destroy the Hero. They represent the face of the dark side, often the home of the suppressed monsters/fears of the Hero's inner world; those dark secrets the Hero may not like about themselves but can't, or won't, admit to.

Vogler observed: Antagonists and Heroes in conflict are like horses pulling in the opposite directions; Villains and Hero in conflict are like trains set on a head-on collision.

7 **Trickster:** This archetype embodies mischief and the desire for change. These characters are primarily clowns or sidekicks, they upset the status quo and provide comic relief.

Vogler sees things more fluidly: archetypes as masks to be worn by a character temporarily when needed to advance a story or character; flexible character functions rather than rigid character types. The Hero, however, remains at the centre of it all.

To appreciate the subtle complexities of Vogler's arguments, you really need to read his book.

## Cast design – some observations

Although, for the most part, you will probably find the four main character types (Hero, Opposition, Mirror/Support, Romance) represented in a script, to see a character as rigidly and permanently locked into that role throughout a story is simplistic and would only do your talent a disservice. As in life, characters are always in flux: an Opposition may end up a Romance (as in romantic comedies), a Support may prove to be an Opposition (as in *Monsters, Inc.* and *Minority Report*).

Try to see your four basic character types as a springboard; add subtlety by, say, examining your characters and script from the Vogler perspective. Do whatever you feel is right to help you create a better story with more believable characters.

When constructing your Cast Design, try asking yourself two questions that will help you understand the nature of the archetype or role:

1 What is its dramatic function in the story?

2 What psychological function or part of the (Hero's) personality does it represent?

# The counter-character chart

When looking at the relationships between your characters, it might help to draw up a counter-character chart like the one shown opposite. When creating this chart, ask yourself what your other characters have to be in order to get the most contrast with your protagonist. Make the traits as mixed and as varied as you can to illustrate the different elements of your protagonist you wish to highlight. If it helps, think in terms of opposites and different degrees of dominance. For example, the chart for the satirical cartoon comedy *Family Guy* might look like this. Can you fill in the spaces?

| Peter Griffin | Male (Husband) | Caucasian (dubious genetic heritage) | Dominant Competitive Dependent | Crass Insensitive Self-centred |
|---|---|---|---|---|
| Lois | Female (Wife) | Caucasian (fiercely) | 'Submissive' Long-suffering | Loving Put-upon Frustrated |
| Meg | Female (Daughter/ eldest) | Caucasian | Assertive achiever Dependent | |
| Chris | Male (Son) | Caucasian | Very dependent | Stupid but loving Easily pleased |
| Stewie | Male (Son/Baby) | Caucasian | Megalo-maniacal Dependent | |
| Brian | Canine (Talking dog) | Mongrel | | Debonaire Artistic Drink problem |

And so on ...

**figure 5.4** counter-character chart

# Character flaws

Take one aspect of your own [writer's] character that you're not particularly proud of and explore that, push the envelope to the limit.

*Kingsley Amis*, author

Try to think of each principal character in your story as being in-complete, as hiding some profound imperfection in their soul. Think of it as a 'hole' going through the middle of their character, like the words in a stick of seaside rock. Perhaps your character needs to be a perfectionist or a control-freak, can't love or trust anybody or must rigidly organize all aspects of their life; maybe they loathe themselves and believe nobody could love them.

When you know or have chosen the flaw, you can begin to see how they have hidden it over the years, probably since childhood. What defence mechanisms have they devised to conceal it? What attitudes and forms of behaviour have grown up to help them survive it? What tentative and probably fearful attempts have they made (or might they make) to heal it?

All characters (just like people) have this hole right through their middle and all of them are desperately trying to hide it and live with it. Grasp this, and you have a powerful tool for developing your character/s even further.

You might trying using this 'flaw' idea, and a character's reconciliation of that flaw, as jumping-off points for creating their developmental arc (page 95) or your theme (page 58).

# Audience identification

People go to the cinema to see themselves on the screen. As an actor, people must identify with you. You cannot hold up a picture and say 'this is me', you hold up a mirror and say 'this is you'.

*Michael Caine,* actor

While it is important to establish your protagonist as early as possible in your script (don't clutter it up with other secondary or minor characters first), it is essential you get the audience 'on the protagonist's side', to establish subconscious links so that your audience sees the world and experiences emotion through that character's P.O.V. – and you must do it quickly. The way you do this and maintain it so that the audience completely identify with the protagonist is a key factor in emotionally affecting your audience.

There are a number of ways of achieving this:

- *Sympathy* is the most often used identification device. Make your protagonist the victim of some undeserved mishap or misfortune (*Edward Scissorhands, Signs, Minority Report, Batman Begins, The Pursuit Of Happyness* even Kenny in *South Park*), preferably in your opening scene(s).
- Put your character in *jeopardy*. We identify with people we worry about, fear for or feel anxiety about, whether the danger is life-threatening or simply loss of face (e.g. the *Indiana Jones* sagas, the *Bourne* films).
- Establish the *likeability* of your character. Perhaps they are nice, highly skilled, hard working, rogueish, a decent honest person or they may make us laugh (*Iris, George Of The Jungle,* Frank Abagnale Jr. in *Catch Me If You Can,* Larry in *Kiss Kiss Bang Bang,* Captain Jack Sparrow in the *Pirates Of The Caribbean* films). An audience will be more prepared to go along with them; a good example is the joke about the astrological tie in *A Beautiful Mind.* But remember, likeability and audience identification are not necessarily synonymous.

- Arouse our *curiosity* in this character: here the character will often be a negative or dislikeable person (e.g. *The Fisher King, Bad Influence,* Merv in *Sin City,* The Operative in *Serenity*), but we are drawn in by the mystery to follow their actions and choices. It is important with dislikeable characters or anti-heroes to give them at least one redeeming feature such as humour or witty dialogue, or to have a likeable secondary character who likes them. Audiences find it difficult to identify with completely obsessive or mad characters. Examine how this was handled in *American Psycho, The Talented Mr. Ripley* and *Falling Down.*
- Establish some element of *inequality.* We feel sympathetic to someone who is unjustly downtrodden (e.g. Thelma in *Thelma And Louise*) or vulnerable (*Birdy, It's a Wonderful Life, Erin Brockovich, Spider-Man*). Examine how they work for Hartigan in *Sin City* and for Jason Bourne in the *Bourne* films.

There are also other subtler ways of approaching the task:

- *Empathy* This is the strongest form of identification, but the most difficult to create and sustain. Generally, it is a combination of sympathy, fear for and likeability (*Wall.E*); we share what the character feels, are involved with them in their life-situation, challenges, failures and dilemmas. The more normal the character (however abnormal their situation) the more chance of empathy there is (e.g. *Field Of Dreams*).
- *Admiration* Courage, determination, luck, intelligence, adherence to their principles in the face of temptation or danger all encourage the audience's admiration. Sometimes this is different from likeability: we may not like someone we admire (e.g. *Patton*).
- *Familiarity* Familiar and recognizable settings induce a feeling of comfort in an audience. Also, giving a character familiar foibles might help: forgetting names, getting up late, mis-programming a video recorder, overeating (*Kung Fu Panda*), dreams of rock superstardom (*Rock School*) etc.
- *Power* A character possessing complete power is intriguing – we all have a fascination with power (*The Godfather, The Krays*). Power can also be shown through feelings (*Dangerous Liaisons, Cruel Intentions*). You might even make your character a superhero (*Superman, Batman, Daredevil, James Bond, Iron Man*). Here you are building on an already established genre and cultural base with its own pre-fixed values system.
- *Omnipotence* Allow your audience only to see events and characters through one person's (the protagonist's) eyes/ P.O.V. (*Maverick, American Beauty, Spider-Man, Goodfellas*).

This is most common in the detective genre (*The Big Sleep, Chinatown, Sin City*). Often it is simply achieved by the use of voice-over.

- Try to introduce your protagonist into the script as soon as possible (*Maverick, Birdy, Spider-Man, A Beautiful Mind, Calamity Jane*). Rather obvious, perhaps, but it needs stating. Later you can strengthen identification by layering on more and more modes.

Again, don't just stick to one of the above, mix'n'match. Play with the possibilities. The stronger the identification between audience and characters (especially the protagonist) the better.

> One thing that makes *Heroes* so popular is the way the audience can easily identify with the characters. They may be heroes but these are fundamentally ordinary people with everyday problems. And it's this ordinariness that makes for its 'identifiably'.
>
> *Tim Kring,*
> creator/screenwriter/executive
> producer: *Heroes*

---

Watch the first few minutes of *Thelma And Louise, Maverick, Tootsie, Butch Cassidy* . . . and *Field Of Dreams*. From that information, describe each film in one or two sentences. Does the end result sound especially wonderful? Probably not. Yet we are engaged by each film. In what ways are we drawn into an intense and enjoyable identification with the main characters (Thelma, Louise, Bret, Michael, Butch, Sundance and Ray)?

---

Now watch *The Talented Mr. Ripley* and *American Psycho* – compare them. Tom Ripley and Patrick Bateman are not exactly likeable characters, but were you interested in them, charmed by them, intrigued by them? Did you feel involved with them or did you feel at the end you wished you'd never met them? Did you *care* about their respective fates? Did you secretly wish that, perhaps, one of them could have gotten away with their misdeeds?

Now do the same for other similar movies, for example: *Falling Down, Goodfellas* and *Taxi Driver*.

In Europe, producers ask: 'Are the characters intriguing, is the protagonist interesting?' In America they ask: 'will the audience like him?' They call it 'rootability'.

*Lynda Miles,*
producer: *The Commitments, The Van*

It's very freeing doing independent or lower-budget movies – your character is no longer bound by the rules of likeability.

*Anthony Hopkins*, actor

Yes, your audience have to relate to your characters; but they don't have to approve of them.

*Christian Bale*, actor:
*The Dark Knight, American Psycho*

# 06

## character goals, growth, motivation and conflict

**In this chapter you will learn:**
• to go deeper into your
  characters – to examine their
  motivation(s) and goals, look
  at how they develop and
  change over the arc of your
  screenplay story and
  examine the various conflicts
  and obstacles they will
  encounter on the way.

# Character growth – the transformational arc

Your principal characters, especially your protagonist, must experience growth in order for your story and characters to have any meaning. (If nothing happens to your protagonist, where's the story and the interest for your audience?) And that growth must occur gradually over the arc of your entire screenplay (no less), never instantaneously. This is termed the *transformational arc* or growth line. If your character has grown all they can after just ten pages, all you've got is a ten-page story.

---

Growth Occurs As A Result Of

Confronting Obstacles

---

And remember, we learn about a character from the decisions they make, often under pressure; decisions about obstacles, decisions about conflict, and how to overcome them.

The greater the pressure, the more 'backs to the wall' the situation, the more we find out the real truth of the person. Hence, growth occurs over the arc of your screenplay in a series of emotional 'beats' (moments or leaps of growth/revelation) within each Act and within individual scenes.

Getting started, you have two kinds of characteristics:

- those your character starts the script with
- those that your character will need at different points to overcome the story obstacles, and the final beat of growth leading to the end goal.

Let's look at *Witness*: if John Book, the protagonist, needs to be more sensitive, trusting and less individualistic by the end of the story, then you can already begin to see the characteristics he will need at the start. This means it is possible to start from either end of the story in order to understand who your character is and where he or she is coming from and going to, just like knowing the end of your story to find its opening. Understanding this will make it easier to chart the growth arc of your character. Once you know what characteristics are needed at a specific stage in the story you can then design the scenes and incidents that help create and reveal these characteristics. Often you will create a scene or incident first and then discover what special aspect of the character and/or growth it is revealing. Writing is a mix of both approaches. Let it happen.

For example, in *Rain Man* we first see Charlie (Cruise) cut off, with no emotional connection to other people, even his girlfriend. News arrives about the father's death and the will. Charlie reacts as he would normally do to get whatever he wants: he kidnaps Raymond (Hoffman). Change comes when he purchases the television set, and we now see Charlie moving from the reactive character he has been to one of anticipating Raymond's needs. Charlie teaching Raymond to dance is a turning point: it is the first unselfish thing Charlie has done for Raymond, the two characters actually touch each other, and we can see Charlie moving away from selfishness. Raymond drives the car (i.e. Charlie is now risking his beloved possession). Charlie goes to the doctor and says: 'You should have told me I had a brother'. Finally, we see Charlie willing to give up his money in order to connect with his brother.

In *Witness,* John Book only achieves his final beat of growth by putting down his gun and exposing himself to Shaeffer's gun – risking his life to save Rachel. In doing this he achieves his final beat of transformation which is necessary to solve the 'problem' set-up in Act I (i.e. calling upon the power of the Amish community to witness what is taking place – whereas in our society so much is ignored, allowing some things to happen), and to take away Schaeffer's power despite his shotgun. In this scene Schaeffer realizes he cannot fight the whole community, that his power as an individual (the power he's always lived by) is not all-powerful. This is Schaeffer's final beat of character growth, which occurs after he has 'won' – defeated Book according to the rules and values of the game as played in big city cop life. It should also be noted that Book is revealed to be a carpenter before becoming a cop. This is significant to the relative ease with which he is seduced by the values of Amish life.

So, as a writer, first you need to establish the values and emotions in the world of your script, then put your protagonist through various crises where their emotions pitch and waver, their values are challenged, and they have to make decisions, and end with them being changed, with an altered value-system and an altered emotional response.

In any script, your protagonist needs a powerful transformational arc to emotionally grip your audience and hold your story together. Someone sitting at home wanting a glass of water is not powerful – they can go into the kitchen and get one; if that person were stranded in the desert for a week and would, literally, kill for a glass – that's powerful and gripping. A weakness in new scripts is that the story of the life depicted is just a collection of incidents strung together (as in real life); the emotional arc is not there. Bio-pics are especially prone to this, taking that person's life chronologically from birth to death (e.g. *Malcolm X*). You need to depict the most dramatically effective incidents to create that arc. *Ali*, for example, concentrated on a specific ten-year span in that character's life (1964–74), and Tim Burton's *Ed Wood* concentrated on the most dramatically interesting period of Wood's life, his backstory integrated into the body of the movie, and his 'afterlife' covered via end-credit captions. Kevin Costner's *Wyatt Earp*, on the other hand, spanned 1848–1929 (and well over three hours!). *A Beautiful Mind* covered 47 years (1947–94) in the life of John Nash Jr., but at least there was a clearly outlined emotional arc to the tale.

> Look For The Emotional
>
> Development Arc
>
> In Each Of Your Main Characters
>
> (Not Just Your Protagonist)

Ask yourself:

- Where does the growth begin? Why? What causes it?
- What changes are they going through?
- How do they react to these changes?
- Where do we first see some indication of change?
- How do we see it?
- What do they make of it?

Finally, do not confuse character growth with theme. They are similar and linked, but growth applies to your character/s and is specific to them, whereas theme applies to your audience – that universal statement about the human condition you want them to take away at the end.

> Now watch *Witness* complete and try to chart out the beats/moments of growth in the John Book–Rachel relationship (the dramatic emotional beats of the main subplot, starting from when they first meet, moving through significant eye-contact, hand holding, not kissing, kissing etc.). Do the same with another film/TV drama. Continue until you feel conversant with this concept of the arc.

# Character motivation

> The goal of the character is the most important thing: what the character wants when the story opens, and the character becomes clever by the number of ways they can find in obtaining that goal. How they go about it is down to who they are and the assets they have. When writing I just say 'I know what this guy wants' and a scene is always about what a character wants.
>
> *Tom Schulman*

If character is the most important element of your screenplay, then it follows that what motivates that character to act is even more important.

Audiences always hunger to know why a character acts as they do. When we read in a newspaper about some horrific but senseless murder, we may be partially interested in the event itself, but our overwhelming interest is not in how he killed his family, but why – the reason. A screenplay character is no different. If you provide this motivational dimension of character, satisfy the audience's natural hunger to know why, then you have already begun to separate yourself from the common herd of would-be screenwriters and those that merely try.

Working on a character's biography and backstory will tell you what generally motivates them in their life. However, you must also know what motivates them in this specific script – their dramatic need/outer motivation/goal in your story. Without this an audience cannot make sense of a character's actions – neither can you.

Motivation in a screenplay is usually defined in terms of 'character-in-action', i.e. we're not interested in characters who tell us what's driving them, we need to see it embodied and enacted.

Hence it is crucial that your protagonist (and your other major characters) have a clear, specific need or goal. They must want to do or need to accomplish something by the end of your script, and their reasons for doing it must be clear, evident and *visual*. This is your character's motivation. It is the driving force of your screenplay, forms the focus of your story and ties it all together. Motivation is what makes it dramatic: the character in conflict and *why* that character will seek conflict.

A character's motivation exists on two levels:

- Outer motivation: their path to their goal, what the story is about and what ultimately determines your plot. It is *visible*, revealed through action and clearly conveys what visibly represents success for the protagonist.
- Inner motivation: *why* your character is pursuing their path to their goal. This determines your character growth and theme. It is *invisible*, hidden and revealed through dialogue and subtext.

For all screen drama, outer motivation or goal is essential. It is the foundation of your entire script. If there's nothing that needs to be accomplished by the end of the script, where's the story? A character's motivation develops over the course of a screenplay's structure in what is called the *motivational through-line*, examined in Chapter 10. Exploring inner motivation, however, is optional, though no less important; even though you may never reveal it overtly on screen, you must be aware of it. Know your character!

Often new screenwriters will employ inner motivation for their dramatic need but dramatic need is the same thing as outer motivation. Consequently, many scripts appear with characters whose goal in the script is to 'become a better human being', 'find themselves', 'rediscover love', etc. But these motivations are not visible, concrete or strong enough to work successfully as a dramatic need – they are internal needs. Internal needs, therefore, often form the basis of a film's theme.

So ask yourself:

- What does my character want or desire?
- Why? both the reasons they know and the subconscious reasons.
- What are they willing to do to get what they want?
- How does this change over the course of the story?
- What could they lose (what's at stake?) if they fail to achieve their goal, fail in their quest or task? If the answer is 'not much', where's the story and the reason for watching? Failure is the basis of tragedy.

For example, at the start of *Glengarry Glen Ross*, the characters are set a challenge. The most successful deal-closer wins a Cadillac Eldorado, the next gets an expensive set of cutlery, the worst gets... the sack. (Note the magical three combination – see page 201).

Knowing your characters (a) have a strong enough need/goal (external motivation) to drive them through your script story and up against powerful, sometimes life-threatening conflict, and (b) that they fear the alternative enough (i.e. not fulfilling their need or achieving their goal) to throw themselves into this conflict and confrontation can only help you reach a deeper understanding of your character. If you can't answer these questions above, go back and rethink your story.

Some important principles apply to character goals within a screenplay:

• The protagonist and antagonist must have the same goal or two aspects of the same goal (e.g. in *Witness*, Paul Schaeffer wants to kill John Book; Book wants to survive). Although ideally your story should avoid having two separate distinct goals, normally this can't be avoided because the main plot goal, which tends to be action based, will not be the same as the main subplot goal, which tends to be relationship based. However, your main plot should stand out and be distinct.

In *Witness*, the main subplot goal is to get the woman (or man) to form a relationship. This is different to John Book overcoming Paul Schaeffer. To leave these two goals distinct and separate would reduce the impact of the story's end, so ways are found to integrate the two, to unify them into one goal. This is usually done by making one of the goals a necessary stepping stone to achieving the other goal.

*Witness* unifies them imaginatively, not just in terms of action but also of theme. John Book is fast defeating his three opponents at the end of the film, but then he must give up his gun and risk his own life to save Rachel. He must go through this self-sacrifice stage (his penultimate beat of growth) in order to reach the final stage. This self-sacrifice enables him to call on the power of the community – rather than the power of the individual – to witness Schaeffer's actions and so take away his power, despite the fact that Schaeffer has the gun. Book has discovered the true power in the world we are watching, with both main plot and main subplot goals unified and fully integrated.

One of the things that makes 'buddy' movies or road movies interesting for us to watch is seeing two mismatched characters forced together and forced to share the same goals (*Training Day, Thelma And Louise, Lethal Weapon,* and even *Fight Club*), but for the most part I would urge you to consider these:

• The goal cannot be shared or divided; there can only be one winner.

- The goal must be strong enough (in the context of the script) to generate the need, and the need must be generated by an equally strong motive; so, the audience must believe that your character really needs this particular goal badly enough to willingly endure whatever conflict lies ahead in their path.
- The protagonist's need (for the goal) must be as strong as the antagonist's need (to prevent them from achieving the goal) so that both are eventually and inevitably forced into conflict with each other.
- A character's strength is gauged by the strength or magnitude of the obstacle(s) they confront. (That is, the magnitude, difficulty or counter-intention must equal the strength of the dramatic need, goal or intention at that point in the screenplay.)

Although the above five principles appear fairly logical and straightforward, it is surprising how rarely writers (beginners and professionals) pay attention to them. Ignore them or try to change them and your script will encounter difficulties.

# Conflict and character

So, the most important component of a screenplay is character, and the most important aspect of character is motivation. However, character and motivation cannot be understood in isolation. You need the third part of the equation: to understand the relationship these have with conflict.

A character has to be *motivated* to meet a particular *conflict*. Go to a dictionary: how does it define conflict?

- a sharp disagreement or clash (e.g. between divergent ideas, interests or people)
- (distress caused by) mental struggle resulting from incompatible impulses
- a hostile encounter (e.g. a fight, battle or war)
- to be in opposition (to another or each other); to disagree.

They say conflict is the essence of drama; certainly, in real life, it is the one thing we all try to avoid. As a screenwriter, you cannot avoid conflict. For you, conflict must be the thing which you seek out, rush to meet head-on, and when you find it, draw it out, shape it, texture it, deepen it. You cannot run away from it. You cannot write a screenplay without it.

Your character may have a goal or outer motivation and even inner motivation, but if there is no conflict there is no drama.

Being confronted by obstacles and problems, and the different ways your character reacts to and tackles them, is how we see the protagonist develop. Hence:

> Conflict Arises When A
>
> Need/Intention/Goal (Outer Motivation)
>
> Meets An Obstacle

## Types of conflict

How many types of conflict do you think there are? Two?

- Outer conflict: whatever stands in the way of a character achieving their outer goal/s
- Inner conflict: whatever prevents the character from achieving inner development and self-worth (or what they *perceive* as such) when pursuing their goal/s and the chosen path to it/them

Wrong. The screenwriter has a choice of three:

- individual against individual (outer): personal conflict with other characters, their different goal/s or counter-intentions
- individual against environment (outer): conflict with the forces of nature (disaster movies: *Twister, Airport, Armageddon, Towering Inferno*); society (*Witness, The Truman Show, V For Vendetta*); the group or system (bureaucracy, the government, the family, etc.) (*An Officer And A Gentleman, Gattaca, My Big Fat Greek Wedding, The Family Stone*); values (*Witness*) or sometimes the supernatural, cosmic or invisible forces (God, the devil, time e.g. *Ghostbusters, The Exorcist, Independence Day, Back To The Future, Groundhog Day, The Others, Clockstoppers, The Orphanage*)
- individual against self (inner): conflict within the character from something they have not acknowledged, confronted or overcome; perhaps they are unsure of themselves, their actions or goal/s (*A Beautiful Mind* powerfully illustrates this).

## Principles of conflict

In screenwriting, a number of very important principles apply:

- Outer conflicts must be personalized as relationships between characters (hence the importance of your cast design)

- Interior conflicts must be externalized in physical manifestations or personal conflicts, or by letting the audience imagine the turmoil (but this relies on clues and information you have carefully set-up earlier in the script)

Michael Hauge noted that the hero's inner conflict is embodied by the antagonist or opposition character, is pointed out by the mirror, and the romance is the reward for overcoming it; hence the protagonist achieves character growth.

As a writer, you will usually begin by working on your outer conflicts. If you have a solid and clearly defined outer conflicts structure to hang things on, then you can move on to your inner conflicts, and they will become all the more believable. Bear in mind, too, that the sooner you introduce conflict into your screenplay, the stronger your story will become.

---

- Consider scenes in your favourite films/TV dramas.
- Analyse those scenes and actions in terms of these principles of conflict and goals.
- Think also of some of the bad films/TV you have seen and analyse those also.

---

## Obstacles

The obstacles which your protagonist must face can take a number of forms:

- physical: e.g. the *Indiana Jones* and *Batman* canons, and including obstacles of nature (*The Mosquito Coast, Earthquake, City Slickers, The Beach, Lord Of The Flies, White Squall, The Perfect Storm, Cliffhanger, Twister*), environment (*City Of Joy, Panic Room, Die Hard*) and distance (*Sleepless In Seattle, Saving Pvt. Ryan*)
- other characters: e.g. *Indiana Jones, Batman, Heat, City Slickers, Thelma And Louise, Seven, Dead Ringers, Hamlet, Die Hard, Spider-Man, Election, Titanic, Saving Pvt. Ryan, The Skulls, The Dark Knight*
- mental: e.g. *Field Of Dreams* (Ray's image of his father), *When Harry Met Sally* (their mutual belief that friends can't or shouldn't become lovers), *Birdy, Hamlet, Cliffhanger, Good Will Hunting, A Beautiful Mind, Mr. Brooks*
- cultural: e.g. *City Slickers, Ghandi, Malcolm X, Priest, Rob Roy* and *Braveheart* (the system as embodied in their English adversaries), *Pleasantville, Titanic, The Skulls, The*

*Crying Game, Singin' In The Rain* (the introduction of the talkies)
- supernatural: e.g. *Ghost, Halloween, Dracula, The Shining, Flatliners, Independence Day, The Sixth Sense, The Exorcist, The Blair Witch Project, The Others*
- time (a time-lock or limit within which a certain task must be completed): e.g. *48 Hours, Scent Of A Woman, High Noon, Apollo 13, 13 Days, 24* (the TV series), *Minority Report, Don Juan De Marco, Don't Say A Word, Around The World In Eighty Days, Seven, Nick Of Time, Flight Plan*, and of course the nature of time itself (*Groundhog Day, Back To The Future, The Time Machine, Clockstoppers, Deja Vu*).

Ultimately, of course, the most powerful or effective obstacle is the counter-intention: someone wants to stop you getting what you want. Their intention and your intention inevitably clash and out of this clash comes conflict.

> Watch a favourite film and try to fill in the Character Motivation Grid (Figure 6.1) like the one below:

|  | Goal/Outer Motivation | Outer Conflict | Inner Motivation | Inner Conflict |
|---|---|---|---|---|
| Hero/ine |  |  |  |  |
| Opposition |  |  |  |  |
| Mirror |  |  |  |  |
| Romance |  |  |  |  |

**figure 6.1** character motivation grid

> Now draw up a similar grid for your own story's characters.

We will return to character motivation in Chapter 10.

# Developing conflict

In the overall development of your screenplay, it is important that each conflict met, each obstacle faced, is greater than the one before it. Consequently, the degree of courage it takes to confront and defeat it is stronger each time: there has to be something that frightens the protagonist, be it a physical threat (harm or loss of some possession) or an emotional one (loss of face, embarrassment). Each time the stakes must be raised higher, with more at risk (Chapter 10 – Raising the Stakes). *Toy Story* has many good examples of this, even within the same scene.

This leads us to two important principles:

- each obstacle should be *different* from the previous one (e.g. physical, emotional, psychological, etc.)
- each obstacle or counter-intention must be *stronger or more difficult* than the previous one (hence the set-back or failure will be progressively stronger and the recovery require appropriately more courage).

This kind of conflict development (i.e. minimal) would be predictable and boring for your audience:

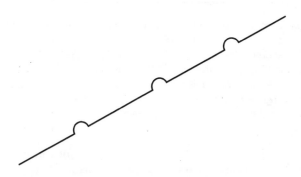

**figure 6.2** increasing the difficulty of the obstacles

So, in order to extract the maximum dramatic effect from each conflict, you need both conflict (which leads to a climax) and a set-back. In the course of a feature script there will be at least three major set-backs:

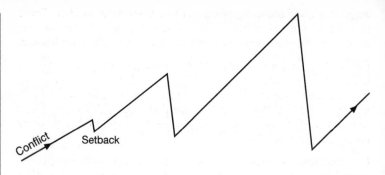

Conflict    Setback

**figure 6.3** crucial setbacks

Notice the scale of the setbacks on the chart.

Also a climax does not necessarily mean a physical action climax, it can be an emotional climax (*Field Of Dreams, The Truman Show, Sleepless In Seattle* and many European films – *Amélie, Life Is Beautiful, Cinema Paradiso*).

---

Now try to draw a graph of your conflict, obstacles and setbacks over the development of your screenplay.

Ask yourself these questions:

- What obstacles get in the way of my protagonist? Remember these can be physical obstacles (other characters/ environment), internal obstacles or supernatural, cultural and other obstacles.
- Why do they get in the way of the protagonist?
- What are these obstacles willing to do to stop my protagonist achieving their goal(s)?
- Is the obstacle greater than the preceding one? How? Why?

---

Hence we return to conflict and character motivation – the motivation of those opposing your protagonist.

## Final comments

As a screenwriter, your essential task – and most difficult challenge – is to create an emotional reality on the page. The key to this is character and motivation.

How often have you sat watching something wondering what the heck the characters are doing and why? As an audience, we always need to know that there's a good reason for a character's actions, a good enough reason to drive them into conflict. There is always something heroic in a character who 'takes on the odds', always something that touches us ... providing we believe.

Emotional realism comes from having strong motivating incidents and personality traits that force the character (reluctantly) into conflict and danger, causing the audience to *identify* with the character *because* they are in danger; a scene with no conflict means there is little or no emotional content or room for identification.

For example, *Tootsie* is emotionally realistic not because it resembles reality but because we are made to believe that Michael would put himself through this ordeal because of his internal emotional needs (inner motivation). At certain points in *Field Of Dreams*, the protagonist Ray steps back in time. Clearly this is actually impossible, but the emotional sweep of the movie has carried us along and to a point where we believe, at that moment, something like this *could* happen. It's all about audience believability – in your characters and their story. (Note: the genre of this movie is called Magic Realism.)

To create emotional realism in a scene and in your screenplay, you must build believable characters that experience conflict, and do so in a way that is economical and dramatically succinct. That means:

> ### Show What Is Absolutely Necessary – And No More!

To show more will dull the edge of the conflict and thus dull the emotional realism you are trying to create. The other essential ingredient here is that the audience most engage totally with the plight and problem/s of the character – hence the importance of identification.

Here is a flowchart you can use, not just in the planning of your screenplay, but whenever you come to write any dramatic scene.

> Now, before you proceed to Chapter 07, where we take a look at screenplay structure, I want you to re-watch *Witness*.
>
> After you've done that, watch any (but preferably all) of these films: *A Beautiful Mind*, *American Beauty*, *Billy Elliot*, *Fight Club*, *Good Will Hunting*, *Maverick*, *Minority Report*, *Monsters, Inc.*, *Shrek* and *The Talented Mr. Ripley*.
>
> View each one in a single sitting, critically, but without making any notes. And don't say 'but I've already seen that one'; make the effort – they all repay another viewing.

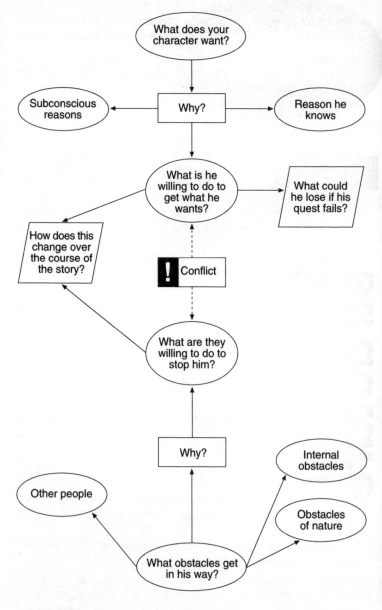

**figure 6.4** character motivation flowchart
source: *Jurgen Wolff*

# 07

## structure

**In this chapter you will learn:**
- about the classic three-Act
  linear structure of most
  screenplays and the various
  marker-points that root your
  story to an architectural
  whole: the hook, the inciting
  incident, the different turning
  points and focus point
  scenes, the point-of-no-
  return and final climax – the
  blueprint that should make it
  all work.

# The classic three-Act linear structure

What's the trick? A good story that catches your attention, good characters that are believable. If those two criteria are correct you're in the top half per cent of screenplays. Then there's good structure.

*Tim Bevan,*
Working Title Films

When you look at a script, you instinctively know where everything is supposed to fall. With a feature script, if your first Act is under 20 pages you know there's going to be a problem. That's why you keep going back to structure. Because nothing else really works, no matter how avant garde your script is, it still has to be in that structure. And when you're reading a large number of scripts, that's one of the first things you look for.

[A Script Reader]

Having decided on your idea, thought through your story concept and worked on your characters, the next step is to look at the overarching dramatic structure of your story development and script. (Remember, character work and plot structure are symbiotic; they feed and drive, complement and illuminate each other.)

A screenplay – and the course of this book – is a series of breakdowns, moving from the general to the specific. The first breakdown creates Acts I, II and III; the next breakdown gives us the beginning, middle and the end of each Act; we can then break down each of those sections into sequences, then scenes, and finally action and dialogue. But in order to create a screenplay in the first place, it is essential to know *how it* breaks down. If this feels like writing-by-numbers, it is – to an extent. But it is also the way screenplays are structured. Why do you think this is so?

There are two classic types of poorly written scripts: understructured (writing exactly how it happens in real life; such scripts are boring – rather like real life) and overstructured (all style: over-complex plotting, many special effects, etc. but no story or thematic content). You are dealing with events that are dramatic, looking for the dramatic moments that will move your story on, building and structuring an emotional experience for your audience and culminating in a climax.

A screenplay is a blueprint for the finished film, it points the way. Most importantly, it lays out a structure, a spine you can hang your visions and dialogue on. A screenwriter's job is to lay out the blueprint.

*Howard Schuman,*
screenwriter: *Rock Follies, Selling Hitler*

Screenwriting structural guidelines have been developed and refined since cinema's early days and were first codified by Syd Field. When looking at the most widely used three-act linear template, it seems presumptuous to say most films follow this pattern, but nearly 90 per cent (especially mainstream Hollywood ones) do to a greater extent. As an experiment, pick a film at random showing on television or from the video store and watch it with the chart on page 114. Does it work?

---

**Important note:**

You should not regard structure as rigid rules set in stone that *must* be followed at all costs. It's an abstract ideal and more about logicality and our eternal need for good, well-structured storytelling: a compelling tale, compellingly told.

---

Perhaps the most important thing to bear in mind about good structure is: you should eventually be able to get to a point where, when writing, you don't consciously think about it. Structure should be innate in your storytelling and eventually second nature to you when writing.

It's a mistake to get hung up on numbers. Writing a script is not a joining-the-dots operation or getting the numbers right. Allow the story to dictate its own requirements. The 'numbers' you get on many courses or in various books should be used to develop your storytelling instincts, to validate your guesses and intuitions, and then forget them. Learn them, then throw them away.

*David Webb Peoples,*
screenwriter: *Unforgiven,*
*Twelve Monkeys, Blade Runner*

Let's recap:

- A television play (of 60 minutes) can be divided by the commercial breaks, usually into three parts/acts.

- Half-hour dramas and sitcoms are divided into two acts (Chapter 08).
- In a feature film, the act divisions are not marked by a break in the action, but they can be seen when the film is analysed. (When a movie is shown on TV, the ad breaks tend to occur at the end of Act I, the half-way point and the end of Act II).

Remember the proportions:

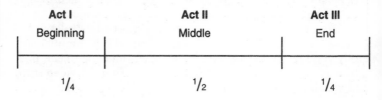

**figure 7.1** act divisions

Thus in your two-hour film (120 minutes) the divisions will be: 30 minutes/60 minutes/30 minutes.

Stick to the accepted rule (Chapter 02) with feature script playing time: one page of script equals one minute of screen time. Hence your feature screenplay should be *no longer than 120 pages* (maximum), your Act division being approximately 30 pages/60 pages/30 pages.

There is no law setting in stone this ¼–½–¼ delineation. Indeed, you may well find variations such as a 90 minute/90 page feature (dividing into 20/60/10 minutes), but we'll be sticking to the 120-page model.

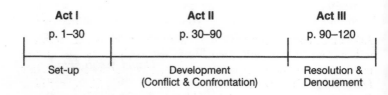

**figure 7.2** act content

When reading this chapter, refer to the template on page 114. Although following this grid is not a guaranteed formula for success (there *are* no guaranteed formulae for success), it will at least help you organize the telling of your story so that your audience grasp more clearly what you are trying to say.

# What goes into each act?

> Now, before you proceed any further, I want you to view another
> batch of films. First, re-watch *Witness*. Next, watch again those
> movies I asked you to watch at the end of Chapter 6: *My Big Fat
> Greek Wedding*, *The Truman Show*, *Erin Brockovich*, *Spider-Man*,
> *Field Of Dreams* and *Cruel Intentions*. Again, view each one in a
> single sitting, critically, but without making any notes.

To restate: in your screenplay, you are working towards one
eventual goal – your final climactic scene in Act III (not
necessarily your last scene). Every piece of description, every
image, line of dialogue, detail of characterization, every obstacle
met, every set-back, and every conflict resolved, should be
pushing towards that final climax to achieve maximum
emotional effect.

Note: The 'writing backwards' strategy you apply to your entire
screenplay also applies to each Act. Before creating one, you
need to know your ending (climax) of that Act; then you can
start working backwards, making sure everything works
towards that ending.

## 1.1 Act I (overview)

> I read so many screenplays that were boring and poorly
> written I could tell within the first ten pages whether the
> script was set up correctly. I gave the writer 30 pages to set
> up a story: if it wasn't done by then I reached for the next
> script.
>
> *Syd Field*

Act I gives your audience all the ingredients from which the story
will be made: the main characters, the setting (the social and
psychological/environmental 'norms'); tone (gritty-realistic like
*Heat, Road To Perdition, Billy Elliot, Fight Club, Gangs Of New
York, Insomnia*; mythical like *The Legend Of Bagger Vance,
Field Of Dreams, The Rookie*; elegaic like *American Beauty,
Hearts In Atlantis*; anecdotal as with *Waiting To Exhale, Don
Juan De Marco*; fantastical/bizarre/surreal like *Pleasantville,
Being John Malkovich*; fairytale as with *Shrek, Edward
Scissorhands, The Lord Of The Rings*; quirky like *Amélie*, etc.);
also the problems; tension; love interest; the timescale (real or
dramatized) and any time-locks (something that needs

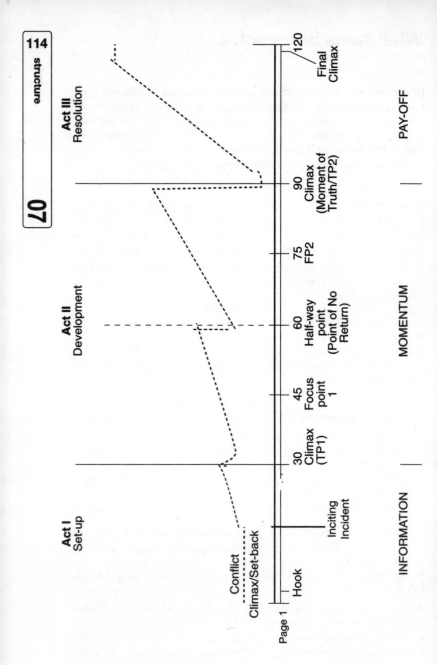

**figure 7.3** the three-Act linear structure

accomplishing within a set deadline – e.g. *High Noon*). *No important elements should be introduced later than Act I* (and most definitely by the opening pages of Act II).

In that short space of 30 pages (Act I), a number of things have been established. Let's examine them in blocks of ten pages:

## 1.2 The first ten pages

> The beginning should set up the 'heartbeat' of your script.
> *Alan Plater*, writer

*Your first ten pages are critical.* All Readers tell you if your script hasn't grabbed them in the first ten pages (some now say five), they probably won't continue with the rest of it. If those pages are predictable they'll assume (rightly or wrongly) the last 100+ will be predictable too. People have a habit of jumping to conclusions: after reading just the first 5–10 pages the Reader will say to themselves 'this is a good script' or 'this is a bad script'. If they read it with a positive attitude, it is more likely their final coverage and recommendation will also be positive. So your first ten pages need to demonstrate your skills. They need to be unique, exciting (or, for a comedy, funny) and, above all, grab the Reader's interest and make them want to read on to the end.

> What's curious about a good screenplay is you can often identify it within the first few pages. One of the key things an opening scene does is present the hero. Having an opening scene that grabs the audience, not necessarily by the throat, it could be a very subtle way; but it has to be something I feel is unusual, something I haven't seen before. But then don't give everything away in the first five minutes. Make me want to turn the page.
> *Norma Heyman,*
> producer: *Dangerous Liaisons, The Honorary Consul, Carrington, Gangster No. 1*

In the space of ten pages you have to *set up your scenario*. Establish:

- who your main characters are, and especially who your protagonist is (i.e. the star)
- what your story is going to be about
- the dramatic circumstances surrounding your story
- the genre you are working with.

Hence you need to show your protagonist in a setting that is normal and natural for them, i.e. before the changes that are about to happen to them in the story occur. (In TV scripts it is even tighter: the first 2–3 minutes are crucial, hence it is your first *five* pages which are make-or-break.)

## 1.3 Openings

The first thing a Reader looks for in a script is a *hook* – that something which grabs the audience's attention, draws them into the story and makes them want to watch or read. Ideally, it needs to be in by page three, certainly by page five.

Powerful confrontation between two strongly contrasting characters will always hook your audience. In William Goldman's script for *Maverick*, we first see Bret Maverick on horseback, his hands tied behind his back, and a noose around his neck which is attached to a tree bough. The horse is moving slowly forward; Bret is going to hang... very slowly. Then the baddies throw a sack at the horse's feet, from which emerges a snake. The horse, further frightened, moves forward, more agitated. Tension – this time he really is going to hang. But we know he doesn't because Bret is narrating (v.o.). His first line is a gag: 'It had been a shitty week for me. It had all started when...'. We know we are about to follow his (the protagonist's) journey. So how does he escape? We aren't told that until much later in the script, but at least we are intrigued enough to follow and see how he did it. We're hooked!

A hook doesn't have to have a knock-you-over-the-head impact (like the daring daylight heist of *Heat*, the gun in Jack's mouth in *Fight Club*, the unexpected car smash of *Erin Brockovich*, or the violent explosion in *Star Wars, Episode II: Attack Of The Clones*). It can be subtle, like an arresting visual (the reverse-developing photograph of *Memento*) or dialogue-driven ('If I could just go back...' of *The Talented Mr. Ripley*; 'Who am I?...' of *Spider-Man*) or arouse our curiosity (the focus on the leather-bound journal in *Cruel Intentions*, the mathematical puzzle solved by a young janitor *Good Will Hunting*). It can be seductive (the cars arriving at *Gosford Park*, drawing us in, arousing anticipation) or intriguing (the light suddenly falling from the sky in *The Truman Show*, the talented pianist Tom Ripley who actually works as a mensroom attendant) or mysterious (the opening 'Murder' montage of *Minority Report*, the body floating in the sea in *The Bourne Identity*, the children's voices calling from afar in *Signs*). It can be sinister (drops of blood turning into nouvelle cuisine in *American Psycho*) or quirky (*Shrek, Amélie, Monsters, Inc.*) and funny (*My Big Fat Greek Wedding*).

Hitchcock's opening for *Strangers On A Train* is a marvellous example of hooks at work: first, the ear-splitting whistle of the train, followed by a tracking shot of the walking feet in strange, two-tone shoes – who is the man? Where is he going? – and by the time we see his entire body for the first time, we are hooked. And for some men of a certain age, the most memorable hook of all time was the opening credits scene of *Barbarella*.

A useful hook device is to have ordinary people doing unordinary things, or unordinary people doing very ordinary things, or pose some question, or have something which holds the promise of more to come.

For the writer, finding the actual opening to your screenplay (the *point of entry*) is often difficult. Most openings are character rather than plot based. Often, a point of entry will see your protagonist at some kind of life-crisis point, a dilemma or decision to face about their life, direction or future: Peter Parker, a parentless wimp going through teenage changes, can't get the girl (*Spider-Man*); Erin Brockovich, struggling to keep self and family together, suffers yet more set-backs; John Nash, a fish-out-of-water in his new college environment (*A Beautiful Mind*); Pastor Graham wrestling with single parenthood and a loss of faith since the death of his wife (*Signs*); frumpy Toula seemingly left on the shelf *(My Big Fat Greek Wedding)*.

One of the deciding factors on where to open may well be revealed when working on your character biographies and, in particular, their backstories. Whatever you decide, you open the screenplay at the *last possible moment*, usually before the dropping in of some vital piece of information we need to know.

Lastly, a tip: if you have a number of characters you need to establish very quickly, a handy device is to have a newcomer join the team and need to be introduced to them, just as Danny Witwer is at the start of *Minority Report*.

## 1.4 The key line

Also somewhere between pages three and five you will need to pose the question you the writer are asking in your script, the issue (personal or universal) you are attempting to confront, explore and resolve within yourself – that is to say what the script is really about and the reason you need to write this script. It's to do with your theme. The issue is addressed in the *key line*: it is spoken by a character and gives the audience clues as to what idea will be explored in your script. For example:

'I was part of something. I belonged...'  (*Goodfellas*)

'You should be proud to be Greek'
(*My Big Fat Greek Wedding*)

'Without scream, we have no power'  (*Monsters, Inc.*)

'Support yourself. Don't look at me, look ahead.'  (*Billy Elliot*)

'You've got history to burn'  (*Sunshine State*)

'Thinking of flying today?'  (said by the radio dj in *The Truman Show*)

'You be careful out there among the English'  (*Witness*)

The line from *Witness* evokes the fundamental truth of the film: there are boundary lines between worlds and to step across them is dangerous.

Sometimes the key line is repeated towards the close of the film (sometimes word-for-word), but slightly changed in its meaning (as in *Witness*) – can you explain just how it has changed, and why?

It is not essential to have a key line (but it helps) and it does not have to be set-up on or even near page three but it helps your audience to understand the context of your story or to have something by which to measure the standards of the world of your story.

---

Watch the openings of *Spider-Man, Erin Brockovich* and *Chinatown*. What do you think are their key lines? (Answers: Taking it further)

---

## Teasers

Sometimes you will find a prologue (or *teaser* scene) situated pre-credits before your Act I starts. Again this is a hook to grab the audience and/or set the scene (*Pulp Fiction, The Piano, Heavenly Creatures*). It happens a lot in TV drama and sitcoms (*Cheers, The X-Files*). In *Hill Street Blues*, the pre-credit sequence would not only hook and set the scene, it established the different storylines to be followed in that episode. In other TV dramas it may take the form of an 'in last week's episode' montage. Sometimes the teaser is run behind the opening credits (*Friends*, *The Sopranos*, *Seinfeld*, *Family Guy*, *Mad Men*, *The Wonder Years*). The teaser is a useful device to quickly establish the premise your story action will be based on.

The pre-credit sequence of vox-pop interviews in *The Truman Show* neatly introduces us to the cast of players we are about to see and establishes the all-pervasive presence of Christof. The video interview that opens *American Beauty* ('Want me to kill him for you?') is an excellent example of the teaser as hook. There are further hooks during the credits: the voice-over 'in less than a year I'll be dead' – a clever echo or nod to the opening of *Sunset Boulevard*; and visually (Lester in the shower).

At the other end of the dramatic spectrum, the teaser sequence in *George Of The Jungle* not only fills in George's complete backstory, it also established the important role of the voice-over Narrator as a character in his own right.

## Repeated images

Somewhere in the first half of Act I, it helps if you can establish a strong visual image of something that will be repeated (echoed) near the end of your completed script. It doesn't have to be brilliantly memorable, your audience only needs to register it subliminally (in *Witness* it is the image of the Amish community emerging over the brow of a hill). When that image is repeated (usually slightly changed) towards the end, it subconsciously indicates to your audience that we are nearing the end of the story. These two images act like bookends.

---

Watch the first 15 minutes of *Witness*. Note its creation of mood, the introduction of the characters (particularly the protagonist), shifts of location (rural to big city), the murder. Ask yourself: how were these various effects created; what does choice of location add to each scene (general information, dramatic value, etc.)? Do you think the murder occurs (at 13 minutes) too late, too soon or just right? What about the introduction of John Book (15 minutes) – too late? Should he have entered any earlier?

Now do the same for *My Big Fat Greek Wedding*, *The Truman Show*, *Erin Brockovich*, *Spider-Man*, *Field Of Dreams* and *Cruel Intentions*. What do they tell you about the nature of the film you are about to see, the characters, settings, genre? Do you agree with some of the decisions the writers made? What were the hook devices used, how were they used and were they effective? Notice the entry point in the story and any life-crisis situation of the protagonist. Did you notice any key lines? (You should already know some of them!)

## 1.5 Act I: pages 10–30 (overview)

In the remaining 20 pages (20 minutes) of Act I, you need to do a number of other things:

- Environment: fill out the background details to the world your protagonist lives in.
- Beliefs: illustrate by action your protagonist's code of conduct, their value-system.
- Subplots: set them up.

Moreover, usually about half-way through this section (i.e. two thirds into Act I and 20 per cent into the overall screenplay) you should have the first major event of your main plot, the *inciting incident*: a scene, incident or line of dialogue in which something happens or a problem is posed to make your protagonist make a decision and pursue the course of action they will follow for the rest of your script. This causes a crisis which leads to your first climax at the end of Act I. Now let's examine things in more depth.

## 1.6 Pages 10–15: character-in-action

Between pages 10 and 15 either the arena, theme or direction of the film should be evident, preferably all of them. The audience need some kind of landmark to pull them through the movie, refine their focus on what to look for and where they are headed. If they don't get that they'll get bored or lost.

> *Steven E. De Souza,*
> screenwriter: *Die Hard I & II,*
> *48 Hours, Beverly Hills Cop III,*
> *The Flintstones, Judge Dredd*

This section of the script usually focuses on the main characters-in-action (especially your protagonist). This deepens their characterization by showing their character problem: a mixture of their attitude and personality interacting with a specific situation you have designed for them. For example, in *Witness*, John Book is portrayed as insensitive, ambitious and a user of people. Yet he must work with a woman and child (Rachel and Samuel) whose world and value-system are the complete opposite.

Moreover, this section also acts as a benchmark by which the audience can measure the character growth (how your protagonist and main characters change through Acts II and III, and at the end). In *Witness* the three drive through the streets, being forced to identify possible murderers. Hence in this section you should try to stay focused on your protagonist in all or most of the scenes.

Remember, you illustrate by action, so your protagonist has to be active – this means making decisions. Keep them active and you will keep your audience engaged. And don't forget to start establishing your major subplot, and any others you feel crucial to your story's development (for example, Book and Rachel meet sixteen minutes into the film).

## 1.7 Pages 15–30: inciting incident

By page 15 your character should have been fairly well established; you've got most of the essential character information out of the way and established a benchmark. So as we move on we are entering that section of the script that will lead us up to the inciting incident and eventually to your Act I climax (Turning Point 1).

In *Witness* Samuel views the identity parades and then identifies the murderer McFee from a photograph, leading automatically to the meeting between Book and his boss Schaeffer, and then to the underground garage shooting attempt by McFee.

Pages 15–25 of a script are often made dramatic by introducing an element of risk to the main character/s. In *Witness* the risk enters when we learn that the murderer is a fellow cop, thus meaning real danger for Book, Rachel and Samuel.

At the risk of seeming too proscriptive – but, these days, Readers are increasingly so – at about page 18 (if not smack-bang on it), you will have your Inciting Incident (also known as a catalyst or plot point).

The inciting incident is a moment or a scene that confronts the protagonist with a problem, it creates a crisis. This crisis forces your protagonist into a decision or choice which then causes a change in that character or story (ultimately leading to a climax at the end of Act I, your first turning point).

At the opening of your script, life is seen pretty much as normal and in balance. The inciting incident comes along and upsets that balance; it creates the 'problem' that your protagonist must resolve or restore over the course of your screenplay. The protagonist must be aware of it (although unaware of the effect it will have on him/her), and react to it (even refusing to react is a reaction). The inciting incident gives your protagonist the general need and desire to restore that balance, thereby creating the (general) goal or outer motivation to aim for; these attempts form the spine of your story and the inciting incident sets them all in motion.

For example, in *Minority Report*, it's the moment Agatha the precog lunges from the pool and John Anderton sees the projected premonition; it's when Billy Elliot tries ballet for the first time; when Shrek discovers the community of toys encamped on his swamp; when Will meets Skylar for the first time, in the bar (*Good Will Hunting*). It's the first appearance of Tyler Durden in *Fight Club*; John Nash in the bar, reaching his 'eureka' moment about Governing Dynamics, his one original idea (*A Beautiful Mind*); when, momentarily, Randall becomes Scare Leader and Sulley's supremacy is threatened in *Monsters, Inc.*; and in *The Talented Mr. Ripley* it's the moment the jazz albums are dropped on the floor and Dickie decides Tom should not return to New York but stay in Italy – from hereon the conspiracy starts.

When creating your inciting incident, ask yourself:

– What's the worst thing (apart from death) that could happen to my protagonist, which could turn out to be the best thing?

– What's the best possible thing that could happen to my protagonist that could turn out to be the worst?

– Does it upset the balance of forces in the protagonist's life I have already established?

– Does it indicate or set-up the incident and images for my Act III climax scene?

Note: If any time-lock is going to be set, it might just be established at the inciting incident. Equally, it might be set later, often at the first turning point at the end of Act I. In *Monsters, Inc.* Mike is given thirty minutes to fix things before the door closes, and that one occurs just before the half-way point. To repeat, these 'rules' are not to be taken as rigid doctrine but as guidelines to be manipulated and applied to the demands and designs of your own individual story. Have you noticed any time-locks in the films you've watched for this chapter – remember, not every film has one (or needs one).

## 1.8 The role of turning points

As your story pushes relentlessly forward, your protagonist energized by the problem or challenge set out by the inciting incident, things are heading inexorably towards a climax at the end of your first Act.

Now, although your inciting incident is very clearly a turning point (for your characters and story), in the overall scheme of your screenplay it is still considered a minor one – albeit a very important and essential one.

For the architecture of your entire story you will have two major turning points: at the end of Act I and at the end of Act II (the *moment of truth*). You will also have several smaller turning points in your script, but these turning points, TP1 and TP2, are fixed. Look at it like this: the structure you create for your story is like a bridge spanning a river; the two turning points are the two main supports that prevent the bridge from collapsing – that's how crucial they are to your screenplay.

A turning point in a screenplay performs a number of functions:

- it *grabs* the story, turns it around and *catapults* it in a new direction by setting up a problem that you protagonist must resolve over the course of the screenplay
- it *pushes* the story forward towards the Act climax (which will then push it into the next Act)
- it *raises the stakes* of the story (increasing risk, danger, level of commitment, etc.)
- it *increases momentum* by raising the stakes, by pushing the story into a new and 'dangerous' direction, by making the achievement of the dramatic need, goal or intention more uncertain. Note: 'dangerous' is relative to *your* screen story.
- it is a crisis point that generates in the audience a 'what are we going to do now?' feeling
- it dramatically *alters* your protagonist's *motivation* (TP1 creates the dramatic need, goal or outer motivation).

Turning points always happen to your protagonist, are character-related, and caused by their actions (remember: decision is action). Inevitably your protagonist will react to that turning point in some way: they will formulate a goal and an intent to act as a result.

TP1 often occurs at a time when the story seems to be over because of the apparent success of the protagonist. In *Witness*, John Book has successfully found out who the murderer is, has a witness, and has told his boss Schaeffer. Feeling very self-satisfied, he makes his way home. The story is apparently over because Book has 'won'. At this precise moment the crisis (TP1) occurs. Suddenly the story is catapulted into a new, different, more dangerous direction.

Lastly, your crisis leads directly to your first climax, at the end of Act I (which creates the momentum to kick your story into the next Act). The climax is the strongest and highest dramatic moment in your first act.

## 1.9 Pages 28–30: Act I climax/first turning point (TP1) and transition into Act II

A climax occurs when a crisis or problem is resolved one way or another. Following the inciting incident, we now see your protagonist (and main characters) reacting and responding to it. Because it has transformed your protagonist's original motivation, their original goal has altered or been forced to alter. Consciously or not they will be compelled to formulate a solution, a new (generalized) goal and a line of action they believe will lead them to that goal. Remember, this is their external motivation – what your character must get or win by the end of the story – the thing that drives them through the script. The formulation of this goal and the specific line of action chosen must be strong and visible to the audience (through not necessarily apparent to the protagonist), and demonstrated by visual action. This climax/reaction creates the energy to finally push us into Act II.

In *Witness*, Book bursts into his sister's house, dishevelled and afraid. He is taking Rachel and Samuel with him to escape the threat from McFee and Schaeffer. This climactic action reveals his decision (i.e. his reaction to TP1). The sense of urgency allows the audience to measure the enormity of the danger he feels they are all in. The bleeding wounds engender audience sympathy, allowing us to forgive him if we might have felt his reaction was somewhat exaggerated.

TP1 in *Minority Report* is the 'Goodbye Crow' projection where the murderer is revealed to be John Anderton, and his 'ball' is created; it's when Billy Elliot shouts 'I hate you' to his father, who has just ordered him to give up his ballet; it's Shrek cutting a deal with Lord Farquaard over Princess Fiona. It's when Sean is approached as the last-chance therapist for Will (*Good Will Hunting*) – their first encounter kicks off Act II; when Jack fights Tyler for the first time and ends with 'We should do this again sometime' (*Fight Club*); it's John Nash's 'what would you like me to do?' said to William Parcher in *A Beautiful Mind*. It's when Boo 'the kid' enters the monster world for the first time (*Monsters, Inc.*); and, for Tom (*The Talented Mr. Ripley*), it's the moment Freddie Miles enters the picture – things won't ever be the same again.

> By the end of Act I, I want to achieve a feeling of closure, that some stuff is out the way. It's not always the audience understanding everything. A mistake is to try to get all that foundation exposition into the early part of the film, that's why a lot of films start to wind down as you go through them...
>
> *Steven E. De Souza*

Now work out the inciting incident and the TP1 in the films you have watched (*My Big Fat Greek Wedding*, *The Truman Show*, *Erin Brockovich*, *Spider-Man*, *Field Of Dreams* and *Cruel Intentions*). Answers at the end of Taking it further.

## 2.1 Act II (overview)

This Development Act tells your main story, shows further your characters in action, and shows the development of those characters through their experiences. All the elements introduced in Act I are now shown working with and against each other: conflict, suspense, tension, action, adventure, passion, romance, murder, mystery, and whatever else you've got.

The nature of this Act, where the problem introduced by the inciting incident is further developed through conflict, is that your characters are operating on borrowed time, underpinned by the existence and nature of the protagonist's solution decided on at the end of Act I. Being a bad or a false solution (even though they don't realize it as such), your protagonist will often find his or herself re-confronting their old problem, though it may take on a new or slightly different shape. They cannot escape the fact that their 'solution' did not solve the problem completely. The audience will of course understand this better than the protagonist. This is the nature of putting the audience in a superior position (we know something you don't) and they know subconsciously that the protagonist will have to deal with this problem at some point later in the film.

In *Witness*, Schaeffer has to deal with the fact he's been betrayed; Book will have to face the fact that running away, for whatever reasons, hasn't solved the problem and has led to Carter's death. This moment of painful realization usually occurs at the climax at the end of Act II (the second turning point or moment of truth) and this leads to a new and more powerful clarity of purpose.

To get a clearer grasp of Act II, it will help if you see it as two equal halves divided by the half-way point. In the first half of Act II (pages 30–60), up to the half-way point (page 60), your protagonist progresses steadily upwards in their quest and things seem to be going swimmingly. But nothing moves forward except through conflict. If all you have is exposition and explanation, things will get boring and your story will lack momentum. Hence you should be building towards a set-back. Indeed, you will probably have two set-backs in this segment of the script: a minor one as you enter the Act and a more serious one at your script's half-way point. Let's look closer at this first half.

## 2.2  Act II: pages 30–45

A *golden rule of screenwriting* is: after a climax, give your audience a breathing space, a pause moment or scene for them to come down, assimilate that climax and all that has happened.

Your protagonist has now fixed their general goal/s and is back on track – or so they think. There is soon a minor set-back but they overcome that and they move steadily upwards. Hence these 15 pages are usually ones of reaction/response and the setting up by the writer of incidents that will lead to further problems and obstacles later in the story (relationships and complications may begin here).

In *Witness*, we see the potential chemistry between Book and Rachel in the nursing scene (the main subplot's first turning point). This is also a serious complication, because Amish customs state it is not possible for a woman to have an affair or marry an outsider. Through no fault of their own, Book and Rachel belong to two different worlds.

## 2.3 Page 45: first focus point

At approximately page 45 you will often find a *focus point* (also called *focal* or *focusing point*). This is a scene or moment which:

- tightens the storyline action
- reminds the audience of the 'problem'
- pushes the story forward helping to keep it on track (and stopping the audience and the writer from getting lost)
- may indicate the first beginnings of character change or growth in your protagonist.

By this stage we have seen some first indications that the protagonist is changing or growing, for example a moment or scene showing a kind of acceptance of the new situation (i.e. your protagonist has adjusted to preceding life-changing events, especially the 'problem' and TP1). It is a marker or 'beat' in the protagonist's character transformation and growth. Up until now they have probably been reacting to events brought on by TP1. The first focus point (or FP1) now sees them making a first significant active move towards achieving their goal.

Forty-six minutes into *Witness*, John Book gives Rachel his gun, even though he knows that somewhere 'out there' McFee and Schaeffer are still after him (a clever integration of main plot and subplot). This is a distinct moment of growth for the Book character in the Book/Rachel main subplot: previously, he would never have done this even if he were not in danger. But here he is already responding to the Amish values around him. In terms of main plot (Book has to find the murderer) it reminds us of McFee and Schaeffer and the 'problem' facing all of them.

As with the two major turning points, there are two focus points (the other comes at approximately page 75) and they are usually related: what is promised/foreshadowed/mentioned/indicated in FP1 is often delivered in FP2. Hence with the first focus point you the writer need to design a scene that essentially *refocuses* on the storyline.

## 2.4 Pages 45–60

This section sees your protagonist begin to fulfil the line of action begun at TP1 and tightened at FP1. The line continues onwards and upwards, almost unhindered, because you are building towards your half-way point which will be a *point of no return* for your protagonist. In other words, pages 45–60 see:

• the obstacles get tougher
• the protagonist get stronger
• the protagonist approach a point after which they cannot quit.

In *Witness*, this segment is where Book, formerly a carpenter but now a cop, is seduced by the Amish life (and later, at the half-way point, by Rachel).

Generally speaking, this segment in your main plot restates the external problem. But we also see the protagonist take their first decisive action towards attaining the ultimate goal of the story. More specifically, they will be moving towards the point of no return/total commitment scene at the half-way point (page 60).

In your main subplot, this segment usually illustrates a change taking place in your protagonist. Up till now we have had an indication of that change, but now we are focusing in on it (e.g. Book helps the Amish build a barn and their communal values are seen in practice; as John falls in love with Rachel, he is also falling in love with the Amish life and values-system).

## 2.5 Page 60: the half-way point

The half-way point or mid-point of your script (approximately page 60), is your protagonist's *point of no return*, their scene or moment of total commitment. Here, something happens which causes them to reassess and consider giving up their quest or journey. Should they give up or push on? Looking at your script logistically, your character having come 60 pages, it would take them the same time to give up the quest and return to where they started (page 1) as it would if they decided to continue the quest to page 120. In *Falling Down*, 67 minutes into the 104-minute film (i.e. 15 minutes past half-way), D-Fens is on the phone to his ex-wife, and says: 'I'm past the point of no return, Beth. You know what that is? That's the point in a journey where it's longer to go back to the beginning than it is to continue to the end' – a screenwriter's in-joke perhaps, but it neatly illustrates the point.

Unlike at other points in your script (i.e. at the end of each act) this half-way point does not necessarily involve any sort of climax or big action scene. It may be the reaction to a perceived serious setback, but for your protagonist it is a point of no return.

Its main purpose is:

- to force the protagonist to reassess their quest
- to make the protagonist consider giving up
- to make the protagonist then decide to continue on (they must do this)
- to make them formulate a new set of more specific or focused goals
- to make them commit to that new goal totally in a way they cannot back out of.

(Remember: we learn about our characters from the decisions they make ... under pressure.)

The half-way point usually tells us something new, something we didn't know before; it can also represent a major moment of recognition for your protagonist, where they recognize what is really going on, particularly between themselves and the other main character/s. It also evolves and adds to the protagonist's motivation: anyone who reaches the point of no return has, by definition, fewer choices open to them and are compelled to adopt a specific line because they can no longer quit or return home. Also, obtaining a significant part of the solution to the problem adds greatly to a protagonist's motivation to remain on the case; there are fewer options but they are now 'addicted' to finding the solution.

Very often in a film with a love story, the point of no return is when the two people either go to bed together or say 'I love you' for the first time. In *Witness* it is the seduction scene in the barn where Book and Rachel dance, touch and almost kiss. After this Book's actions and options are narrowed: his attraction to Rachel, a woman who could be ostracized by the community, limits the choices he can make. The pair (and audience) realize they are on a path of no return, or what seems like no return; an emotionally dangerous course for both of them.

In *Minority Report* it is John Anderton's eye transplant operation; it's Billy Elliot's decision to turn up at court and show family solidarity, causing him to miss the important local ballet audition; it's Shrek's decision to remove his helmet and reveal to

Princess Fiona that he is not Prince Charming but an ugly ogre. It's the session in which Will and Sean discover a common bond in baseball (*Good Will Hunting*) and Sean recalls how he first met his wife; it's when Lou tries to shut down Fight Club – after this, the franchise starts; it's when John Nash tries to escape during the Harvard lecture, only to be confronted by Dr. Rosen, then arrested and sedated (*A Beautiful Mind*). In *Monsters, Inc.* it's when Randall realizes it was Mike – and Sulley – who were responsible for letting 'the kid' into Monstropolis; and for Tom Ripley, at the opera and wearing Dickie's clothes, it's when he first meets Peter Smith-Kingsley and there is very evident mutual attraction (*The Talented Mr. Ripley*).

Returning to *Maverick*, the mid-way point cleverly takes us back to the opening hook of the hanging scene. We discover how Bret escapes and now realize he *must* pursue his quest. We also realize that the first half of the film has been solid backstory in flashback: the audience has been cleverly manipulated – conned, in fact – which is the essence of the film. (It also subconsciously prepares us for further manipulation to come; all the more effective when we discover, at the final climactic twist, we have been wrong-guessing all along.) Even in something as vast as Spike Lee's *Malcolm X* (see Chapter 08) the half-way point occurs ninety minutes into the 205-minute story with his conversion to Islam. Up until then Malcolm has been an aimless, self-destructive mass of anger and disruption.

I urge you to watch the British film classic *If...* from 1968. The key mid-point moment is the brutal caning, shown in one unbroken eight-minute sequence. The three main characters (especially Travis) change from unfocused, passive, wannabe-troublemakers to focused, active, anarchist-aggressors.

After this mid-point the protagonist will hold to their commitment and be driven along a certain course *because* they have committed to that line in a particular way. From now on your protagonist cannot return to their former life and ways.

---

Now return to *My Big Fat Greek Wedding*, *The Truman Show*, *Erin Brockovich*, *Spider-Man*, *Field Of Dreams* and *Cruel Intentions*. What are their points of no return? (Answers: Taking it Further). Notice also how many minutes into the film they occur – are they half-way through? Do they (and your script) fit any of the following criteria? (see overleaf)

| Before | After |
|--------|-------|
| *Before* | *After* |
| not in control of their life | • taking more decisive control |
| a victim | • hitting back |
| puzzled by the mystery or 'problem' | • on track to the solution |
| uncommitted | • committed |
| hunted | • hunter |
| living the dream or fairy tale | • dealing with the reality |

## 2.6  Act II second half: pages 60–90 (overview)

Your protagonist, having made the decision to continue, and with a new, more focused set of goals in place, progresses onwards. But in this section the stakes are raised, so that now more is at risk, more in danger of being lost (immediately, or in the long term). Raising the stakes also shows us the enormity of what must be committed in order to succeed.

Script Readers have noted that if a script is going to show signs of flagging, it always tends to be in the second half of Act II. Sometimes, to combat this, you might find the script exploring one particular subplot or shifting location from the script's main setting. (Both these happen in *Tootsie* during the 11-minute sequence at Les's farm.)

In the section between pages 60 and 75, the direction of your protagonist is very clear: they are holding to (or being held to) that commitment made at the half-way point. That point has added some element of compulsion (from within themselves/other people/outside events) where they are compelled to choose more and more specific lines of action to achieve their ultimate goal. The nature of character motivation in film is not allowing your protagonist to do what they want to do, but compelling them to do what absolutely must be done.

## 2.7  Page 75: second focus point

This second focus point (FP2), at approximately page 75, performs many of the same functions as FP1 (at page 45):

• it moves the story forward
• it keeps it on track

- it pays off FP1 by delivering on some promise or suggestion made at that earlier point
- it may add another significant clue to the solution of the 'problem' or mystery
- it tests your protagonist's new growth.

This last function is the most important one.

In *Witness*, it is when Rachel is washing herself, half undressed, and turns to find Book in the other room. Without dialogue and with little physical action happening we see that very powerful decision-action of John *not* to make love to her. At the same time, John's growth (transformational arc) is being tested: if he makes love, it will be because the 'old' John Book is still in charge, the old rules still controlling his actions and choices. His 'success' at passing this test proves that concrete change has taken place in his character; he is a new person. However, it is not only the audience that discovers it; the protagonist himself realizes he has changed and moved on. Book now knows who he truly is. This moment of self-realization is important, and it must be powerful.

Remember the FP1–FP2 linkage: if FP1 plants/indicates the beginnings of change in your protagonist, then FP2 shows proof that they have indeed changed.

The most interesting and engaging type of FP2 is where your protagonist is tested to almost breaking point. The audience must be gripped to genuinely believe that the outcome could go either way (Book might make love to Rachel or he might not).

Sometimes (actually quite often) after this second focal point you will have a long expositionary speech, usually told in the form of a story to someone, which illuminates the real reason for your protagonist's journey, their real inner motivation. By now your protagonist has probably recognized this inner motivation, although it may be someone else who tells the actual story. Go back to the four films you have watched. Does this happen? Ask why the decision to include or exclude it was made. Was it placed later and if so, why?

## 2.8 Pages 75–90: complications

The second focal point has tested our protagonist's growth, they've come through it, and we are seeing a new person. The audience now needs to see the true (dramatic) vindication of this test – and this vindication lies in the second turning point (TP2), the moment of truth and the climax to your second Act.

As with pages 15 to 30, this screenplay section is principally concerned with setting up TP2. This is done in two ways:

- TP2 must be strong and well-integrated and the set-up for it clear
- at the same time, your protagonist will usually experience a sense of failure just prior to TP2.

This sense of failure is the crisis point for the whole film story and is your protagonist's crisis.

In *Witness*, the set-up for TP2 is begun early in the screenplay: when Book punches out the punks (TP2/Act II mainplot climax), he is wearing Amish clothes – yet for him to get to this crucial point, we must have been able to see John's interest in Rachel and Amish values and their subsequent influence on him. But what is also necessary in this scene is that Book should reach a crisis point which will generate a sense of failure and despair. This occurs when Book learns that his partner, Carter, is dead. Book himself has run away, is living in relative ease on the Amish farm, falling in love, etc. and yet ultimately because of his activities, Carter has been murdered. This sense of failure and despair causes Book to become very angry. The punks choose this moment to annoy the non-violent Amish and Book seizes this as an opportunity to express his anger: he beats them up – but by being dressed in Amish clothes, he draws attention to himself. This information is passed to a police officer who informs Schaeffer and thus we are catapulted into Act III. Note too this is also a crisis point in Book's transformational arc: he has resorted to violence, his old ways – a step backwards. This is part of the story's theme. It also reinforces the idea of the difficulty of crossing into a new world and remaining there, thus foreshadowing the end of the film when Book returns to his own world (albeit changed).

## 2.9 End of Act II, pages 85–90: second turning point/TP2 – moment of truth

By the end of Act II your protagonist reaches that second turning point (TP2) somewhere between pages 85 and 90 of the script. It is a major setback and forms the second act climax (or leads directly into it). Here they meet the biggest obstacle in the story, and are defeated by it (although not permanently). This immediate crisis for the protagonist will give them a sense of failure, of having been abandoned or isolated, and of having realized at last (and now being forced to face the fact) that the decision or action taken at the TP1 was false, weak, unprincipled or a terrible mistake. Hence this turning point is called the *moment of truth*.

This creates a new and yet more powerful clarity of purpose for the protagonist, a clearer goal, which accompanies them as they enter Act III. Now, knowing exactly who they are and having faced up to (and possibly accepted) their bad decision or false solution made at the first turning point, they are ready for the final showdown at the end of Act III.

TP2 (the moment of truth) performs the same functions as TP1:

- it involves the protagonist
- it leads logically to and 'causes' the final confrontation scene (and the final climax in general).

In *Witness*, Book beats up the punks and we are thrust straight into Act III. The actions of the active protagonist almost always *cause* the climax. This is the nature of characters in films: they bring about those events which may cause their own downfall and destruction.

In *Minority Report*, it's the scene where John realizes Crow is not the man he's after, decides not to kill him, yet still sees him fall to his death; it's Billy Elliot's audition in London, now with his father in support, which culminates in Billy's speech about 'What does it feel like when you're dancing?'; it's when Shrek mis-hears Fiona's 'Princess and ugly don't go together' speech and he is convinced he doesn't stand a chance. It's the therapy session in *Good Will Hunting* where Will has to finally confront the question 'What *do* you want?'; in *Fight Club*, after the car crash, Tyler walks out the door leaving Jack alone, but in a house that is still Planet Tyler ('I am Jack's broken heart'); and in *A Beautiful Mind* it's where John Nash finally decides that Alicia should go to her mothers and she leaves (although not for long). It's when Sulley re-enters Monstropolis and saves Boo from the scream chair; and it's when Tom types 'Dickie's' suicide note, removes all traces of the man's existence and, as Tom Ripley, escapes to Venice (*The Talented Mr. Ripley*).

Remember that in Act I, just when we thought the story might be over, the inciting incident came along, created or posed the 'problem', and caused the TP1, which then spun the story off in a new direction. TP2 often occurs when the story seems to be over for the opposite reason: the protagonist has failed and despair has overtaken them (not all films will follow this format – follow the demands of *your* story). At this precise moment there is a breakthrough, a clue revealed, an inner strength found or (as in Book's case) an action taken precisely *because* of the despair and sense of having failed (his partner Carter's murder); the action causes him to give away his identity and his whereabouts. It also creates the energy and momentum to catapult us into Act III. (Note that the climax to the Book/Rachel main subplot is when they kiss.)

> Now return to your six films: can you work out each one's second turning point? (Answers: Taking it further)

## 3.1 Act III: pages 90–120: final push and climax

The climax is the principal part of the story and for which ... all the machinery of planning and constructing has been set in motion...

*Syd Field*

Your Act III needs to do three important things:

- have a strong **climax** to the story action
- **resolve** the problem or task and the relationships you established in Act I
- provide a satisfying **ending**.

In Act III you have to tie up all your loose ends, answer all remaining questions, show how the characters have changed, show what has been achieved or what disaster has struck *and* send the audience away feeling ... however you want them to feel.

So, as we enter Act III, your audience will be experiencing that pause moment or scene after Act II's climax, thus giving your protagonist a chance to regain their stasis, pull themselves together and go for that one last do-or-die attempt. After that, from now on, everything should accelerate towards that final climax.

Your protagonist usually enters Act III with a greater clarity of purpose about who they are (from FP2) and knowing more clearly (usually for the first time) what they really need to do (from TP2) – hence a new and clearer goal is usually formulated and chosen.

After the ending of Act I the protagonist had a general overriding powerful goal: what they believe they need to get in the film. But the character goes through transformation, and is challenged to grow. This has consequences for the character's goal, because if they change and grow, then so will the nature of their goal – the old goal no longer satisfies them. So they are given a new goal at the half-way point and a yet more focused goal at the moment of truth. Each time can mean an alternative goal, or simply the old goal with something added to it. The events of Act II have *almost* led to complete disaster and to a sense of personal failure in the protagonist. Indeed, the low point that follows the Act II climax is usually the protagonist's darkest moment in the script (hence the moment of truth) – a realization that comes *only just in time*. Act III provides the arena in which to redeem these negative situations.

In *Witness*, John Book's main plot goal is to survive and protect Rachel and Samuel. But as he enters Act III it is no longer just his physical survival, but also the survival of his new Amish values and beliefs. In order to save these he is actually forced to put his physical survival at risk by laying his rifle down and stepping in front of Schaeffer's weapon. So physical survival is no longer the main goal, otherwise why risk it for 'something else'? Surely that something else is now the main goal? Survival now not only involves survival of his new value-system (which includes the importance of the community above that of the individual); the *method* of survival is also crucial: it must be done without the gun, by using the power of the community. In the main subplot, Book's goal is a relationship with Rachel. The second focal point illustrated that this goal was already changing and by the end of the film his goal is to allow each of them to remain in their separate worlds.

Note that in this 'final push' segment you will often find a chase – not necessarily fast cars and screeching tyres – but at least a pursuit of some kind. In *Witness* it is the stalking of Book in the granary silo.

It's there in most of the films you've watched for this chapter: *Fight Club, Minority Report, Monsters, Inc., Shrek, American Beauty, Billy Elliot, The Talented Mr. Ripley*. In *Tootsie*, for example, after the unmasking on live TV, Michael Hoffman is in the bar with Julie's father. Michael decides to leave the bar, go to the studios and try to talk to Julie. She initially brushes him off and goes along the sidewalk, Michael follows her until they finally talk (the climax) and resolve matters.

Also note that pacing (Chapter 10) is very important in Act III: it is the fastest-paced of all the acts, with more 'crises-per-page' and little let-up. In this segment, incidents will happen fairly quickly and lead inexorably to the final climax. This is also why third acts are often built around a single major sequence. The last acts of *Witness, American Beauty, Field Of Dreams, Good Will Hunting, Insomnia* and *The Legend Of Bagger Vance* are single sequences. Sequences will be covered in Chapter 09.

## 3.2 Pages 115–120: final climax

The climax happens between approximately pages 115 and 119 of the script. It is always a scene (sometimes the final scene) in which the protagonist faces the greatest obstacle of all – the final confrontation with the opposition – and one of them 'wins', the other 'loses' (though note that by winning they may lose, and vice versa). Whatever, this must be seen on-screen. It cannot happen off-screen, or be reported. We want to see it. And this climax must *integrate* three elements:

- resolving the main plot
- showing through action the new transformation in the protagonist
- playing out the Theme of the script.

The climax caps off the process begun in Act I: a goal was set but we often discover it was a false or insufficient goal; at the end of Act II a truer goal was set, but at the end of Act III a real or concealed goal is revealed (*Field Of Dreams* powerfully demonstrates this).

It is important to understand that this climax is the *peak emotional moment* of your screenplay (where your theme comes forcefully into play). It may be the screen kiss (as in the ending of *Speed* or as in most romances/romantic comedies – *Four Weddings and a Funeral, Sleepless In Seattle, Groundhog Day*); the big belly-laugh fate of the telephone box in the comedy *Waking Ned*; the quirky cliff-hanger of *The Italian Job* and *Lock, Stock And Two Smoking Barrels*; or much subtler – the tenderly erotic exchanged kisses of *Amélie*; Rannulph and Adele dancing together, united again, in *The Legend Of Bagger Vance*.

In the films you've watched for this chapter, we've covered a whole spectrum of different types of climax: from a gun going off (John's nemesis Lamar dies in *Minority Report*; Jack finally achieves separation from Tyler Durden in *Fight Club*); through erotic murder – Tom caught in a situation where he has to kill the thing he loves, Peter, in *The Talented Mr. Ripley*; to a screen kiss ('But you *are* beautiful' in *Shrek*); and friends reunited (Sulley's splinter reopens the door to Boo's bedroom in *Monsters, Inc.*).

Interestingly, the three 'subtler' endings seem to be a series of rising and linked climaxes: Billy Elliot, having bonded with his father at the graveside, leaving town, his future ahead of him/culminating in his first adult performance in front of an approving family; the pen ceremony in *A Beautiful Mind*, moving through John's accommodation of his own condition ('I still see things, I just choose not to acknowledge them' leading to his Nobel speech 'only in the mysterious equations of love can true logic be found'. In *Good Will Hunting*, it starts with Will's emotional breakdown ('It's not your fault'), the acknowledgement of 'That's it. You're a free man', to ultimately his letter to Sean and the recognition that Will is now a constructive, focused individual and following his heart.

Lastly, the brilliant twist at the end of *Maverick*, a film about conning people, makes the viewer realize that the biggest confidence trick of all has actually been played on them. (It also cleverly unites the generational audiences: one who accepts Mel Gibson as Maverick, and those who grew up with James Garner as that character).

John Book entered Act III of *Witness* no longer solely worried about his physical survival, but now more concerned about the survival of his Amish values and less individualistic ethics – all of which are played out in the ending (in the way he now goes about trying to achieve his new goal). Schaeffer, by capturing and threatening Rachel, is also threatening these new values. Book is forced to put down his gun, expose himself to Schaeffer's gun, and then call upon the power of the community to defeat Schaeffer. (This ending powerfully integrates the thematic elements with the main plot action climax.)

Read again the climax quote on page 135 and think carefully about it. This climax is the point towards which you build your screenplay. The value of any incident or character development point in the story is measured in terms of this climax: does it move the story forward to the climactic scene, or not? The question you should ask yourself when creating each and every scene is: how does this scene relate to this climax? As I said earlier, screenplays are written backwards.

Lastly, what comes after a climax? A pause to let the audience come down. Hence...

## 3.3 End of Act III: resolution/denouement

Having got over that final climax – the biggest of your entire screenplay – you must again give your audience a chance to come down from all that emotion. Your protagonist has faced their biggest challenge and either won, or been defeated by it yet still won, or defeated by it and lost (although they've learnt something about themselves and therefore still 'won').

In *Witness*, Book contacts the authorities, the police arrive, take statements and examine the site, and depart. Book then approaches Rachel and they say their silent farewell. In *Field Of Dreams* it is the simple rising crane shot revealing a stream of car headlights ('they will come'). Can you work out the denouement moment/s for the other films you've watched?

This tapering-off period in your script should also tie up all the loose ends, and any subplots that have not already been resolved in and by your final climax.

This is a moment (or moments) where your protagonist re-evaluates their situation, of how life has changed for them, as if they were setting up a new design for their new life to come (after your screenplay ends). So your story needs to create a sense of an *afterlife*: a feeling that the lives of the characters go on after the story has finished, after your audience has left the cinema. Hence the importance of creating fully three-dimensional characters: if your characters haunt you the writer, and live in your head after the writing is complete, then you're on the right track.

Incidentally, don't forget that resonating visual image (and possibly resonated key-line) near the end of your script, that image or line which is similar to and relates to the one you set up in your opening pages. Here it will be slightly changed or adapted, allowing the audience to measure how much that main character has changed over the course of the story. It does not have to be as obvious a bookend visual as, say, the feather in the wind of *Forrest Gump* or the gun in Jack's mouth (*Fight Club*) bringing us back to the opening hook. A more subtler version can be found in *The Talented Mr. Ripley*; or the ariel shot of the drive in *Gosford Park* with, first, the cars arriving and, finally, the cars departing. In *A Beautiful Mind*, the bookending is both visual (the pen ceremony) and in dialogue 'Are you scared?/ Terrified, petrified, stupefied...' etc.); and with *Spider-Man* we have the voice-over of Peter Parker. In *Witness* it is much subtler – if you've read this far, you should know what it is.

## 3.4 Endings

Finally, a fundamental consideration you *must* address: what effect do you want to create on your audience after they have experienced your screenplay?

> When we previewed *Four Weddings...* in New Jersey, by the end we knew we had a good film, but we were still convinced it would be a small, quiet, almost arthouse, British film. Then one of the US studio heads came up to me and said: 'This movie's gonna make you fifty million dollars.' I said that was ridiculous. Then he said: 'Look at the faces of the people coming out: they're smiling, they've just seen a great movie, they feel good – and that feeling is gonna spread.'
>
> *Richard Curtis,*
> writer: *Four Weddings And A Funeral,*
> *Notting Hill, Love, Actually*

I'm not necessarily saying give it a happy ending, but give it a *satisfying* ending. The endings of *American Beauty, The Talented Mr. Ripley, Philadelphia, Gladiator, Sunset Boulevard, Spider-Man, Cinema Paradiso, Shakespeare In Love, Romeo And Juliet, Titanic* or even *Witness* aren't exactly happy, but they are at least satisfying. Can you think of others?

Ideally, the audience should feel that there was a reason for your film. They shouldn't be shaking their heads and asking 'why the hell did any one make *that*?' Again, this comes down to your ending, your theme and their integration.

---

Now try to watch *The Sixth Sense* and *Enemy At The Gates*, paying particular attention to their endings. Compare their endings to, say, *Fight Club*. How did you feel about them? Were they surprising and imaginative, predictable, baffling or 'so what'? Were they linked to their main Theme (as you perceived it)? Were they satisfying? Did you care?

---

> I'm very keen to get right the opening five minutes and closing five minutes of a film – they are crucial.
>
> *Steven Spielberg*

The last 10–20 minutes of a film is often what most affects a cinema-going audience. It is also where those vital three elements of Act III (page 139) all come together. The ending is where your theme is integrated into the final action and often makes sense of it – it *unifies* the whole film. What this means in practice is: your choice of ending and how it is played out must be *informed*, *influenced* and *symptomatic* of your theme.

So, get the last twenty minutes of your script right, the ending right... and write a brilliant screenplay too!

When thinking about structure in relation to your own screenplay or any story you may think of, try approaching it like this:

1 First decide on an end for your story

2 Then design the opening: your first ten pages; then your first Act

3 Ask yourself:

- does it set the story in motion?
- does it establish my protagonist?
- does it indicate what my story is going to be about?
- does it set up the situation?
- does it set up a problem or an obstacle that my character must confront and overcome?
- are my protagonist's needs, goals or motivations clearly stated?

If you leave this movie unsettled, disturbed, afraid that this could happen here – Good. You *should* be afraid. That is the whole point. To scare you. To make you not want to be another mindless, thoughtless follower.

> *Fight Club* review by *Harry Knowles*
> (ain't-it-cool-news)

## Some observations

- Most 'journey' films are geographically plotted. That is, each act takes place in a separate geographical location. In *Rain Man*, Act I takes place in Los Angeles and Cincinnati, Act II in the desert, and Act III in Las Vegas and L.A. More obviously in *Speed*, each act is a separate story: Act I – The elevator (25 mins); Act II – The bus (64 mins); Act III – The Subway (17 mins). In *Maverick*, Act I is set in the town; Act II (first half) on the plains, (second half) on the riverboat; Act III back on dry land. Are there any Act/location correlations in the films you watched for this chapter? Also try viewing *Sideways*, *Oh Brother, Where Art Thou?*, *Y Tu Mamá También* and *Finding Nemo*. Ask why these choices were made (or not).

- Looking logistically at the overall three-act structure, one's overriding feeling is of symmetry and balance (the half-way point being a pivot). Remember too that bridge spanning the river with two central support columns: the two turning points.

- Try to see a film in terms of energy: every scene is a burst of energy; conflict produces energy; new insights or directions produce energy in the audience's mind. The first burst of energy is the hook (it grabs and carries us into Act I); the next is the inciting incident and TP1 which carries you into Act II; the energy that sustains us through Act II comes from the protagonist's realization that they've had to compromise their values, have chosen badly or wrongly; this realization (the moment of truth/TP2) is another burst that drives us into and through Act III and towards the climax.

Of course, you will be able to find exceptions and other approaches to this chapter's template (e.g. Christopher Vogler's 'Hero's Journey' construct – examined in the next chapter), but the three-act 'paradigm' is the basic foundation of all good storytelling – just ask Aristotle! What you should be asking is how and, especially, why any exceptions might differ.

---

To reiterate: when examining structure in any film or TV drama, it is too easy to interpret any guidelines as rules that *must* be followed (if your inciting incident isn't on page 'X' your script is rubbish, etc.) The things in this chapter are not set in stone; they are there to help you organize and focus your own script.

---

Remember, you should aim to reach that point where you don't consciously think about structural rules any more.

I do get worried when people get so obsessed about structure in a formulaic way that they forget about character and dialogue and telling a good story – the things that actually do matter most. I would rather a writer came to me with a script that was structurally all over the place but was full of wonderful ideas and characters and sparkling dialogue. Structure you can work on after. What

I don't want is something that fits the formulae but actually has no significance, life and energy.

*Lynda Myles,*
Pandora Productions/Pathé Films

Ultimately, your story dictates the positioning, style and magnitude of your climaxes and turning points.

---

### Trust Your Story

---

To hammer home for the last (I hope) time: Please don't get 'hung-up' or obsessed about structure and/or its perceived rigidity, especially when actually writing. When seeing a movie – or reading a script – for the first time, it should be the story and the characters that propel the audience through this journey – the structural points should not call attention to themselves. These things only emerge or become evident once you sit down and start analysing or studying the movie. It is a theoretical construct – a template, if you like – by which Readers and the industry 'suits' can come to grips with a screenplay (and probably criticize it). For the writer, these points are there to help you when constructing your script, not to restrict your imagination.

Remember the rule – there are no rules.

*Jim Sheridan,*
director: *My Left Foot, The Field,*
*In The Name Of The Father,*
*In America*

There are no rules, but you've got to know them before you can break them!

*Adrian Dunbar,*
screenwriter: *Hear My Song*

You read all about these rules and these how-to things. You pick what is relevant for you, add your own unique perspective and voice and create your own smorgasbord of rules and guidelines.

*Dominic Dromgoole,*
Theatre director

You will find some excellent script analyses of the major blockbuster movies at Richard Michaels Stefanik's site: www.themegahitmovies.com

# 08

## structural variations

In this chapter you will learn:
- about other approaches to and adaptations from the classic three-Act template: the Hero's journey; multi-plotting; two-, four-, five- (and more) Act structures; and what they call 'portmanteau' films.

# The Hero's Journey approach to three-Act structure

Let's return to Christopher Vogler's book *The Writer's Journey* (see Chapter 05). Taking as his starting point Joseph Campbell's work on myth in storytelling (specifically the book *The Hero With A Thousand Faces* – see Taking it further), he saw screenplay structure as a series of 12 stages and called it The Hero's Journey (some call it the Monomyth):

Act I (1) The Hero is introduced in their ORDINARY WORLD where

(2) they receive the CALL TO ADVENTURE.

(3) They are RELUCTANT at first or REFUSE THE CALL, but

(4) they MEET WITH and are encouraged by a MENTOR to

(5) CROSS THE 1st THRESHOLD and enter the Special World where

Act II (6) they encounter TESTS, make ALLIES AND ENEMIES.

(7) They APPROACH THE INMOST CAVE, crossing a second threshold

(8) where they endure the SUPREME ORDEAL.

(9) They take possession of their REWARD and

Act III (10) are pursued on THE ROAD BACK to the Ordinary World.

(11) They cross the third threshold, experience a RESURRECTION, and are transformed by the experience.

(12) They RETURN WITH THE ELIXIR, a boon or treasure to benefit the Ordinary World.

... and he laid it out across the three-Act Structure like this:

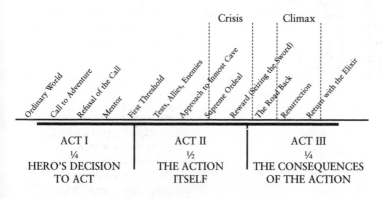

(Note: the Act lengths remain the same: ¼ – ½ – ¼.)

**figure 8.1** the Hero's Journey

**1 The Ordinary World:** This shows our Hero in their ordinary, mundane world – something against which we can compare the new world they are about to enter. For example, it's Luke Skywalker, the bored farmboy in *Star Wars* before he sets out to tackle the universe.

**2 The Call To Adventure:** The Hero is presented with a problem, a challenge or adventure to undertake. Once presented with this Call To Adventure, they can no longer remain indefinitely in their comfortable Ordinary World. It's the kidnapped Princess Leia's holographic message to the wise Mentor figure Obi Wan Kenobi, who asks Luke to join in the rescue quest.

This Call To Adventure may take the form of a new case (in detective stories) that a private eye takes on, a case which has upset the order of things. It may be a wrong that needs putting right. It may be the first encounter with that special someone the Hero will be pursuing and sparring with throughout their journey.

The Call To Adventure establishes the stakes of the game and makes clear the Hero's goal: to win the prize or lover, to right a wrong, gain revenge, achieve a dream, confront a challenge or change a life.

[One might see this as equivalent to an Inciting Incident.]

**3 Refusal of the Call (The Reluctant Hero):** This is all about fear. The Hero may baulk at the threshold of adventure, either expressing a reluctance or Refusing The Call.

At this point, the Hero has not yet fully committed to the journey and may even consider turning back. Hence some other influence is required to get them past this turning point of fear: a change in circumstances, a further upset to the natural order, or encouragement of a Mentor, for example.

It's when Luke refuses Obi Wan Kenobi's Call To Adventure and returns to his uncle's farmhouse, only to discover his relatives have been killed by the Emperor's stormtroopers. Luke is no longer reluctant and now eagerly undertakes the quest; he is motivated because the evil of the Empire has now become personal to him.

**4 Mentor:** By this point in the story a Mentor figure may well have been introduced. This relationship has powerful symbolic resonances: the bond between parent and child, teacher– student, doctor–patient, God–man.

The Mentor's function is to prepare your Hero to face the unknown. They may offer advice, guidance or magical equipment (when Obi Wan Kenobi gives Luke his father's light sabre) or give the Hero a swift kick in the pants to get the adventure going. ... But a Mentor can only go so far with a Hero...

**5  Crossing the First Threshold:** This is the Turning Point between Acts I and II. The Hero finally commits to the adventure and fully enters the Special World of the story by Crossing The First Threshold. The Hero agrees to deal with the problem or challenge posed at the Call To Adventure – and face the consequences of dealing with it. It's the moment the story really takes off: having committed to the journey (overcome their fear, decided to confront the problem and take action) there is now no turning back.

**6  Tests, Allies and Enemies:** Once across the First Threshold, your Hero encounters new challenges and Tests, they make Allies and Enemies, and begin to learn the rules of the Special World they have just entered.

Interestingly, Vogler has observed the useful role of the saloon or seedy bar in this stage of the story (and not just in Westerns). They can present a handy scenario where friends and villains are introduced, where manhood and determination are tested, where the Hero can learn more information and new rules of this new world entered. But, of course, not all tests/alliances/ enmities take place in bars.

In *Star Wars* the cantina is the setting where a major alliance with Hans Solo is formed and an important enmity with Jabba The Hut made. But we can also watch some character development in our Hero Luke Skywalker and his companions as they react under stress (an important catalyst in any development). Moreover, Luke's tests continue after the cantina scene: Obi Wan teaches Luke more about The Force, makes him fight blindfold, the early laser battles with the Imperial Fighters – all tests successfully passed.

**7  Approach the Inmost Cave:** The Hero finally reaches the edge of a dangerous place, where the object of the quest is hidden. Often it is the headquarters of the Hero's greatest enemy, the most dangerous spot in the Special World – the Inmost Cave (not necessarily deep underground).

When the Hero enters this fearful place they will cross the second major threshold, hence the Hero will often pause at the gate to prepare, plan, and outwit the villain's guards. This is the Approach phase. In *Star Wars* this Approach is when Luke Skywalker and his group are sucked into the Death Star where they will meet Darth Vader. Approach covers all the preparations for entering the Inmost Cave where the Hero will confront extraordinary dangers or even death.

**8   The Supreme Ordeal:** This is when the fortunes of the Hero are at their lowest in a direct confrontation with their greatest fear. It is a life-or-death moment in which the Hero or the Hero's goals are in mortal jeopardy; they are pushed to the brink and the audience, not knowing if the Hero will live or die, are left in suspense.

For Luke Skywalker and his companions, it's when they are trapped at the heart of the Death Star; Luke is pulled under the sewage by the monster and held there – it looks like he will not survive. The concept of the Hero tasting death/dying/appearing to die (and subsequently reborn with renewed vigour) is a critical stage of the Hero's journey.

[You can see how this can be interpreted as the Mid-point/ Point of No Return]

**9   Reward (Seizing the Sword):** Having beaten the monster and survived death, our Hero (and the audience) have cause to celebrate. The Hero takes possession of the treasure they have been seeking, their Reward. While it might literally be a special weapon or elixir, it might just as easily be some special knowledge or experience that leads our Hero to a greater understanding of, or reconciliation with, the hostile forces.

For example, Luke Skywalker rescues Princess Leia and captures the plans of the Death Star, which he will need to defeat Darth Vader. Vogler observed that at this point the Hero may also settle a conflict with a parent (as Luke does with Darth Vader in *Return Of The Jedi*).

As a result of having survived the Supreme Ordeal, the Hero may also appear more attractive, for they have taken the ultimate risk on behalf of their community and earned the title 'Hero'.

**10 The Road Back:** ... But our protagonist is not out of the woods yet. As we now cross into Act III, the Hero starts to deal with the consequences of confronting the dark forces of the Supreme Ordeal. If any reconciliation with parents/gods/hostile forces has not taken place, they may come raging after our Hero

– hence, many a good chase sequence might occur at this point: the Hero is pursued on The Road Back by the vengeful forces who have been disturbed by the Seizing The Sword (reward/elixir). Thus Luke and Leia are vigorously pursued by Darth Vader as they escape the Death Star. This stage marks the Hero's decision to return to the Ordinary World; a realization that not only must the Special World inevitably be left behind, but that there are still dangers/temptations/tests ahead.

**11 Resurrection:** Having 'soiled their hands' by entering the Special World, our Hero needs a process or ceremony of purification before he returns to their Ordinary World. This cleansing usually comes in the form of a second Ordeal of death followed by a Resurrection.

It is almost a replay of the life-or-death/death and rebirth scenario of The Supreme Ordeal. The forces of darkness get in one final, desperate last shot before finally being defeated. It's like a final exam the Hero must pass to demonstrate they have learned the lessons of the Supreme Ordeal.

You can see how this stage might be interpreted as your TP2 (from the linear template): the Hero is transformed by these death-and-rebirth moments and is now able to return to ordinary life reborn as a new being with new insights.

The original *Star Wars* trilogy constantly plays with this element. All three contain a final battle scene in which Luke is almost killed, appears to be momentarily dead, then miraculously survives. Each ordeal gains him new knowledge and command over The Force; each time he is transformed into a new being by his experience.

**12 Return with the Elixir:** In this final stage the Hero Returns to the Ordinary World – but the journey is meaningless unless they bring back some Elixir, treasure or lesson learnt from the Special World. Again, it doesn't have to be as specific as a magic potion to heal the world our Hero is returning to; it may simply be knowledge/self-knowledge or experience that could be useful to the community someday. It's when Luke Skywalker defeats Darth Vader (for the time being) and restores peace and order to the galaxy.

Sometimes the Elixir is a treasure won on the quest, but it may be love, freedom, wisdom or even knowledge that the Special World exists and can be survived; it may be just coming home with a good story to tell.

Unless something is brought back or gained from the ordeal in the Inmost Cave, the Hero is doomed to repeat the adventure. Many comedies use this ending where the foolish character, refusing to learn any lesson, embarks on the same folly that got them into trouble in the first place.

---

As with my words on the three-Act linear structure about taking it as a template rather than rigid rules that must be followed at all costs, Vogler stresses:

> The Hero's Journey is a skeletal framework that should be fleshed out with the details and surprises of the individual story. The structure should not call attention to itself, nor should it be followed too precisely. The order of the stages outlined is only one of many possible variations. The stages can be deleted, added to, and drastically shuffled without losing any of their power.

It is the values of the Hero's Journey that are important. The images of this blueprint (Heroes seeking magic swords from old wizards, knights risking death to save a loved one, etc.) are just symbols of universal life experiences. These symbols can be changed to suit the story demands and the needs of the society. Modern day Heroes may not enter caves or labyrinths to fight mythical monsters, but they do enter a Special World to reach that Inmost Cave and return, whether they venture into space, into the modern city (or the Amish community as in *Witness*) or into their own hearts and souls.

## Comment

Inevitably, this has been a brief summary of Vogler's structural template. In order to understand it fully (and the character archetypes he outlines) you really need to read his book.

In truth, you may well find that many (if not most) movies will stand analysis by both the three-Act linear and the Hero's Journey paradigms. After all, these *are* theoretical constructs.

To stress again: trying to write a screenplay with some structural grid to the fore in your mind will not work. Any well-integrated script should sweep an audience along with its story and characters, and any structural template used should not be obvious for an audience or call attention to itself. But if using such templates can help you enhance your storytelling powers or help you better tap into your Theme (very important), so much the better.

…And lastly, two books for you to investigate:

Stuart Voytilla: *Myths and the Movies*   [Vogler's 'Hero's Journey' construct applied to 50 movies]

James Bonnet: *Stealing Fire from the Gods: a dynamic new story model for Writers and Filmmakers* [He claims to take you beyond Classical Story structure and the Hero's Journey]

(both published by Michael Wiese Productions)

## Blake Snyder's 'Beat-Sheet'

Yet another perspective on the three-Act linear structure has arisen more recently from Blake Snyder in his book *Save The Cat: the Last Book on Screenwriting you'll ever Need*. He posited a very clear 15-point series of 'beats' which are fairly self-explanatory if you've been following the linear template outlined in Chapter 07.

**Note:** Snyder works on a 110-pages script length:

| | |
|---|---|
| OPENING IMAGE | page 1 |
| ESTABLISH / STATE YOUR THEME | pages 1–5 |
| SET-UP | pgs 1–10 |
| CATALYST / INCITING INCIDENT | pg 12 |
| DEBATE - HALF COMMITMENT | pgs 12–25 |
| BREAK INTO ACT 2 | pg 25 |
| 'B' PLOT INTRODUCED | by pg 30 |
| FUN & GAMES (and PUZZLES) | pgs 30–55 |
| [you get to play with your characters before the serious 'throwing of rocks'] | |
| MIDPOINT / TENTPOLE / REVERSAL | pg 55 |
| BAD GUYS CLOSE IN | pgs 55–75 |
| [serious throwing of rocks] | |
| ALL IS LOST / LOW POINT | pg 75 |
| DARK NIGHT OF THE SOUL (Darkest Decision) | pgs 75–85 |
| [this section often references Death in some way, sometimes symbolically] | |
| BREAK INTO ACT 3 | pg 85 |
| FINALE / CONFRONTATION | pgs 85–110 |
| [AFTERMATH pgs 107–110] | |
| FINAL IMAGE | pg 110 |

# Multi-plotting

What happens if you are writing an ensemble piece – a lot of main characters, each with their own story to tell (e.g. *Independence Day, Nashville, Magnolia, Sunshine State, Love, Actually, Short Cuts*)? Quite simply, you take it Act by Act. If you have, say, six sub-stories, you have effectively six subplots of equal weight, and you set them up and develop them, one block at a time ...

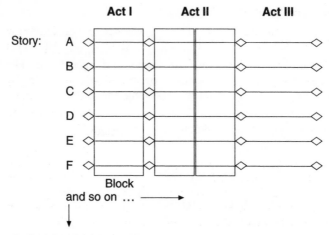

figure 8.2 developing subplots

... and you arrange the order of the scenes and plots within each block in the most dramatically effective way possible (you may still find, however, that one sub-story is more prominent – effectively a main plot). Multi-plots happen more often in television drama series (*Band Of Brothers, C.S.I., The West Wing, The Sopranos, Mad Men, The Wire, Caramel, Sin City*) where there are lots of story strands happening at the same time (but often one particular story will be set-up, developed and resolved in that episode); you may find that the different story strands in an episode are linked in some way, built around a single thematic idea – guilt, rape, trust, etc. (for example, *Traffic*). Multi-plotting is also enhanced by all the stories taking place in either a single environment, preferably restricted (*Gosford Park, Airplane*), or over a short time-span (*American Graffiti* – one night; or *24* – twenty-four hours).

Take a look at *Gosford Park* – both script (Julian Fellowes) and directing (Robert Altman) display master craftsmen at work.

The overarching main story – the thing that links the strands together – is the murder of Sir William. It has a hook (first sight of the poison bottle), an inciting incident (the white-tie evening soiree begins), TP1 (a knife goes missing), a half-way point (the stabbing itself), TP2 (revelation of who wielded the knife), climax (the poisoner revealed and the reasons for their actions and decisions) and denouement (the poisoner keeps the secret and the guests depart).

Yet the real focus is on the subplots, the way they criss-cross (and the subtle interplay between the classes):

Upstairs: the stories of Lady Sylvia (Kristen Scott Thomas); Freddie Nesbitt (James Wilby); Mr. Weissman (Bob Balaban); Lady Constance (Maggie Smith), etc.

Downstairs: the stories of Denton (Ryan Phillippe); Parks (Clive Owen); Mrs. Wilson (Helen Mirren); Mrs. Croft (Eileen Atkins); Mary the maid (Kelly Macdonald); head housemaid Elsie (Emily Watson); Mr. Jennings (Alan Bates), etc.

And nearly every subplot has its own establishment, inciting incident, developments, turning points, mid-point, final climax and resolution. These climaxes and turning points may be the tiniest of events – a decision made, a glance exchanged, an expected reaction not executed – but each is significant within the context of its own subplot (and it's often where the subtext – see Chapter 09 – comes powerfully into use). For example:

Denton's story runs something like this: approach to house, arrival downstairs, questions about everything (establishment – development); his first encounter with Lady Sylvia – 'Trouble sleeping, m'lady?' (I.I.); he delivers the milk (TP1); he reveals his true identity (mid-point); his second visit to Lady Sylvia, unhooks her top (TP2); the milk spilled in his lap/is later told 'you can't play on both teams at once'/departs house (climax – denouement).

Parks's story runs: arrival (establishment); during the meal downstairs he reveals he is an orphan (I.I.); the chat with Mrs. Wilson, who sees the photograph of his mother on the side table (TP1); the stabbing (mid-point); the revelation to Mary 'can't a man hate his own father?' (TP2); it is revealed, from Wilson's subplot, who his mother is (climax); he departs unaware (denouement).

Mrs. Wilson's story: organizing the new arrivals (establishment); first mention of Parks's name (hook); the meal downstairs and the orphan revelation (I.I.); brief chat with Parks where she sees the photograph (TP1); she brings Sir William his coffee (mid-point); revelation of the poisoner (TP2); revelation of her relationship to Parks and Mrs. Croft and her decision not to disclose – 'He'll never know me' (climax); everyone, including Parks, departs (denouement).

... and so on. Can you continue outlining the other subplots?

Another multi-stranded drama, *America Beauty*, has numerous subplots: wife Carolyn and Buddy; daughter Jane and boyfriend Ricky; Ricky and his father; Angela's story; Angela and Jane. Yet all are subordinate to the main driving story: Lester Burnham's quest to divest himself of all forms of responsibility and achieve complete 'freedom'; and his storyline crosses with all these subplots. Try working out the various turning points and climaxes for yourself, and remember, these things may be the subtlest of events or lines may intersect from another character's subplot.

---

Now watch the Australian film *The Dish*. Again, try working out each subplot's and each character's developmental template. Here are some clues: the overarching plot is the story of the moonlanding itself (lift-off/I.I.; the power surge/TP1; the Ambassador visits the dish/mid-point; the moon landing/TP2; the magical moon walk/climax) – the role of television, in fact.

And the subplots take place in two locations: at the dish (Cliff's story; Mitch and Al; Glenn and Janine; Rudi the guard); and in the town of Parkes (Mayor Bob; Bob and wife May; Bob and son Billy; daughter Marie and cadet Keith; Bob and the Ambassador; Bob and his assistant Len, etc.)

How did you feel at the end?: confused and distanced or warm and full of wonder?

Now do the same for the movie *Magnolia*. How many subplots can you detect? (There are at least nine disparate stories that I can see.) Was there a focused overarching narrative thrust and a clear sense of a developmental architecture? How did you feel at the end of the marathon?: stimulated and admiring or bored and beaten into submission?

List five more examples of multi-plotted dramas. Watch an episode of each. Do any similar patterns emerge?

# Plot variations

There are, of course, other ways of approaching plot structure. For example, when the television detective series *Columbo* started out, it was very innovative. It showed us at the opening who did the murder (using its Act III conclusion as the hook). But the story that drew the audience in was how that murder was actually committed, the backstory that led to it, and how Columbo pieced the puzzle together.

As the adoption by mainstream Hollywood of the linear three-Act structure template 'rules' has become more doctrinaire, independent-minded writers/directors/producers have become more wilfully inventive in their approaches to plotting and structure. Perhaps it is no wonder you are most likely to find them in the independent film sector or in more innovative contemporary TV drama.

*The Usual Suspects* is a very fine example of what some call *interleafing* (or *interleaving*), and although the term itself hasn't really 'taken off', it neatly describes the technique. Here subplots which juggle with flashbacks and flashforwards intersect and complicate the overarching linear main plot and are run as parallel action (see also *Pulp Fiction, Lone Star, The Weight Of Water* and *Courage Under Fire*).

*Memento* is a challenging and ambitious example of this technique. It runs two simultaneous storylines: one (in black-and-white) is linear beginning/middle/end, but the recounted tale (in colour) is run backwards. It demands that we re-examine our received concepts of 'traditional narrative', while neatly capturing the disorientating nature of the protagonist's memory condition.

Kurosawa's 1951 film *Rashomon* is a story of rape and murder, but seen from four different viewpoints/P.O.V.s – a technique also used by Costa-Gavras in his movie Z. And in the TV series *Boomtown*, each week a crime is enacted, then replayed through different P.O.V.s. The British film *Lawless Heart* follows three separate characters' stories/P.O.V.s, each time 'looping back' to an opening scenario of a funeral reception. Similarly, *Amores Perros* explores three disparate tales, all linked by a single horrific car accident.

Todd Solondz's *Storytelling* consists of two separate story segments: '*Fiction*' and '*Non-Fiction*', yet both explore the same themes of sex, race, celebrity, exploitation and our basic need to tell stories. You can call it a portmanteau movie if you like (see later) or a Two-Act movie, yet each segment still has a beginning, middle and end.

Warren Buckland's book *Teach Yourself Film Studies* (Hodder Education) contains some excellent analyses of different film and storytelling structures and is a recommended read.

# The two-Act structure

This linear form is found in half-hour (mostly TV) dramas and sitcoms, the act division coming at the ad break. Similar to the three-Act linear structure, the conflict starts in Act I and, by a series of climaxes and setbacks, escalates to the highest point of conflict at the end of Act II.

In the two-Act structure, the acts are generally of equal length, with three or four main scenes in each act (with perhaps one or two additional transitional or establishing filmed external scenes).

In TV, it is the first two or three minutes which are crucial, hence the hook is in the first three pages and the main plot established early in the first scene. If you have a subplot (you will rarely have more than one – the length cannot sustain overcomplication), it should be introduced, or at least foreshadowed, in your first scene (or second, if your first is short). Prologue 'teasers' (page 118) are an established shorthand for this.

You will, of course, find examples of two-Act templates with a number of subplots (*The Simpsons, Friends, Malcolm In The Middle, Frasier, South Park*), but these are very sophisticated vehicles, honed to perfection, often involving a writing team – and mostly American, where they have it down to a fine art.

At the end of Act I, instead of an obvious climax, there is some cliffhanger moment of tension (strong enough to hold your audience over the ad break and return for Act II). There is no need to follow it with a pause moment, the break itself will do this. Entering Act II you continue building the action until your moment of truth which in this case is half-way through Act II (i.e. 75 per cent into the drama – like the three-Act structure). The remainder of Act II is your resolution.

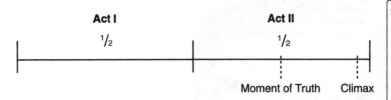

figure 8.3 two-Act structure

Now watch three randomly chosen sitcoms. Do they fit this template? If not, why?

## Four- and five-Act structure

You will discover that longer films (e.g. *Goodfellas, Malcolm X, Gone With The Wind, Magnolia, Pearl Harbor, Braveheart, Schindler's List, Casino, Titanic, The Lord Of The Rings, Ben Hur*) may well break down into four, sometimes five acts (each act being generally of equal length). However, the key turning points are still there and similar to the three-act proportions: first turning point at 25 per cent, point of no return at 50 per cent and moment of truth at 75 per cent.

## Portmanteau films

These are the types of film which have a number of separate stories running back-to-back to make a full-length feature and are more director-generated. Most of them, however, do display some kind of through-running link, either the same character/s (*Pulp Fiction, Mishima, Four Rooms, Mystery Train*), the same location (*New York Stories, Grand Hotel, Four Rooms, Asylum,* the Iranian film *Ten*), the same theme (*Aria*) or author (*Quartet, Trio* and *Encore* from Somerset Maugham), similar storylines (Hal Hartley's *Flirt*), or the same linking prop (*Tales Of Manhattan*) or the same event (*Amores Perros, 11' 09" 01 – September 11*). And, of course, each mini-story has its own beginning, middle and end. Mixing your genres within the overall fabric of your feature does not help (*New York Stories, Four Rooms*); that way lies confusion.

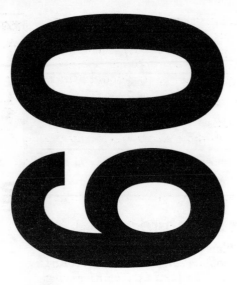

# 09

## 'deep structure'

**In this chapter you will learn:**
- to break down the overall architecture of your screenplay into smaller, more manageable, units – sequences and scenes
- about writing dialogue and examining what goes on underneath the words, the subtext.

Having looked at the overarching structure, let's now examine what is called *deep structure* (or *sub-structure*) – the elements used to dramatize your story. As you go from the general to the specific, you are moving closer to the heart of your screenplay and nearer to the actual writing of your first (exploratory) draft.

In writing your screenplay you have two devices:

- *scenes* – the individual incidents
- *sequences* – the arrangement of those scenes into meaningful clusters of development.

Your tools are:

- *visuals* – the actions your characters enact and your selection of visual images (into an image system)
- *sound* – principally dialogue, but also the other sounds and effects around them.

By now you should have a clearer idea about the overall structure of your intended script and about certain specific moments in your story. But before you can proceed further, you need to know five key things about your story: where you begin; what your inciting incident and TP1 are; your Act II climax/moment of truth (TP2); your final climax and your ending. List them. From there you can go on to fill in the template by dividing it up in terms of sequences as you flesh out your storyline.

# The sequence

The sequence is an important concept to understand; it is the organizational framework of your story.

There are two types of sequence:

- *dramatic* – a series of scenes linked together or connected by a *single idea* that, in themselves, form a self-contained unit of your screenplay (and end in a sequence climax)
- *bridging* or *transitionary* – mini-sequences used to link dramatic sequences or to establish character (early in Act I). They do *not* culminate in a dramatic event.

The *dramatic sequence* is probably the most important element of a screenplay. If structure is the spine of your screenplay, sequences are the rest of the skeleton, they hold everything together; they are the microcosm, foundation and blueprint of your script. This block of dramatic action held together by one idea can be expressed in one or a few words: escape, chase, arrival, departure, a certain character, a reunion, murder, whatever. For example, towards the end of *The Graduate*, racing to track down Elaine, finally finding her at the church (pursuit); in the wedding sequence that opens *The Godfather*; the extended Opera House sequence that climaxes *Godfather III* (it's pretty much an entire Act in itself); or the Terence Mann sequence in *Field Of Dreams* where Ray researches, seeks, finds and almost loses Mann.

Sequences are the pegs attached to the washing line of your structure from which you hang your story. Every dramatic sequence has a definite beginning, middle and end – a unit of dramatic action complete within itself – each sequence mirroring the overarching structure of your screenplay. Moreover, each sequence (dramatic or bridging) overlaps slightly with the one next to it, creating continuity and momentum.

A screenplay can have any number of major sequences – however many your script needs – and is related to the pacing of your story. A relaxed, contemplative drama such as *Field Of Dreams* has nine, the brooding *Rebel Without A Cause* seven; *Speed, The Fast And The Furious* and *xXx* are exciting, fast-paced, fast-edited, hence more sequences – and shorter ones. Try to work out how many sequences in *Speed*; it's very clearly plotted. Then try delineating the sequences in the films you watched for Chapter 07. Ask why there were so many (or so few).

Tip: DVD versions of films are broken down into 'chapters'. These chapter cues are often the actual sequence or part-sequence. Think about this the next time you watch a DVD (and consider your own screenplay).

Let's examine *Thelma And Louise* (total length = 123 minutes) in terms of sequences:

1 *Opening sequence* (escape) runs approximately from 2 minutes to 11 minutes into the film:
- Louise phones Thelma (need sets goal)
- kitchen: Thelma/Darryl confrontation (problem/obstacles: Darryl's domination, etc.)
- Thelma makes decision (solution: wait till Darryl leaves)
- Thelma packs (action)
- Louise picks up Thelma, they drive away (climax and result).

2 *Bar sequence* (bridging) (at 11 min)

3 *Fugitive sequence* (18 min):
- (19 min) attempted rape (problem posed by inciting incident: motivates all that follows, gets complicated later)
- (20½ min) shooting (action, crisis)
- escape (resolution).

4 *Transitional (1st) running away sequence* (21 min):
- driving: no plan (problem)
- hotel room: make plan (problem resolved).

5 *Losing money sequence*:
- (45 min) pick up Brad Pitt character
- detour to avoid cops; Jimmy meets Louise in hotel (obstacles in her path)
- (60 min) Thelma and Pitt make love; Jimmy and Louise say goodbyes
- realization: money left in room (crisis)
- (66 min) discover Pitt has stolen their money (climax, resolution) – major set-back.

6 *Thelma takes control sequence*:
- (71 min) Thelma robs convenience store – major set-back: point of no return.

7 *Heading for Mexico sequence* (structured around rude trucker):

- (74 min) first encounter with trucker
- Pitt in cop station
- Thelma phones Darryl, realizes cops are there (problem intensified)
- driving through night
  (this part of the sequence totals 15 min)

- (89 min) second encounter with trucker
- Thelma asks Louise if she was raped in Texas
- cop chases them for speeding
- lock cop in trunk
- Thelma and Louise discuss being on the run
- Thelma phones friendly cop again
- Thelma and Louise talk about never going back
  (this part of the sequence totals 16 min)

- (105 min) third encounter with trucker
- (108 min) they shoot up his truck – climax to this entire sequence.

8 *Final chase sequence:*
- (111 min): cops start chasing them
- they are cornered on cliff top
- (120 min): they drive off cliff.

You can see a distinct pattern within each sequence:

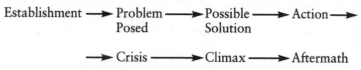

Establishment ⟶ Problem ⟶ Possible ⟶ Action ⟶
                    Posed         Solution

⟶ Crisis ⟶ Climax ⟶ Aftermath

## Sequence goals

In each sequence, the central character will have a specific goal, which they believe is a definitive step towards achieving their overall screenplay goal (and fulfilling their dramatic need). This does not mean that there aren't also character development goals which contribute to their transformational arc. Hence:

- the sequence goal is derived from the overall goal
- it is different to all the other sequence goals
- it must help escalate the action (be stronger than the previous sequence goal).

In the sequence, each attempt to get the goal meets an obstacle, which usually fails the first time, then a new attempt is made. Each new attempt will involve your character formulating a new strategy or approach. At the end the attempt either fails, succeeds or is interrupted. Hence the main part of any dramatic sequence is the struggle to reach the sequence goal. Struggle is caused by intention meeting obstacles and conflict.

## Sequence setbacks

Sequences generally use setbacks, or reversal, as a burst of energy to move into the next sequence. These setbacks may not alter the story direction but they change the fortunes of the characters, causing them to dramatically alter their strategy for getting their goals. These setbacks will also usually indicate the direction which your next sequence will take. Go back over the *Thelma And Louise* sequences and see how that works.

## Revelation

After a setback, a moment or process occurs where the character realizes their strategy and/or sequence goal must be abandoned;

it may not be conscious but is often embodied in some significant action indicating the abandonment.

## Context and content

While there is no rule about how many or few sequences you need for your screenplay, you do need to know the *linking idea* behind each sequence (the context). You'll then find content will follow.

---

Let's create a sequence around the idea of departure. The setting: a young man is flying far away to take up a new job. Beginning: we start with your protagonist getting up in the morning, shaving, dressing and packing their bags and leaving their home. Middle: they load their bags into a car and drive to the airport, perhaps dropping off at a friend's to say goodbye, then arriving at the airport. End: at the airport they check in their baggage, collect their tickets, maybe say their final, tearful farewell to the family and disappear from the departure lounge, onto the plane and fly away . . . but something is wrong. What? You decide.

---

Suddenly you have created a series of five or more scenes in each of the three sections and fleshed out that sequence. You've created the content – and about six to eight pages of script.

---

Now create the next sequence (beginning/middle/end) based on the idea of flying, journey or arrival.

---

Now break down your own script story into sequences, using the points outlined in this section. Imagine it was being prepared for a DVD release: what 'chapters' would you create and what would you call them?

---

# The scene

> If you want to understand the structure of a scene, go get Stanislavaky and read what an actor looks for in a scene. What does each one of these people want? Where are the points of conflict between them? Where does the scene change and go in a different direction?
>
> *Larry Ferguson,*
> screenwriter: *The Hunt For Red October,*
> *Alien 3, Maximum Risk, Rollerball* (2000)

The *scene* is the single most important element in a screenplay, the basic building block. It is where something happens, something *specific* happens. It is a distinct unit of action – the place you tell your story and the setting you design for dramatic conflict.

Think of a favourite film; what do you remember? Not the entire film, but great scenes: *Psycho* – the shower scene; *Butch Cassidy And The Sundance Kid* – the pair jumping off the precipice; *Casablanca* – the 'Play it, Sam' scene or the airport departure scene; *Reservoir Dogs* – the ear-severing accompanied by happy pop music; *When Harry Met Sally* – the faked orgasm scene; *Apocalypse Now* – the entry of the helicopters or the explosive ending; Tom Cruise hovering over a computer, suspended from the ceiling (*Mission: Impossible*); the tango dance in *Scent Of A Woman*. Great scenes make great movies.

By definition, *a new scene occurs whenever there is a change of location or time.*

The purpose of a scene is to *move the story forward*. A screenplay is composed of a large number of scenes – the number isn't important. Your screenplay must have precisely the number of scenes it needs to tell its story dramatically and effectively – no more, no less.

Likewise, a scene is as short or long as it needs to be. It may be one sentence, one line, or just a couple of words. It may also be many pages long. However, Readers frown on scenes longer then three pages (three minutes). Novice screenwriters always include too much dialogue and detail, often failing to find the opening and ending. Your story will determine how long or short your scenes will be, so trust your story.

However, a scene is much more complex than this. It is also part of a whole, a component in a larger structure – the screenplay. Think of a carburettor in a car: its purpose is to assist the functioning of that car; remove it, the car will not operate. In a script, take a scene out and the screenplay will be (should be!) damaged. And just as a carburettor has its own internal mechanism, so does a scene. So look at your scenes in terms of this dual function: as an individual element and as a functioning component of a larger entity.

Scenes come in three types: visual (where something happens visually, with no dialogue – like an action scene or a bridging/transitional scene); dialogue (for example, a conversation between one or more characters); and dramatic scenes (a combination of visuals and dialogue).

Visual scenes are usually very short and undramatic, their single purpose to connect other scenes and act as a bridge or transition between different sections of the action. For example:

EXT. PHILADELPHIA STREETS – DAY
John's car passes by on the way home

. . . or they can act as an establishing shot for the next dramatic scene. For example:

EXT. HONG KONG. MARKETPLACE – DAY
Crowded. Filled with Oriental and British merchants. You can buy anything here. Electronics. Furniture. Food. Anything.

. . . or sometimes they can do both.

Such scenes have little or no internal structure and therefore do not build towards (or open with) a crisis leading to climax. Their purpose is simply to move your story or character(s) from A to B without jolting the audience.

The thing to remember when writing dialogue scenes is: you are working in a visual medium. A solely dialogue-driven scene can only sustain itself for so long. So don't let any of your dialogue scenes last longer than three pages (three minutes); script Readers don't like them and it shows a lack of professionalism about the arena you are entering. Of course you will find exceptions, but most individual scenes tend to last from between a quarter to three pages – remember those assemblages of 'snapshots'.

Conflict is drama, true. But a good dramatic scene could be written over an argument about who does the dishes as much as a train crash.

*Mal Young,*
Head of Drama Series, BBC

Dramatic scenes are, if you like, the 'ideal' scene, with a beginning, middle and end – though not all of this may be shown on screen; *you* decide. These scenes advance your overall plotline and illustrate character. They escalate the already rising conflict in your story and reach a crisis point followed by a climax.

Each dramatic scene contains:

- text ('the business' or 'the blackstuff'): what the characters are doing
- dialogue: what they are saying
- subtext: what is really happening beneath the surface or apparent meanings of the action and speech.

Remember, in your script, every image, every piece of description, and especially every line of dialogue must either: (a) advance the action of your plot, (b) illustrate character, or (c) preferably do both. If it doesn't perform any of the above, you should question whether it could be expressed in a better (more visual?) way, or whether it need be there at all. Examine a well-crafted script (like *Witness, L.A. Confidential, Out Of Sight, Tootsie, Misery, Maverick, The Usual Suspects, Speed* or the films you watched for Chapter 07) and you'll see how every line is there for a reason and justifies its space on the page. It's down to what you choose to show and what *not* to show, both the scenes themselves and within each separate scene.

A scene is made up of two factors:

- the general *context*
- the specific *content*.

The context consists of when and where your scene takes place, i.e. *location* and *time*.

- location: EXT. or INT.
- time: stick to DAY or NIGHT (Chapter 02)

This gives us

INT. KITCHEN – DAY

or

EXT. STREET – NIGHT

A change of either place or time means you have a new scene.

As for content, every scene reveals *at least* one element of necessary story information to your audience. The information it receives is the purpose of that scene. Even if it's just a bridging scene, it denotes we are moving to a different location.

Just like your screenplay and a sequence, each dramatic scene has a beginning, middle and end – but you decide which part of it to show. You are looking for the maximum dramatic impact. Again, there is no rule; your story tells you what to do.

> I never enter scenes until the last possible moment i.e. before the ending of some specific action in the scene. As soon as it's done, I get the Hell out of there!
>
> *William Goldman*

Tip: When you have written a scene, try this standard technique most screenwriters use: cut out the beginning of it and the end of it. Then, condense the remaining information. Your scene may now be only half its original length, but it should be twice as tight. If it isn't, cut front-and-back again, condense the remainder, and go on until you're happy with it. Treat each scene as you would a party: arrive late, depart early.

## Creating a scene

As with sequences, first create the context (the purpose, place and time) of your scene, then content will tend to follow. To create context, ask yourself:

- What *happens* in this scene?
- What does each character in this scene want, want to happen, or prevent happening by the end?
- Where does the scene take place?
- At what time does the scene take place?
- What is the *purpose* of this scene?
- Why is it there?
- How does it move the story forward?
- What happens in it to move the story forward?

An actor will approach a scene by finding out what their character is doing there; where they have been and what they have been doing since their last appearance in the script; what they did immediately before this scene happened; where they are going and what they'll be doing after this scene; what their purpose is in this scene and why they are there. As a writer, you have to know all this too.

It is important for you to know what happens *within* scenes (in real time), but also what happens *between* scenes (omitted time) – which you choose not to show. Be aware that the decisions you make regarding which scenes you choose to omit can be as important as those you make about the scenes you decide to show. You leave out what the audience can deduce (Chapter 01). You're in control of this, remember! So ask yourself:

- How did my character get from the end of that scene to the start of this one?
- What were they doing all the time?
- While I've been concentrating on characters X and Y in this scene, what are the other characters doing while this scene is being played out?
- What are the other characters doing between the scenes?

You should know, too, why all your characters are in this scene and how their actions or dialogue move the story forward. If *you* don't know, who does?

The flowchart opposite might help when you approach the construction of a scene.

### Location

The location you choose should help dramatize the events taking place there; if it doesn't then it's the wrong location. Always look for conflicts: add tension by making something difficult, and then more so.

- Look for the unobvious, the most dramatic setting for your scene. For example, in *Edward Scissorhands*, Edward is frightened not on a sofa (a neutral choice – with limited action potential), but on a waterbed: a place that is not only visually interesting and humorous but also the place where his hands can create most havoc. So if you wanted to create a love scene, where would it be most dramatically interesting to set? In the bedroom, on a garage forecourt, in a box at a concert hall, at the zoo in front of the lions? Look for the unobvious – the original. Note that a constricted location or controlled environment (submarine, spaceship, airplane, tube train, car, warehouse, etc.) – somewhere the character can't escape from – is highly dramatic (*Speed*, *Crimson Tide*, *Escape From New York*, the pub in *Shaun Of The Dead*, *Panic Room*, *The Others*). *Glengarry Glen Ross* neatly

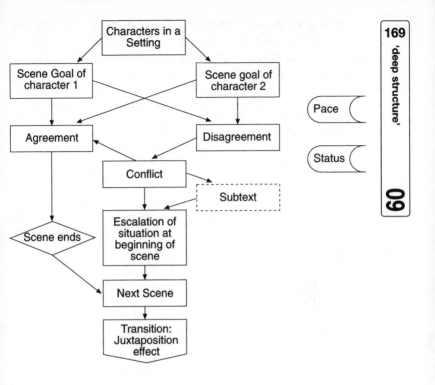

**figure 9.1** scene construction flowchart
source: *Jurgen Wolff*

exploits the claustrophobic/paranoiac potential of both the
office and the bar; *Cherish* has a protagonist forced to wear
an electronic tag which means she cannot leave her
apartment; the metal cage that drops down enclosing the
wrestling ring in *Spider-Man*.

- Can you dramatize this scene 'against the grain'? Your couple
  decide to make love in their concert hall box; they are about
  to kiss, suddenly another couple enters and occupies the other
  seats; your first couple have to stop. Do they stay to watch
  the concert or continue their scene elsewhere? You've added
  conflict, made something difficult, and then made it more
  difficult and added tension to their decision: should they stay
  or leave?
- Can you heighten the emotion by using weather and the
  elements? Notice how many scenes of high dramatic or
  emotional content take place in the pouring rain (*Apocalypse*

*Now, The Piano, Spider-Man, Road To Perdition, Witness*, the final scenes in *Breakfast At Tiffany's, Four Weddings And A Funeral*, the entire third Act of *American Beauty*). Rain is very dramatic – as are gales, thunderstorms, hurricanes, sandstorms, restless seas, etc. Think of the cold, stark bleakness of the Winter landscapes in *Fargo, Misery, Affliction* and *Insomnia*. Can you think of other scenes where weather plays a significant role?

## Content

By creating context you determine the dramatic purpose of your scene; you can begin to build that scene line by line or action by action and create the content. So how do we go about that? First find the components or elements within that scene. For each character in your scene, ask the following:

- What aspects of this character's life (professional/personal/ private) will be revealed?
- What is their goal in this scene? What do they want to do or achieve? What do they want to happen or prevent from happening?
- Is there agreement? (If so, your scene ends and you move on to your next scene.)
- Is there disagreement? If so is there conflict? What is it? What type? What's the subtext? Does the scene escalate the situation at the beginning of the scene? (If so, move on.)
- Are the stakes raised by this scene? In what way?
- What has changed at the end of this scene from when we first entered it?

Also ask yourself these questions about your character's attitude:

- What is my character's general attitude within the overall screenplay?
- What is the character's attitude in this specific scene, both at the start and by the end? Has it changed, and if so, how?

Now ask yourself those last two questions in relation to each character's status within that scene.

Lastly, ask yourself if this scene moves your protagonist a step (large or small) nearer to their goal at the end of the screenplay (and the sequence). How does it connect to that Act III climax?

If it doesn't do any of these, drop it, no matter how brilliant it is.

## Crisis and climax

As mentioned, a dramatic scene is internally structured. It moves to a crisis then a climax – indeed, there may be a series of smaller internal crises before the major scene crisis arrives. Let's recap the definitions:

- Crisis is a moment in a scene that forces a decision and causes a change in the character or story.

After the crisis the forces operating within the scene or Act are realigned. A major crisis, therefore, is a turning point.

- Climax is a moment in a scene that resolves a crisis one way or the other.

## Character revelation

In most scenes your character will discover something, realize something or have something revealed to them. They will gain knowledge. This will affect the storyline or their character development or both. The revelation may be dramatic or merely significant; it depends on your story.

## Scene causality

Understand that each scene 'causes' the next one (more or less) and, of course, events within a scene 'cause' the subsequent incidents. Causality is an essential element in constructing your screenplay; it helps you define or even possibly construct your plot, and is a tool in creating powerful momentum (Chapter 10). Remember that 'burst of energy' analogy I made at the end of Chapter 07.

## Scene ends – writing backwards

Just as it is important to know the end of your script before writing it and to know the end of each Act before entering it, so it is equally important to know the end of your scene. The writing of each scene is, nevertheless, almost always an act of exploration. Once you discover the end of your scene you will probably find yourself going back to rewrite it in the light of your new knowledge.

Finally, consider the effect you create (or want to create) by juxtaposing your scene with the previous or following scene. Are you trying to create a transition, a contrast, conflict, humour, irony, what? (see Pacing, page 192).

## Flashbacks

*Flashback* is a technique of showing past happenings in order to expand an audience's comprehension of the present story, character or situation. It's very tempting to slip into flashbacks in a script, but for the Script Reader it usually suggests either sloppiness or problems in your script. Try to execute your story through *action*, not flashbacks; if you do use it, use it sparingly and effectively. The same applies to flashforwards.

> Traditionally, flashbacks were taboo. Hopefully with *CSI*: we broke that taboo. We have flashbacks and what we call 'versions': a flashback is a standard one that shows what happened; a version is flashback that shows that character's POV or take on what they say or claimed happened.
>
> *Anthony E. Zuicker,*
> Executive producer: *CSI: Crime Scene Investigation,*
> *CSI: Miami, CSI: NY*

---

The scene is a hi-tech office block. Richard is an accounts executive: 43, industrious, trustworthy, rather shy and weedy. His boss, Steve, is a thrusting high-flyer: 28, ruthless, driven, focused, fit, he hates older people and thinks they're slow. Somebody has made a grave error in accounts: Richard knows it's not him, suspects his boss, but somebody has to take the blame. Steve is in his office 'discussing' the matter with Richard. Write the scene.

---

Now relocate this scene (preferably within the building) and texture it using conflict (direct and indirect – think subtext) to complicate, tighten and enrich the action. Draw out the contrasts between the characters, their relationship, reveal more about each of them to us, anticipate further conflict down the road. What must you show? How can you dramatize it? What scene goals does each have? Can you do it without dialogue? Use the location potential.

---

If you have already written some scenes for your own script, try this scene relocation exercise on them too.

# Dialogue

*Dialogue* is verbal action which pushes the story forward and which is derived from the character's needs within the scene.

> Sometimes you steal dialogue you hear. But normally the way I write dialogue is: I have an idea of how long the dialogue should be – one page, two, three pages, how much the scene will support, and how many points I have to make in that dialogue – either information points or character development points. Then I just start working out conversation . . . using what seems natural to get from one point to another.
>
> *Paul Schrader,*
> screenwriter: *Taxi Driver, Affliction, Mishima,*
> *Raging Bull, Bringing Out The Dead*

Dialogue is the easiest way to impart story and character information. Hence, most new screenwriters will tend to over-emphasize dialogue above the other elements, but the sources of information in a screenplay should be shared by all the script's components.

Screenwriting is about learning how best and most appropriately to use *all* the means of expression: visual action (physical and decision), props, sounds, setting, context, subtext, etc. In general, dialogue should be the last resort of the screenwriter after all the other means of expression have been tried and found wanting.

Did you notice how spare the dialogue was in *Witness*? Did it work against your appreciation and understanding of the story and characters, or did it say more by saying less?

> Never let an actor talk unless he has something to say.
>
> *John Huston,*
> director

Film is primarily a visual medium. Images, not words, are your basic currency. Hence the accepted rule is: *show, don't tell.* Despite the popularity of Quentin Tarantino's clever and entertaining 'plotless dialogue' (he's also a director, remember), it is still always preferable to show someone exhibiting a trait rather than telling it in dialogue. Even though TV is more dialogue driven than feature films, the TV writer should still conceive their script visually. Think visual: visualize your character, their behaviour details – body language, gestures, unconscious looks, habits, etc. – as you write your dialogue. And remember, characters interact.

Dialogue performs certain functions:

- providing information
- advancing the story onward and upward
- deepening the characters by revealing emotion, mood, feel, intent (via subtext) and by telling us what would be difficult, time-comsuming or ponderous via character action
- revealing incidents and information (especially motivation) from the past, i.e. from the backstory, so that dialogue can avoid the need for flashbacks
- adding to the rhythm and pace of the script by the ambience it contributes to each scene and contributing to the style of the script (snappy and witty like *Butch Cassidy And The Sundance Kid, Pulp Fiction, Shrek, Maverick*; sparse like *Witness, Death In Venice*; distinctive like *Blade Runner, Fight Club, Memento, Brazil*); naturalistic (*Billy Elliot, Good Will Hunting, Sweet Sixteen*) etc.
- connecting scenes and shots by providing continuity
- suggesting the presence of objects, events or persons not seen by using off-screen (o.s.) dialogue.

Ideally, all the dialogue your characters speak should be caused by their need to get something in that scene or in a later scene. The true nature of good screen dialogue is that it comes from, is caused by and is driven by the immediate needs of your character at that specific point in the scene and that juncture of the plot, and also by their longer-term needs of the screenplay story.

Screen dialogue is not everyday conversation. What you strive for is *effective* dialogue, to give the *illusion* of real conversation. Effective dialogue sounds natural; it conveys the sense of real speech even through it is more structured than the wanderings of everyday speech. Effective dialogue has more economy and directness than real-life conversation.

Make a recording of people conversing, then listen to it; their dialogue is full of half-completed sentences, 'ers' and 'ums', hesitations and repetitions, rambling, overlapping and rarely focused – the *tone* is conversational, non-literary.

As in conversation, effective screen dialogue is essentially oblique (see subtext), more naturalistic than, say, stage dialogue.

Screenwriting uses all the hesitations, half-sentences, etc. of everyday speech, but the dialogue is condensed. For example, examine the many dialogue exchanges in *Good Will Hunting*. While it reveals the improvisatory techniques Matt Damon and Ben Affleck used when creating the original scenes (and, latterly, with Robin Williams when filming), the finished product – the scene itself – contains the key information that needed to be imparted in that scene at that point: scene goals had been very clearly thought-through.

Screenwriting is typically lean and economic. Effective dialogue is sparsely written, with short sentences of simple construction, using simple, informal words. Speeches are brief and crisp. Screen dialogue is written for the ear, to be listened to, not for the eye to read. The basic principle of dialogue (as with all screenplay description) is:

---

### Say More With Less

---

Dialogue *can* convey what a character thinks or tell us what is going on in their mind, but it can also be one of the dangers; it encourages novice writers to be lazy.

Screen dialogue words are used more for their implicit rather than explicit meaning. What is important in dialogue is not the literal meaning of the words used, but the meaning being conveyed in the circumstances of that scene. What is not said, or is left unsaid, can be as important as what is spoken (see subtext, page 179).

Dialogue should fit the character, their mood and emotions in the particular situation, with a rhythm and individuality of expression typical of that character. Make your dialogue sound like the character, not the writer. One test is to take the dialogue in your scene and try swapping the speeches around and get those words spoken by your other character. If they can be switched with little evident distinction, then your characters and dialogue have probably not been effectively individualized.

Dialogue works best when it is underwritten and understated. Excessive emotion and spouting platitudes lead to melodrama. And when you *do* get to an emotional dialogue scene, it must be in keeping with the character and their own personal speech patterns. Likewise, avoid clichés and stock phrases, unless they are part of the way that character always speaks.

Most screen dialogue exchanges are short and snappy, speeches bounce off each other like ping-pong, with one piece of dialogue hooking into or causing the next line, building up a momentum. Long single speeches stretching on and on for half a page or more will only alienate your audience. A Reader, upon their initial flick-through fanning of your script, will notice any great slabs of dialogue. It turns them off; to them it indicates that the writer does not understand the accepted rules of writing screen dialogue. If you must have long speeches in your script, you had better have a good reason for them, as in the 'My name is Maximus…' declaration in *Gladiator*. Alec Baldwin's powerful motivational speech at the start of *Glengarry Glen Ross* is not just a statement of that character's ethos, it embodies the entire environment in which these other characters inhabit, and it sets up the main goal/s of the story itself. (Again, note the use of the 'Rule of Three'.) Likewise, Gordon Gekko's 'greed is good' speech in *Wall Street* is his whole philosophy of existence. So avoid long speeches; cut them out or into groups of smaller speeches. If you must, use very sparingly.

Be aware too of the role of silence: what is not said in a scene can be just as important as what is spoken. Actors and directors learn to use silence as a tool in their box of effects – so should you. Remember, dialogue can be used off-screen (o.s.), or without sound (M.O.S.) – see Chapter 02.

The one thing you don't want your dialogue to do is get the response that Harrison Ford said to George Lucas, upon reading the first draft of the *Star Wars* script:

You can type this shit, George, but you can't say it.

---

Watch *Rififi*, paying particular attention to the 30-minute heist sequence; then view the first 40 minutes of *Absolute Power*. Both are played out mostly without any dialogue. Watch and learn. Does one 'work' better than the other? Ask yourself why and how?

---

## Voice-overs

Modern films have seen a noticeable increase in the use of voice-overs to the extent it almost seems an accepted screen norm these days. However, it is essentially a literary device and usually indicates the original source material. My advice is either try to avoid or at least use sparingly and with extreme care.

Voice-over narration *can* be used effectively to set the story and illuminate it:

- If the narrator is a character – often the protagonist – it can supply a personal touch or establish quickly the script's P.O.V., especially at the point of entry (*Field Of Dreams*, *Spider-Man*, *The Great Gatsby*, *L.A. Confidential*, *Rounders*, *Bridget Jones's Diary*, *About A Boy*, *Out Of Africa*, *American Beauty*, *Goodfellas*, *The Quiet American*, *Fight Club*, *Sin City*, *300*, *Gone Baby Gone*) – how many of those can you detect were from literary sources?
- If the narrator is not a character in the script it can supply a certain objectivity (*The Lord Of The Rings*, *Tom Jones*) or create counterpoint (e.g. humourous – *George Of The Jungle*; quirky – *Amélie*).
- Some stories need a narrator to supply a unifying structure to the story (*Goodfellas*, *Edward Scissorhands*, *Croupier*, *Trainspotting*, *Stand By Me*, *The Wonder Years*, *Little Big Man*, *Kind Hearts And Coronets*, *84 Charing Cross Road*).
- It can be used if you need to create a pause moment or give a reflective/contemplative feel to your narrative (*Badlands*, *Memento*, *Sugarland Express*); see Chapter 10 – Pacing.

When writing your script, and you are tempted to throw-in some v.o. narration, ask yourself: could the information I am trying to impart not be done better, more creatively – more visually?

Watch the film *Election*. It has a total of five different characters' voice-overs/P.O.V.s. Was it confusing overkill or was it well handled?

Any guidelines on dialogue can only be suggestions. Follow any rules too rigidly and you may find your dialogue becoming mechanical or artificial. Ultimately, to learn to write good dialogue, you must *learn to listen*: listen and observe how meaning is expressed, both verbally and non-verbally (in real life and on the screen), listen to the meaning beneath the overt sense of the words – the subtext; listen to the voice, the expressions, even the gestures. Above all, learn to listen to your characters. If you've done thorough work on a character you will know them so well that they will have developed a reality and presence of their own, with their own speech patterns –

their own personal grammar. You will find them starting to write their own dialogue, but talking through you.

> Dialogue cannot be taught. You either have an ear for it or not.
>
> *David Edgar*

Some tips:

- Try to avoid 'passing-the-time-of-day' dialogue: greetings, polite nothings, goodbyes, etc. Tarantino can get away with it. You should be looking to create your own characters' speech patterns.
- Don't repeat information in dialogue that has already occurred elsewhere in the dialogue; beginners' scripts are full of these repetitions.
- Avoid dialect and writing phonetically: tell the Reader when you introduce the character they speak with a Scots/New Jersey/whatever accent. The occasional 'gonna' or 'ain't' is fine but don't overdo it. Script Readers don't like reading phonetic dialogue – write it in readable English and let the actors do their jobs.
- If you want to create emphasis try to do it without using exclamation marks; never italicize dialogue; don't use capitals (except rarely); an occasional underlining is okay.
- Not every question asked in dialogue needs to be answered. The use of silence, a reaction, or non-reaction can be as/more powerful than dialogue (e.g. *Witness*). Not every question needs to be answered with the most obvious reply. An oblique open or indirect answer may reveal more about the state of mind of the responding character.
- Expletives: They may appear to be more acceptable in a modern script, but if you *are* going to use them, they should always be in context: of character, setting and situation. Otherwise, it might indicate to the Reader a lack of imagination from the writer, or just take up valuable space on the page. Use expletives sparingly and when they *are* used they will be more effective (e.g. *American Beauty*).
- Speaking directly to camera: an increasing device (e.g. *Malcolm In The Middle*, *Shakespeare In Love*) but it is difficult to bring it off successfully without seeming 'stagey'. Shakespeare could do it, but you should handle with extreme caution.

- Select a favourite film which is not purely action driven.
- Work out its Act I division. (If you find an entire Act too daunting, try it for a short 30-minute TV drama, or just the first ten minutes of the film).
- View Act I repeatedly, noting down each and every scene and what goes on in that scene, what information is imparted, etc. until you are thoroughly conversant with that act. Better still, work from the script if you can get it.
- Working from your notes (or script), try to rewrite the entire first Act as a silent movie, with no dialogue at all. Force yourself to describe and develop character and meaningful action visually.

Why do this exercise? Because I can guarantee that by doing it you will learn valuable insights into portraying characters by showing us who they are and what they're feeling, not by *telling* us. Think visually and you will start to write visually.

## Subtext

Script editors and actors will tell you that great drama is all about subtext. Think of the classic eating scene in *Tom Jones*, the unbuttoning of the glove in the carriage in *The Age Of Innocence*, the finger caressing the hole in the stocking in *The Piano*, 'Annabella Smith' unrolling her stocking while handcuffed to Richard Hannay in Hitchcock's *The 39 Steps*; what are they about? Eating? Hosiery? No – the subtext is mutual seduction.

As in real life, the actual meaning lies behind the apparent surface meaning. This is subtext – what is being communicated beneath the text lines or action; the real meaning being conveyed, the real intent (conscious or unconscious) of the character. For the writer, subtext expresses the hidden agenda of a character.

Examine the party scene early in *Tootsie*. Sandy holds up a baby saying how much Michael loves and adores babies. She says this to Michael as he passes; he simply grunts out 'yeah' without even looking at the baby. What subtext is being communicated here – for Michael and for Sandy? How is it used?

Now do the same for *Witness*: examine the scene where Rachel is nursing John's wound and their final departing scene.

You can use subtext in a number of useful ways:

- You can *set an agenda* for your plot and state to the audience what the characters need to do. (Very useful in thrillers, adventure, detective stories and teen romances.) It allows you to believably put together disconnected bits of information.

- You can give the audience more information than the protagonist knows, thus putting them in a *superior position*. It lets the audience know about impending disaster round the corner before we watch the character/s turn the corner and confront it.

- You can *pose a question* that the audience and the characters need the answer to. In *Godfather II*, Michael and Alfredo are discussing their futures. Michael is waiting for his brother to confess his part in the killing of a gangster; he is waiting but Alfredo never gets round to it. We know this is actually a tense death-sentence scene although nobody is killed. Note that this only works because earlier Michael had said 'I could forgive him if he'll confess'.

- You can *establish obstacles,* set up expectations in the audience's mind of the problems your protagonist will encounter. The drama comes from the knowledge that we know these obstacles are waiting to be confronted – this is linked to the 'superior position' (above).

- You can *create an enigma* by denying the audience all the key information until the very last moment. You can drop in tantalizing information and unexplained moments that set up the subtext that says implicitly 'if you stay with this long enough, it will all become clear'.

All the above are linked: you are *creating expectations* in the audience's mind – and that's why subtext works (see page 191). Subtext can be used as part of creating a deception: a character says one thing but means another. Another character might not read this subtextual meaning (although they may sense it), but the audience must be aware of the subtext.

As a writer, when writing, you must not only be aware of how a character reads a scene (understands what is going on in that scene, what is said and done), but also how an audience reads a scene. Try to enter the mind of the audience.

Often the subtext constitutes a more enriching emotional experience for the audience than the surface movements of the story, both in main plot and subplots. But what is most revealing are the two levels of meaning integrated together. Screen dramas with appropriate and successful subtext are remembered long after the others have faded in the public mind.

> I don't make epics in the normal sense. I make emotional epics.
>
> *Mike Leigh,*
> director: *Secrets And Lies,*
> *Topsy Turvy, All Or Nothing*

---

When actors rehearse a scene, they try techniques to reveal subtext. First they speak the line as printed, then follow that by voicing what they feel the subtext is. Do this yourself. Take a scene from a film you like, preferably a scene with some meaty dialogue and some action or movement. Watch it, then write down the dialogue and action in that scene (ideally get the script and work from that). Under each line of dialogue and action, fill in what you imagine the subtext is. After you have done this for a couple of film scenes, try doing it for your own scenes. Another technique is to try reading your scene and subtext into a tape recorder. Play it back and ask yourself: 'Is the subtext clear to an audience in the lines I have written on the page?'

---

With screwball comedy especially, there's lots of fast-paced dialogue, but it's what's between and beneath those lines – the relationships between the characters – that is important.

> *Renée Zellwegger,* actress: *Bridget Jones,*
> *Down With Love,*
> *Leatherheads*

Some tips on writing dialogue may be found at this website:

fictionwriting.about.com/od/crafttechnique/tp/dialogue.htm

...and some books to browse:

Tom Chiarella: *Writing Dialogue* (Story Press Books)
Rib Davis: *Writing Dialogue for Scripts* (A&C Black)
Jean Saunders: *Writing Realistic Dialogue* (Allison & Busby)
Lewis Turco: *The Book of Dialogue* (University Press of New England).

# 10

## enhancing emotion

**In this chapter you will learn:**
- how your characters and plot take an audience with them to travel the journey of your story
- how to enhance emotional responses from your audience.

Having broken the screenplay down to its micro-elements, let's return to the overarching perspective and consider how certain events on the screen register in the mind of the audience. By understanding the processes you can begin to manipulate these according to your needs as a storyteller, enhancing emotion *in the audience* and *on the page*. It's down to the decisions the screenwriter makes about what to show and what to exclude.

## Character motivation and structure

The driving force of your screenplay, and what makes it dramatic, is character in conflict and the reasons *why* that character will seek out conflict.

Generally speaking, main plots are fairly simple and straightforward, though they may contain many twists and turns. The main plot of *Witness* is basically: John Book tries to solve a murder but instead becomes hunted by the murderers who are fellow cops. Doesn't really grab you, does it?

What deepens, complicates and enriches this simple storyline is character. Character influences, alters and deepens the main storyline. It travels through your screenplay affecting every incident and person it comes into contact with, kicking the storyline into new directions, into new and often unexpected territory. Character is the element that engages us most deeply and is an essential component of establishing a film's *momentum*, because without character we have no link with the mind of the audience (via their identification with the character).

Rachel's influence on John Book in *Witness* causes him to accept the wearing of Amish clothing which becomes crucial in the second turning point scene where Book beats up the punks, thus drawing attention to himself *because* he is wearing Amish clothing. Hence Schaeffer learns where he is and searches for him in Act III. Rachel's earlier influence also causes Book to hand over his gun, also allowing us to understand that change is taking place in his character. So character deepens and affects the main storyline, making it more interesting and more engaging for an audience. And what makes a character do whatever it is they do? Motivation, which is *character in action*.

Now, armed with your knowledge of structure, we can begin to see how character and growth work within structure. When we first see a character, they have a set of motivations based on their biography and especially backstory. This set of motivations will be assaulted and transformed by you the writer. Indeed, each of the three (or four or five) Acts reflects a distinct phase in the central character's motivation.

Character action follows a distinct path: a character encounters (or creates) a 'problem' which is uncompromisingly threatening; this generates an urgent (dramatic) need or intention to get or do something to cure the problem, which formulates a goal – the external movitation. Having decided what it is, they set out to get it (action) but things don't go smoothly and they reach a crisis. At the point they overcome the crisis (or accept they won't overcome it), their motivations are altered; this is the climax or change point. From this we can draw up a *character action equation*:

$$\underset{\substack{\text{problem} \\ \text{(motive)}}}{\text{problem}} \longrightarrow \underset{\substack{\text{/need} \\ \text{(goal)}}}{\overset{\text{intention}}{\text{/need}}} \longrightarrow \text{action} \longrightarrow \text{crisis} \longrightarrow \underset{\substack{\text{climax/} \\ \text{change point}}}{\overset{\text{result/}}{\text{climax/}}}$$

This equation happens not just over your entire screenplay, but within each Act (important), usually within each sequence and often within each major scene.

Using this, and remembering the transformational arc, you can begin to construct the *motivational through-line* for your character and screenplay. For example, Act I of *Witness* runs:

| | | |
|---|---|---|
| problem | = | the murder |
| need/goal | = | to catch the killer |
| action | = | investigating |
| crisis | = | the killer is a fellow cop |
| climax | = | the shoot-out scene: betrayal |

Can you work out the equation for Acts II and III?

## The motivational through-line

This motivation line is another level on which you can structure your screenplay: at the point of entry, the first kind of motivation that compels your character to act often comes from the backstory. The character may find themselves in a life-crisis situation – even if they don't realize it themselves. By showing your character at some crisis point in their life you are putting them in a state of vulnerability. It is then much easier to shift them in new directions. Ideally, they should be ready to move, virtually begging for something new to happen to them.

For Rachel, in *Witness*, her husband has just died. This makes her vulnerable, open to new influences; it also supplies a believable reason for her to travel to Philadelphia (on her way to visit her sister). Given Rachel's background, we need a crisis in her life to shift her, not only physically out of her environment, but also out of her mental environment, so that she could actually consider falling in love with someone like John Book who, on the surface, seems to represent everything that is opposite to her communal Amish life and beliefs. Can you find any life-crisis situations in the other films you watched for Chapter 07?

This life-crisis device can be used at any point in your screenplay, but it is particularly useful in Act I. So: open with a crisis in your protagonist's life, then throw in the inciting incident like a bomb, and the resulting explosion will catapult your characters into the story. The inciting incident creates the 'problem', starts your story, brings all the crucial main characters together, and provides added and more powerful motivation for your character's actions.

At the beginning of *Witness*, the backstory motivation for Book is that he is an ambitious cop (we *see* he wants to catch crooks and advance his career). Rachel's backstory motivation comes from her Amish community values and her loathing of all things and people who represent violence. The two sets of backstory motivation come into almost immediate conflict as soon as the pair meet. They are both affected by the murder (and Samuel's witnessing of it). This heightens Book's motivation, who clearly sees it as a career advancement opportunity. For Rachel, it motivates her to work with Book (and men who live by violence), however reluctantly, in order to get the matter over with as quickly as possible and return to her life. The motivation line of Act I moves up through the inciting incident, first plot crisis to climax. This is a moment the audience knows will intensify the story and the character's motivation (when Samuel points to the photograph of McFee and they/we realize the murderer is a fellow cop). The protagonist's decision to act tightens the story, its direction, and usually adds more risk. The next major event that intensifies the motivation line is the Act I climax, where the protagonist creates their/your script's goal, external motivation or dramatic need (e.g. John Book needs to survive and protect Rachel and Samuel).

The goal of your character (the most powerful motivation in your story) forces the character into conflict with their environment, with other people, or with themselves. It also links the structure of your screenplay from the first turning point to the ultimate climax in Act III. So always ensure that the audience sees, understands or can clearly deduce the motivation of the main character/s.

Over the course of your screenplay, each of these moments adds something to or strongly affects the motivation line:

Backstory ——→ Point of Entry ——→ **Inciting Incident** →
(life-crisis)

——→ Plot ——→ **Act I Climax** ——→ Focus ——→
Crisis 1        (Turning Point 1)      Point 1

——→ **Half-Way Point** ——→ Focus ——→ Plot ——→
(Point of No Return)           Point 2           Crisis 2

**Moment of Truth**
——→     Act II Climax ——→  Act III Climax
(Turning Point 2)

The four elements in bold are the most crucial; they are the major points on your character's motivation line. The other points shift or intensify the line without necessarily turning it in other directions or creating a point-of-no-return situation.

Remember, external motivation must be very clear and strong in the audience's mind – so it must first be clear in yours. If you are confused, your audience will be too.

---

Now write down the events in your screen story which correspond to the points in the above chart and picture how your protagonist's motivation line will be changed by each event or situation.

---

Now do this for all your main characters.

---

## Momentum: building tension

Momentum is the forward movement necessary for any screen story. It is the effect your screenplay has on the mind of the audience, and it's all linked to creating and building tension. Almost every scene in your script should contain tension: it is the energy that propels and sucks the audience through your story. Tension is created when the audience hopes and/or fears that something will happen to the characters.

At its simplest: tension = conflict + contrast. Opposites create tension, (opposite forces, opposite characters and opposite expectations) for your characters and audience; opposite expectations generate hopes and fears in the audience's emotions.

There are a number of devices you can use to create tension:

- anticipation
- suspense
- subtext
- raising the stakes.

## Tension: building anticipation and suspense

Suspense is the hidden energy that holds a story together. It connects two points and sends a charge between them. It doesn't have to be all action. Emotions can create their own suspense. And secrets are a great way of generating tension.

Frank Cottrell Boyce, screenwriter:
*God On Trial, 24 Hour Party People*

Anticipating that something is going to happen causes the mind of the audience to move forward: they anticipate getting to the goal and the only way of getting there is to mentally move forwards to it, to want it, to hunger for it, etc.

Imagine a small child on her birthday. At 9 o'clock one morning you tell her that today at 4 o'clock there will be a surprise birthday party for her with lots of friends, stacks of food, presents, etc. Congratulations, you have just destroyed her day. That time between 9 and 4 no longer exists for her because her mind is now racing forward and reaching for the time the party starts – but you've told her everything and spoilt the surprise. The audience's mind works in the same way: so give them *only* the information they need at the time and don't spoil the surprise.

When considering how your audience reacts to the dramatic incidents you design for them, remember two things:

- There no one-to-one link between actor emotions and audience emotions. You cannot create specific reactions in your audience simply because you create them in an actor; just because an actor portrays sadness doesn't mean the audience will feel sad. The way you manipulate audience reactions and feelings is via the personality of the character, the situations you put them in, what the risks are, and the degree of audience identification.

- One of the most powerful ways of manipulating audience reactions is via the dimension of future time and its inherent uncertainties – 'What's going to happen next?' 'Will it happen?' 'When will it happen?' It is this future dimension that allows you to affect the audience.

In screen drama there are three dimensions of time: past, present and future. When building anticipation and suspense, the most important of these is the future. This is because the future dimension contains the two elements of *uncertainty* which past and present never can: of not knowing *if* an action will take place or *when* it will take place.

So, how do you create those audience links to the future?

### Anticipation

We anticipate something will happen either:

- because it has always happened (it is a normal pattern of life, like the sun rising in the morning)
- because the screenwriter has established it as a norm in the world of your script (for example, in *Logan's Run* everybody accepts death at 31 because of overcrowding), or the norm in that particular character (i.e. it is normal for this character to smoke in bed, beat his wife, rob banks, drink under stress, etc.).

Creating *surprise* is one way of manipulating your audience anticipation: this maintains audience interest by telling them that things are unpredictable, that their expectations will not normally be fulfilled. However, an audience cannot be surprised by an event unless they anticipated a different event taking place. That's why, for Truman Burbank, the light falling out of the sky is such an unexpected event in this perfect world.

Anticipation, like intention, must be completed: either fulfilled, contradicted or interrupted. You cannot create anticipations and then leave them hanging; loose ends dissatisfy an audience, they feel cheated.

## Suspense

Making the outcome of an event uncertain places the audience in suspense. Suspense causes them to hurry towards the end of your story wishing to get through it as quickly as possible, because suspense is a state of discomfort or pain. But is is also a pleasurable kind of pain like entering the horror house at the fun fair – you are alarmed by the scares and screams but as soon as you get out the other side you want to go back in again.

Think of the murder scene in the men's toilet in *Witness*, a very suspenseful scene full of tension; Samuel came very close to being caught and killed. Did you feel a sense of relief after that scene? Probably.

Both these elements are psychological processes and happen *in the mind of the audience*. They cause the mind of the audience to move forward because the audience craves to see the future become the present so that they can reach the anticipated event, or so they can get out the other side of the tense scene and breathe again.

Suspense occurs when an audience becomes uncertain that the goal of your character will be achieved, and it applies to the screenplay as a whole. (You can also, of course, create it at *any* point in your script.) Let's consider the elements in this process:

- to have suspense you must have a character who forms a *need* or *intention* that is vitally important to them
- from that need, the character conceives a *goal*
- if the goal is easy to get then there is no suspense because there is no *uncertainty*
- for the goal to be uncertain there must be difficulties. Not just any difficulties, but difficulties *powerfully challenging* to the goal.

Suspense is also created when we do not know the outcome of a particular action. Here your audience must be made to feel two emotions, hope and fear:

- *hope* – that the outcome will occur (but fear that it won't)
- *fear* – that the outcome will occur (but hope that it won't).

Usually, to generate these emotions you must create that linkage between audience and characters which is audience identification (Chapter 05).

Hence suspense equals *doubt*. The choice you have is: *certainty of outcome* vs. *uncertainty of outcome*.

A strong, clear goal is therefore vital: as well as helping establish motivation, it gives direction and meaning to your story and to the actions of your characters. If your audience doesn't know the character's goal it cannot measure the strength and quality of the difficulties and cannot know if they are challenging enough to make the getting of the goal uncertain or doubtful. And without uncertainty and doubt there is no suspense. The audience must know the goal *and* the difficulties in getting it.

Suspense starts when you have three ingredients, and not before:

- an intention (setting a clear, strong goal)
- difficulties, especially a counter-intention, that creates . . .
- uncertainty as to the outcome.

Normally, as soon as you have conveyed the intention you will convey the difficulties as quickly as possible and this will create the uncertainty. Suspense is best maintained for as much of your screenplay as possible. So you need to establish the intention and the difficulties as early as possible and maintain the suspense for as long as possible. Suspense ends immediately after the final climactic scene because this represents the success or failure of your hero or heroine after which there is absolutely no doubt or uncertainty as to the outcome. This is another reason why you need to end your screenplay as quickly as possible after the final climax, because the suspense is integral to moving the audience through the story, and once it has gone there is no longer any momentum. Any part of the script without these three ingredients will lack suspense.

You should also understand that suspense is something you create on all levels of a screenplay: for the script as a whole, for each Act, for each sequence and for each scene. All these overlap and form part of each other.

Note that suspense need not always be life-threatening. Love stories have their own suspense. In *My Big Fat Greek Wedding*, the suspense is: will Toula and Ian, despite their differences (and other obstacles in their paths) get married and live happily ever after by the end of the film? What is the suspense in *Sleepless In Seattle*?

Watch *Seven*, an excellent example of generating suspense and anticipation through audience engagement. What elements does it use and how does it use them? Why do we not see the last two murders? Are they all the more effective for our not seeing them?

# Subtext

Re-read page 179. Remember, what we *don't* see is often more effective than actually showing something. Watching the reactions of a character standing outside a door listening to the passionate love-making going on inside is more emotionally effective than actually seeing the event. In *Shallow Grave* or *Frailty* the murders are all the more effective because we only *hear* them being done, or see the bodies being disposed of in darkness. In *Dumb And Dumber* we don't see Lloyd urinating into a beer bottle, we only hear it and see the end result. Think of the severing of the finger in *The Piano*, the strangulation climax of *The Talented Mr. Ripley* and most of *The Blair Witch Project*. The audience deduced it – just as it deduced the ear-severing in *Reservoir Dogs*. Admittedly, a lot is down to the director's decision, but it's also down to what you choose to show and not to show, and the ability and power of subtext to affect an audience's imagination. Hitchcock understood this superbly.

# Raising the stakes

This means increasing the risk to your characters as they progress through your screenplay, that is, the characters must have something to lose, or something bad would happen to them if they fail (or if they go through with their present action). This risk personalizes the 'problem' for them and, through identification, becomes a problem for the audience. Once again your are manipulating the audience through their hopes and fears. *Changing Lanes* is a very good example of stakes being raised steadily throughout the story.

At the start of *Minority Report* the stakes are: although the public trust John Anderton because of his loss, his pain is actually jeopardizing the entire Precrime initiative; increasingly the stakes become more personalized until he eventually loses his freedom and ultimately, possibly, his life. In *Armageddon* the stakes underlying the characters' actions could not be more obvious - if the meteor is not stopped, the world would be destroyed. In *My Big Fat Greek Wedding* the stakes are that Toula and Ian will never finally get married, be accepted by their mutual cultures and thus end up living incomplete lives of mundanity and probable loneliness. What do you think are the stakes in *Witness*: for John Book, for Rachel, for the community?

Now while a screenplay has major stakes, it should also have minor stakes: risks underlying individual scenes, sequences and Acts.

Rising conflict demands that the stakes are raised higher and higher as the story progresses. This is only logical: if the dangers are at a certain level at the end of Act I, it is inconceivable they will lessen thereafter till the end of the screenplay. The audience's interest would also lessen.

An essential ingredient in raising the stakes is (again) identification. If the audience doesn't care about your character, they will not care about the risk; the more they care about the character the easier it will be to put that character at risk because the audience will experience hopes and fears attendant to that character.

So anticipation, suspense, subtext and raising the stakes are all devices to create *tension* and building tension creates *momentum*.

Insufficient tension is a regular problem with scripts. Are you creating tension in your use of each device? So for every scene you should ask yourself:

- What is the audience *hoping* for here, but simultaneously *afraid* of?
- Are these hopes and fears strong enough to keep the audience engaged and move them on to the next scene?

---

Watch *The Usual Suspects, L.A. Confidential* and *Chinatown*: how are the four elements of tension used in these dramas? Why at certain points are certain elements used and not others?

---

## Pacing

Pacing means the overall feel of your screenplay, and relates to the flow and rhythm of the climaxes, reliefs and pauses, the highs and lows, the 'crises-per-page', and how they contribute to the 'heartbeat' within that larger structure.

All drama needs variety within its overall structural unity; moments of crisis, confrontation and climax need to be interspersed with moments of quieter reflection – pauses. Audiences need those lulls when characters open up and reveal themselves, when a mood is established, so an audience can catch its breath before being taken to another high. *Minority Report* moves between the fast-action (mostly chase or pursuit) sequences and John Anderton's comparatively quieter moments (at home, with Dr. Hineman, with his wife in the countryside, etc.). Similarly, *Road To Perdition* moves between two main settings: urban (associated with violence, corruption, tension and claustrophobia) and rural (aligned to freedom, tranquillity, honesty and reflection). Even films which from frame one sweep you up and move along in a seemingly relentless romp (*Speed, Ed Wood, American Pie, xXx*) have their comparatively quieter moments. A drama constantly at the same level of intensity (high as in Spielberg's *1941*, or low as in some 'art' films), or with a continuous build like this:

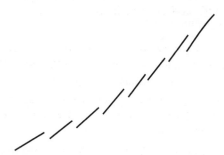

**figure 10.1** a gradual build of intensity

... with no variation, will lead to your script getting dull and lose your audience's interest. To give your script movement (and evoke responses in your audience) you need to have a proper balance of high and low points. And, as with your conflict and setback graph, your highs and lows need to be paced in a saw-tooth construct like this:

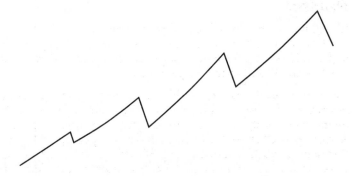

**figure 10.2** climaxes and reliefs

To create your script's rhythm you can use the following contrasting *elements of transition* between scenes:

- fast vs. slow tempo scenes
- short vs. long scene lengths
- plot/dramatic scenes vs. theme/character/mood scenes
- scenes presenting information/mood vs. emotion
- day vs. night; light vs. dark
- interior vs. exterior
- dialogue vs. non-dialogue (descriptive vs. action) scenes
- dynamic vs. static activity
- expansive vs. intimate settings
- light (or comic) tone vs. serious tone
- subjective vs. objective P.O.V.
- quiet vs. noisy (raging sea/industrial/rock music etc)
- variations in real time and flashback/flashforward.

Note that pacing is a function of where you enter and leave a scene. Remember, a scene is a fragment of a larger fragment of a larger segment of continuous action. You enter late and depart early. Hence pacing can also be increased or decreased by the amount of time we spend in a scene.

You will find the pacing of your overall script also determines the pacing of your sequences – the faster the pace or the more accelerating nearer to a climax you get, the shorter your sequences will become. This is especially important in Act III, which should have the fastest pacing of all your Acts with incidents happening fairly quickly leading inexorably to your final climax.

Tip: If you want to have a pause moment or give a reflective feel to your script, you might try using voice-over (page 176). For example, *Badlands* is generally a fast-paced action-based story, but there are interludes of voice-over which give it a reflective pace in parts, thus varying the mood, creating light and shade, peaks and valleys. What other films or TV dramas can you think of that employ voice-over in this way?

Scenes do more in the overall context of a screenplay than just satisfy a story function. They interact with each other to contribute to the formal structure (the flow and rhythm, the movement) of your script. The way you interweave these elements – contrasting, complementing, varying, balancing them – contributes to the overall rhythm of scenes. You should consider pacing when you reach the step outline/filing cards stage of your screenplay development (page 204), and the concept is actively used during the rewrite stage.

So, first work out the overall feel of your screenplay: is your script slow-paced and reflective like *The Straight Story, The Man Who Wasn't There* or *The Rookie*, light-paced as in comedies, romantic comedies and romps, fast-paced and action-driven with fast-cut scenes like *The Fast And The Furious, Fight Club* or *Thelma And Louise*, or does it start slowly and gradually speed up as it unfolds towards its final climax like *Misery, American Beauty* or *The Talented Mr. Ripley*, most Hitchcock films and the horror genre? Working out this overall feel will help you determine the pacing of your scenes, sequences and final screenplay.

---

- Hitchcock's films are skilful manipulations of subtext, pace and mood, lulling the audience into a sense of security and then springing on us a sudden shock or surprise – learn from them. (Brian De Palma and M. Night Shayamalan certainly did!)

---

Watch *Panic Room* and *Falling Down*: what elements of transition are used to vary the pacing in these films? Are they skilfully handled? How is it done, and why?

---

Watch *Reservoir Dogs*: is the pacing gripping for you? Do the lengthy scenes engage or bore you? How does it do this? Why?

---

Watch Martin Scorsese's *Casino*. Does its use of voice-over work for you, or does it have a distancing effect on the audience? Is it over-used? How does its use differ from that in *Goodfellas*? Was it better employed there? How and why? What elements do both films use to create pacing?

## 'Upping the ante'

To get the maximum emotion from a scene or moment of high drama, you should:

- before a scene or moment of great joy or relief, precede this with a scene or moment of extreme tension or jeopardy

or

- before a scene or moment of great drama or heavy tragedy, precede this with a scene or moment of extreme release, fun or tranquility.

For example, in *Four Weddings And A Funeral*, Gareth's death is immediately preceded by two ante-upping devices: we see him dancing vigorously and joyously and he is given one of the wittiest and most memorable lines in the film (about Oscar Wilde's fax number) which not only makes us laugh but also warms us to him all the more. There is a very brief 'pause' moment, then Gareth collapses – an effective juxtaposition of opposites.

# Information in the screenplay

There are many means of expression in a screen drama, and each of these generates *elements of information*. You need to understand both the nature and the effect these elements have on the mind of the audience. Remember, you control the release and arrangement of this information, both in a scene and in the overall screenplay.

Information reaches the audience by:

- what you choose to *conceal* from them
- what you choose to *reveal* to them
- *how* you choose to reveal it.

Also, the way in which you *combine* elements of information together in a scene generates extra information but also creates certain effects upon an audience. They make links, automatic assumptions and deductions when presented with individual elements of information.

You must therefore try to *enter the mind of the audience* and decipher what goes on there when viewing your screen drama.

Tip: Wherever you do your writing, try sticking a card on the wall in front of you. On that card draw what you would see if you were sitting in the cinema stalls: the blank screen, the drapes, the backs of people's heads in front of you. Every time you write, try to visualize what that scene would look like when shown on the screen. If you can enter the mind of the audience you can protect yourself from sending out incorrect or unintentional messages. You can also manipulate the process to send out exactly the messages you desire.

- One of the underlying *principles of information* in a scene and screenplay is: once you have established an element of information and given it to the audience, the audience will assume that information remains true for the rest of the screenplay, unless told otherwise (i.e. unless you contradict or update that information).

So whatever they are led to believe, they will go on believing for the remainder of the film. This also means there is no need to repeat information (unless you are deliberately reinforcing or changing it for some reason). Therefore as the story progresses your audience will accumulate a body of information about the world of this story and the people living in it.

The existence of this body of information means that any information which enters later in the script will be affected (informed or corrupted) by all the information the audience already has. For example, in *Witness,* if Samuel had pointed at the photograph in the very first scene, this would have little meaning and he would simply go on his way. But pointing to it *after* the murder sequence gives the photograph scene a whole new and sinister meaning.

- Hence, the second principle of information is: The *order* in which the audience receives information is crucial to the way you want them to understand the information *dramatically*. This is particularly relevant when writing suspense, horror and murder mysteries.

# Revealing and concealing information

It is important you know who has information in a scene or in a script and who has not. The basic possibilities are:

- both the characters and the audience have the same elements of information
- the characters have information which the audience does not
- the audience has information which the characters do not
- some characters have information which other characters do not; the audience may be in either position
- misinformation.

Each variation creates a different effect in the mind of the audience and on their emotions; curiosity, surprise, stimulation, deep emotional involvement, comic impact, shocked surprise, etc. It is your job to work out and work with these effects, to create them in the audience for the purpose of telling your story dramatically.

Problems you should be aware of are:

- Until a character gets an element of information they cannot act on it.
- If the audience knows something the character doesn't even though it places the audience in a superior position, the character will have to be given the information eventually. From the audience's P.O.V. this is a kind of repetition, since it already has the information.
- If a character knows something the audience doesn't, then this information must be given to the audience eventually. (Try bringing on a character who hasn't yet received the information and give it to them.)

Overall, you need to know the effects you are creating within the mind of the audience by the way you release, reveal and conceal information.

## Plants and pay-offs

This is also called *foreshadowing*. Remember, everything in your script is there for a reason. Likewise, if you plant something (object, piece of information, characteristic) it must be put there to be paid off later in your script: every action has a consequence, every piece of information has repercussions. If a gun is planted in a scene it has to be used at some later point – within that scene or some later scene. Think of the death grip in *Kung Fu Panda*. The use of videotaping the scare simulations at the opening of *Monsters, Inc.* is instrumental to the entrapment of the true villain at the end. In *Gosford Park*, the bottle of poison, the missing knife, the photograph of Parks's mother: all have vital parts to play in the unfolding drama. In fact, the plant that effectively determines the course of all that follows is the passing mention of Parks's name that is recognized by Mrs. Wilson. And the climax of *American Beauty* would be meaningless to an audience without the (half-way point) visit to the gun cabinet.

The use of the embroidered handkerchief throughout *A Beautiful Mind* is an emotional touchstone that grows in significance as the story develops. And in the opening 'arrest' sequence of *Minority Report*, John Anderton deduces from the left/right images that the child is on a roundabout; it cleverly sets up the idea for the opposing water eddies in the later film of Anne Lively's murder. Even in *Dumb And Dumber*, every plant (from urinating into a bottle to selling the dead parakeet to a blind child) is paid off sooner or later.

Now try examining the role of Sebastian's journal and of Kathryn's cross necklace in *Cruel Intentions*.

Even if the pay-off does not happen until after the final credits (e.g. the inflatable doll-kite in *Priscilla, Queen Of The Desert*, the waiting cab passenger in *Airplane*), the plant *has* to be paid off. If there's no pay-off, what is the point of planting the information in the first place? You're only wasting valuable script space.

> If a set-up is too obvious, it can announce a pay-off. But if a set-up doesn't signal something, it doesn't generate any suspense. The trick is to create expectation but fulfil it in a completely unexpected way.
>
> *Frank Cottrell Boyce*, screenwriter:
> *Millions, A Cock And Bull Story*

Also, when you plant or set-up the information in your script (the stuff the audience needs to know), it should be dropped in at its most natural or believable moment; more importantly, the pay-off has to be used at the most dramatically effective moment for that piece of information, that is, held back until the last moment possible. For example, the use of the son's asthma inhaler and the baseball bat trophied/atrophied on the wall in *Signs* – both planted very early and both have powerful inputs into the film's final confrontation. In *My Big Fat Greek Wedding* the running gag about Windex almost has its own developmental arc, but it all builds towards that final mention in the limousine, making its use even more emotionally powerful (see also the next section: Image Systems).

---

In *Four Weddings And A Funeral,* examine the way the David character (Charles's deaf mute brother) is handled – he has a critical role in the final wedding; we first see him only in passing, standing in the background at the first wedding reception. We next encounter him outside the cinema, and only then do we realize just who he is – and we are already one third into the film. Why was this held back for so long?

Now watch *Road to Perdition* and note the recurring use of Michael Jr's illustrated book of The Lone Ranger.

# Image systems

An *image system* is a category of images which repeat throughout your script, acting as resonators and reinforcers to the main subject or theme of your story.

Modern audiences are very visually literate, even if they don't realize it; they read something symbolic into every image. And there is a common pool of recognized and accepted symbols, and a more private pool.

- *external imagery*: images which mean the same inside your film as they do outside (the Stars and Stripes, a crucifix, a set of furry dice)
- *internal imagery*: an object which means one thing outside your film (maybe positive or life-affirming) but which means something else – whatever *you* decide to make it mean – inside your story construct (possibly negative and life-destroying).

Some examples:

*Tootsie*: images and icons of femininity and masculinity

*Spider-Man*: images of spider webs (naturally), but also the complex tangled webs of human relationships; webs of scaffolding (on buildings, bridge structures and cages); of entrapment; of identity – masks and mirrors.

*Minority Report*: images relating to sight v blindness; vision and foresight; science v religion; technology v nature; perfection v human frailties; predisposition v choice and self-determination.

*Chinatown*: four image systems woven together – political corruption as social cement, sexual cruelty, water and drought, blindness and sight.

> In an early draft of *The Fisher King*, the Holy Grail was originally a salmon. I changed it because I realized the Grail was a more universally accessible symbol.
>
> Richard LaGravenese,
> screenwriter: *The Horse Whisperer,*
> *The Fisher King, A Decade Under The Influence,*
> *The Bridges Of Madison County*

Your script must operate in both pools, and in a balanced way; operating heavily or exclusively in one will only alienate your audience. The trick is to choose the image(s) carefully and feed them into your screenplay very subliminally: clearly enough for the Reader to pick up, but the audience in front of the screen must never realize they are being fed these images.

> The image of the dancing plastic bag is one of the key moments in *American Beauty*, it pivots that entire film.
>
> *Sam Mendes*, director

* choose one of the films covered in Chapter 07
* work out their image system/s and list them
* break down those lists into external and internal imagery
* now do it for your own screenplay.

## The rule of three

There seems to be something magical or mystical in our attachment to threesomes. Watch most dramas and you will see a pattern in the protagonist's quest to defeat an obstacle: tries once – fails; tries again – fails; tries again – succeeds. This applies not only in the overall screenplay but sometimes within a single scene. (The protagonist, antagonist and reflection-or-romance is a threesome.) Also, major dramatic speeches tend to be built around taglines (page 56), which includes the rule of three. Alec Baldwin's lecture to his office at the start of *Glengarry Glen Ross* not only embodies the cultural ethics of that working environment, it neatly establishes the overt goal of the screenplay's characters and what's at stake. He offers three prizes: a Cadillac Eldorado; next, a set of expensive steak knives; lastly, unemployment.

Now examine Gordon Gekko's 'Greed is Good' oration in *Wall Street*. Are there any threesomes there? Can you think of other examples where action or dialogue is built around the rule of three or contrasts?

What about your script?

A very useful website to visit is:

www.whysanity.net/monos [Colin's Movie Monologues: there they are, hundreds of them, arranged alphabetically.]

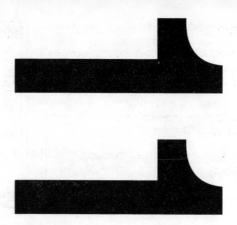

the next step

**In this chapter you will learn:**
- how to distil your story and characters down to a one-page synopsis
- what a step outline is
- how to express your script as a prose document – a treatment.

# The one-page synopsis

Your next step is to write the *synopsis*. This is a one-page (essential) brief factual telling of the entire screenplay story, in prose and in the present tense, typed (singled-spaced) on A4. It shows:

- the twists, turns and final climax of your plot
- the significant characters and their interactions
- an indication of the style of your script.

You write this synopsis for your own use, to get a clearer overall picture of your screenplay. It is not essential to write one, but it can be useful as a diagnostic tool to identify any suspected weaknesses in your plot – and certainly which bits can be cut without losing the core essential story. Sometimes the weakness(es) jump off the page at you.

For example, the synopsis for *The Third Man* might run thus:

> Holly Martins, an engaging but rather seedy writer of Western stories, arrives in Vienna to work for his friend, Harry Lime. He is told by a cold, disillusioned British police officer that Lime, a notorious racketeer, has been killed in a street accident.
>
> Unbelieving, Martins begins to track down all those who knew his friend: the lonely, frightened actress who forged papers who was in love with him; two acquaintances, the effete Kurtz and the shifty Popescu, who witnessed the accident; his porter and his doctor.
>
> These investigations lead him to the heart of seaminess and corruption in Vienna, to the discovery that Lime (a shameless scoundrel) is still alive, to a struggle with his conscience which ends with the eerie pursuit of his friend, who most aptly retreats to the sewers of the city – and the final showdown.

You might find some neatly delineated film synopses in the reviews of the trade magazines (Chapter 19), and for television in the TV reviews of broadsheet newspapers and listings magazines. Press kits for each production also have neat summaries if you can obtain them (try phoning the press and publicity offices of the relevant production companies).

Do not confuse this one-page synopsis with the one-pager (also called a *synopsis* or *proposal*) which is used as a selling document in your pitch or by a producer to pitch an idea (Chapter 19).

---

Now write your synopsis – and on *one* page, so be ruthless.

# The step outline

By now you should have a pretty firm grip on the jigsaw of your script. The next move is to do a *step outline* (also called a *scene-by-scene breakdown* or *step sheet*).

For this you will need a set of 3″ × 5″ (7.5 × 12.5 cm) index cards. Each card represents one scene of your script (even bridging scenes), so at the top of each card write the scene heading (slug line). Then on each one proceed to describe the action and substance of each scene in, brief, clear notes; include snatches of dialogue if it helps. Pay attention to how you start and end each scene, and how it develops in the middle. Why must the cards be 3″ × 5″? Because industry ethos states if you can't fit it onto one side of the card, your scene is too long.

These cards will help you organize your scenes into sequences and Acts, examine how each scene juxtaposes with the next one, examine your story and character developments and get an idea of your pacing, and where your climaxes occur.

Once you have written out your cards, spread them out in front of you – on the floor or blu-tack them to the wall – and study them. You will start to feel a great sense of control over your entire script. Shuffle the cards around, take out and discard some scenes, insert new ones; if you feel like colour-coding your characters or plot and subplots with marker pens, do it. Do whatever you have to do to get the best dramatic effect in your screenplay. You may find the following guidelines helpful:

## Structure

Mark your most dramatically important scenes. Check how they are spaced out over the entire drama. These are your story's highlights. Ask yourself:

- Does the progression of these major scenes move the story forward at an effective pace?
- Is the overall dramatic suspense of the story maintained?
- Are there enough surprise elements (unexpected twists) to keep the audience interested and involved?
- Do my story crises occur at reasonably spaced intervals over the script or are they bunched up? (Expect some bunching in Act III.)
- Am I 'upping the ante' before each crisis or happy incident? Are they sufficient?

- Are the pause or relief scenes used when needed (i.e. after a climax or heavily dramatic moment)?

Start to get a sense of the rhythm and flow of your scenes and how they interrelate. If you don't, start rearranging the cards around, try different running orders, cut or add, etc. Don't be afraid of doing this or any other new approach that works best for you.

## Characters

You should know each character's goals, both overall and within each scene. Look at the function of each scene, its purpose in the script.

- look at when the different characters appear
- are they credibly presented throughout in what they say and do?
- are they consistent throughout?
- is their development a believable arc?
- do characters appear appropriately throughout the script or does one (or more) 'get lost' for too long, only to crop up again as an afterthought or for the convenience of plot?

## Weak spots

Look for the screenplay's weak spots you can correct:

- Are action high points bunched too closely together? Try inserting a 'break', a dialogue scene illustrating more of your character, or a mood scene, or some delay in the suspense build.
- Not enough exciting high points? Insert some additional crises, build up your suspense more carefully to keep your audience engaged or add some surprising twists.
- Too active or too melodramatic? Add more scenes revealing character or relationships between characters. It gives the audience depth – more time to know your characters instead of continuous scenes of constant high points.

## Scene structure

Look at each scene and its internal structure. If the scene doesn't 'work':

- Are you clear about your beginning, middle and end?

- If the scene builds, is the pay-off or high point appropriate?
- Are the characters and the actions in the scene credible?
- Are the characters believable; would they act in that way in the given circumstances of that scene?
- Is the scene basically interesting?
- Is the scene really necessary to the story?

The writer has many tools to use when writing a screenplay, many elements of expression in a scene – organization, structure, characters, relationships, setting, tone, P.O.V., dialogue, props, clothing, sound. Use them. Think visual: images (not words) are your basic currency. You are not trying to make it real, but *alive*.

Your next move is to write . . .

## The treatment

**What is it?** A prose document (approximately 12–15 pages for one hour TV and up to 25–30 pages for features), typed, single-spaced, on A4 paper (one side), telling your plot as it happens chronologically in your screenplay. Some treatments are available to buy (see Taking it further) but, generally speaking, existing treatments are notoriously hard to obtain.

**What is a treatment for?** It has two functions:

- Initially, as a device for the writer to organize their own thoughts and develop the texture of their script.
- Later, and a treatment's major function, as a selling document used to sell your story to a producer (Chapter 19).

So, for your own private use, a treatment can be as long as you need.

**What should a treatment do?** It should:

- tell the story clearly, identifying both main plot and subplots, but not be solely plot-driven
- concentrate on the main overall dramatic structure
- tell us what we *see*: the characters, their actions
- impart some of the mood, atmosphere and feel of the script
- be written crisply; short paragraphs (try one paragraph per scene), in the present tense, using *active* verbs and *descriptive* nouns to capture the action, verve and pace of your script. Pace is important (try applying the 4 2 4 dimension to your treatment also)

- include some brief character details (two or three sentences) of your main players. Incorporate these into your text as they enter the script (the first time they enter, their names are in capitals or upper case, thereafter in lower case). You don't need a separate sheet of characters and their backgrounds; you are selling a story, not a cast list family history
- use dialogue extracts if it helps. But only if it adds colour or helps impart the 'smell' of your script – and do it sparingly
- avoid camera directions or music suggestions

**Is a good treatment easy to write?** No. Indeed, many writers (and agents) believe it is harder to write than a good script. It may even take half the time that writing a script takes. Writing a treatment is a separate skill in itself.

There is no right way of writing a treatment. These tips are accepted guidelines; each script is special and you must impart that specialness via the treatment.

**Is it essential to write one?** No, but it's a very important step along the way. Why?

- A treatment exposes any weaknesses in the planned script. It tells you whether it is worth continuing. If everything is fine, you can move quicker to the next stage – the exploratory draft. If your treatment causes you problems, leave it for a week or more, work on another project. Get a distance on it, then return refreshed. Never write your exploratory draft until you are happy with the treatment.
- Eventually you will need a treatment to send to a producer and catch their interest (it's quicker to read than a full script). Not all screenplays made have had a treatment attached. Ultimately your script should sell itself.

> Treatments can be a poisoned chalice. They are enormously difficult to write, a nightmare, and they can only give you a sense of the movie. The problem is: you can't write a script before you write a treatment.
>
> *Adrian Hodges,*
> screenwriter: *Tom And Viv,*
> *The Lost World, Lorna Doone*

Try to get hold of some well-written treatments (see Taking it further). Compare and contrast their variety. Note how they imparted the energy and feel of the finished film or TV production.

> Now write your treatment. Use all and any devices you have to hand: the filing cards, ideas, images, your own storytelling skills, to impart that original and gripping tale.

The few books on treatments available are:

Kenneth Atchity, Rebecca J. Donatelle & Chi-Li Wong: *Writing Treatments that Sell* (Owl Books)

David S. Freeman: *Writing the Killer Treatment: selling your story without a script* (Michael Wiese productions)

Michael Halperin: *Treatment Pack* [Eight assorted, self-penned Treatment templates (www.beyondstructure.com)]

... and a few websites you might find of use:

LawrenceGray.com [Click on Screenwriting 101.5 tab, in the drop-down link you will find an article: 7 Basic Problems with Treatments]

screenplaytreatment.com [This will lead you straight to the Creative Screenwriting magazine website; click on their Screenplay Treatment tab]

... or you could try entering into your search keywords like: Screenplay, Treatment, Buy or Tips.

# 12

# the actual writing

In this chapter you will learn:
- how to write the first draft of
  your script – in one big
  energetic, emotional push.

I approach my exploratory draft like I'm doing a multiple-choice test: if I come to a tough bit I just write something really rough, carry on to the end, then go back to it after. The problem with new writers is they keep rewriting all the time and lose the spontaneity. Just get it down. It's not like this is the only time you can write it.

*Tom Schulman*

## The exploratory draft

You've now finished the pre-writing 65 per cent. Now to tackle the next 5 per cent: writing the *exploratory draft*. You do this in one burst of activity – try spending no longer than ten consecutive days of solid work on it. Using your filing cards as a blueprint to construct narrative and dialogue, just sit down and *do it*!

Set yourself a strategic plan: if your goal is 120 pages, write a minimum of twelve per day. Don't be afraid to overwrite – your task is not to get perfect copy, but to get it all down on paper in screenplay form.

Tip: If writing longhand, try doing it on squared paper and keeping to the appropriate script layouts (Chapter 02). It will give you a better idea of length (one page = one minute), timing, and pacing.

*Don't* go back over your previous day's work wanting to rewrite it – that comes later.

Try to:

- avoid clichéd images and phrases
- avoid writing 'on the nose' (description or dialogue phrases that stick out as being obvious)
- be clear: avoid lengthy or wordy language (especially in dialogue)
- keep dialogue short and dramatic
- express action and reaction
- write visual images
- think visual – show, don't tell
- make it vivid, affective, memorable and (hopefully) an *easy read*.

Of course, you won't accomplish all these in this draft, but bear them in mind. Now put this book down, take up your cards, go away and *do it*!

### The final full stop: the end or the beginning?

Having emerged from the tunnel of writing this draft, you will feel: 'That's it, I've done it, I can't get it any better'. Wrong! You can – and you will, during the rewrites. But first you need a breather. You've been working closely on your script – too close to get any objectivity on it. You need to *get a distance*.

Put the typed draft on the shelf – for a week (minimum), hopefully a month and forget about it. Work on another project, perhaps from your ideas file (don't feel guilty, most writers work on more than one project at a time). Only return to it when you feel you can read it in an objective, unemotional, critical way. Only then are you ready to enter the rewrite stage (the final 30 per cent), which is where a script *really* comes together.

Writing is Rewriting. The first draft is not important, it is something to work on.

*Graham Lineham*, creator and co-writer:
*Father Ted, The IT Crowd, Black Books*

# 13

## the craft of the rewrite

**In this chapter you will learn:**
- about the various stages and types of rewrites you need to go through with your screenplay – and where everything really starts to come together.

A good writer is not someone who knows how to write –
but how to rewrite.

*William Goldman*

You write from the heart; you rewrite from the head.

*Viki King*,<br>screenwriting tutor and author

With *Sense And Sensibility*, when it came to having to do
a major rewrite, and I've done several, there were tears,
actual tears.

*Emma Thompson*

— — — — — — X Weeks Later — — — — — —

Your exploratory draft is the one written with passion and
urgency, the reason why you were fired up to explore that idea
in the first place. Rewriting is where you apply your knowledge
of the technical craft points covered so far to that draft. The
trick in making a good script great is to marry the two without
losing that sense of energy and drive that originally excited you.

There's no true learning without making mistakes, and writing
and rewriting are all processes of making mistakes: confronting
dead ends, discovering alternative and better routes, shortcuts –
and doing it *your* way.

So, having got a distance on your exploratory draft, now read it
afresh in one go at one sitting, without stopping or making
alterations or notes (however great the temptation); get a sense
of the script as a whole. Then ask yourself the questions in the
checklist on pages 214–15, making notes on a separate sheet of
paper. (These questions are based on several checklists given to
script readers by their production companies.)

Try giving the script and checklist to someone whose opinions
you respect (not close friends or relatives) and ask them to make
notes.

At the end you will have many notes on many aspects of your
script. Separate the notes off into categories: structure, plot and
subplots, sequences, characters, dialogue, images, etc...
however many you need.

A common mistake often made when approaching the rewrite
stage is to assume you can fix it all in one massive swoop of a
rewrite. *Wrong*. There are many rewrites you can go through –

# HANDY CHECK LIST FOR SCRIPT ASSESSMENT

## 1 CHARACTERS
(a) Did you believe in them?
(b) Is the speech pattern of each character (i) individual, (ii) true, (iii) consistent?
(c) Do we know enough about everybody important to understand them fully? Are they written at sufficient depth?
(d) Are their motivations clear?
(e) Do they develop or do they end the piece the same actual people as when it began?
(f) Do they have a life of their own or are they puppets manipulated by the writer for his own purposes?

## 2 CONFLICT
(a) Is there any?
(b) Is the conflict something vague in the background ('Fred v. Life') or is it personalized?
(c) Is the background too much in the foreground?
(d) Is anything of importance to the characters at stake?

## 3 ACTION (Not to be confused with mere activity)
(a) Do people do things?
(b) Does anything happen?
(c) Does anybody <u>make</u> anything happen?
or (d) Is it all a business of people chattering about things?
or (e) Is it a mere portrait of (i) an individual or (ii) a group?
(f) Does the screenplay mark time while the characters unburden themselves?
(g) Do people actually get to grips with things or is it all shadow boxing?

## 4 PLOT
(a) Is the story a mere succession of events (e.g. 'A day in the life of...')?
(b) Is it full of cause and effect?

## 5 CONSTRUCTION
(a) Is there sufficient variety of pace?
(b) Are the climaxes right?
(c) Does the plot develop at the right speed?
(d) Does the end work?
(e) Are the audience's expectations satisfied?

## 6 CONTENT
(a) Is the theme implicit or explicit?
(b) Is it clear what the piece is actually about?
(c) Do the characters know?
(d) Should they know?
(e) Is the theme clearly illustrated or brought out by the plot?
(f) Does the writer bring to his theme an individual point of view?
(g) Is it the right length for what he wants to say?

## 7 PRACTICALITIES
(a) How expensive does it look?
(b) Are all the characters necessary? (Are there enough?)
(c) Are there too many sets? Could we actually fit them into a studio?
(d) If film is suggested, is it necessary?
(e) Do exterior scenes add to the visual and/or emotional content?
(f) If it is (intentionally) an all-film piece, is it containable?

## 8 THE OBJECT OF THE EXERCISE
Discounting your own personal prejudices on its theme or subject matter and regarding it only as an artefact:
(a) Did you want to turn the page?
(b) Did you <u>instinctively</u> like or dislike it? Or were you just bored?
(c) Does the writer know his stuff?
(d) Has he got the vital spark?
(e) Would you want to work on it?
(f) Would a wide contemporary audience of ordinary men and women (i.e. the same audience that Shakespeare was aiming at) be entertained.

THE FOREGOING IS A MERE CHECKLIST. IT DOES NOT ASPIRE TO LAY DOWN A SET OF UNBREAKABLE RULES, BECAUSE THERE AREN'T ANY. IF THE SCRIPT FIRES YOU IN SPITE OF BREAKING EVERY 'RULE' IN THE BOOK, THEN SAY SO.

as many as you feel you need – each time looking at different aspects of the script and tackling different questions on each rewrite. All the time you are working towards making your final screenplay stronger. It is a complex task and the final 30 per cent of the writing process, so don't try to tackle it all in one go.

I suggest at least six stages:

First rewrite: Understandability
Second rewrite: Structure
Third rewrite: Characters
Fourth rewrite: Dialogue
Fifth rewrite: Style
Sixth rewrite: Polishing

The idea of the rewrite is to look at common problems that happen in any script and address them in a *focused* way. The point of the rewrite is to decide what stays in your script and (more importantly) what goes. The true craft skill here is cutting: cutting the unnecessary, the redundant, the insipid, without lessening the passion and urgency. These are hard decisions to take but they are necessary. Learn to '*kill your babies*' – cut out your most favourite line of dialogue, description or scene if it doesn't fit, do a job or earn its space on the page.

> First cut out all the wisdom, then cut out all the adjectives. I've cut some of my favourite stuff. I have no real compassion when it comes to cutting: no pity, no sympathy. Some of my dearest and most beloved bits of writing have gone out with a very quick slash, slash, slash.
>
> *Paddy Chayefsky,*
> screenwriter: *Network, Being There*

## First rewrite: understandability

A common problem when you read your exploratory draft is: you don't understand why certain things happen or why a character does something. The reason usually is: the story or character may exist in your mind but you've not put those important elements, reasons or bits of information down on the page.

Ask yourself:

- Is the story I've chosen the most dramatically and emotionally affective one? (page 44 – How do I choose my main story?)
- What are the pieces of information my audience needs to know in order to understand the story fully? Have they been dropped in at the most dramatic or effective moment? (page 198 – Plants and payoffs)
- Can I make it better by referring to its genre type? (page 49) For example, if your swashbuckling romance lacks enough romance or danger, perhaps the ending doesn't fit the genre of story you're writing
- Do my characters do uncharacteristic things for no explainable reason? See page 77 – Character Checklist. If you don't have a believable answer, change it for the better
- Is the chosen structure type (three-act, multi-plotted, etc.) best suited to this script? Can it be told better by using a different structural approach?
- Whose story am I telling, whose point of view is the audience experiencing it through? (page 54)

A tendency with many exploratory drafts is understructure (page 110) – it indicates insufficient pre-writing work: for example, of your 120 pages, the first 70 are spent wandering, and the real story action is crammed into the last 50, so you end up discarding the first 70. How do you stop such wandering? Make sure you've got your ending (page 43 – Story Concept).

Now ask:

- What is original, different or distinctive about this story? Keep asking yourself throughout the rewrites. Originality is not just one element, it's a mix.
- What is its dramatic structure? Not just the overall three-Act structure, but the smaller internal ones found within it?
- Flashbacks and flashforwards: are these used dramatically, not just as a device to add another piece of information? Tip: construct each one as a complete dramatic structure in its own right. Now that *you* know why one thing follows another, decide which bits are needed for use in your script.
- What are the surprises? And where? If they are predictable your script won't grip the audience.
- Information: are things held back from the audience until they need to know it? Only give it to them when it makes dramatic sense, when it will be most effective and surprise them most.
- Is it the right length? Does the story fit the chosen length? Is it too cramped or too stretched? (page 69)

- Have you started and ended the script in the right places?
- Theme (page 58): what is the real message of your screenplay? Do you truly know it? (These are questions you *have* to face.) Once you know your theme, it will help you sort out just what your plot and subplots (especially main subplot), images, metaphors, cast design, etc. are going to be about, in order to resonate or contradict your theme. Theme is what integrates the Acts and character development (especially in Act III) and unifies the entire story.
- Why do you want to write this story? Like theme, you often don't discover this until after your treatment or exploratory draft. Decide on the why and you can start deciding on your plot and subplots.

## Second rewrite: structure

I don't necessarily believe in the three-act structure when actually first writing something. However, I do find it a useful diagnostic tool during the rewrite: to go back over your draft to see if and where anything might have gone wrong or become unclear.

*Tom Schulman*

Put the sex right on the spine of the movie.

*Robert McKee*, screenwriting tutor

Every action in your screenplay (physical, emotional, verbal, psychological) must advance the overall storyline and be tightly linked to it. This storyline is, of course, the process of your protagonist trying to reach their ultimate goal within the film – their outer motivation. Without this relationship an action should be cut. Also, a correct action should be carefully orchestrated as part of the script's rising conflict. Thus, the overall storyline must be advanced and gradually escalate towards the Act III climax.

Consider the elements of each Act:

### Act I
*Purpose:* essential story information; introduce main characters; establish conflict, tone, visual style, settings (physical, social-psychological); build theme and mood.

*Elements:* point of entry; critical life-crisis moment; time frame; character-in-action; dramatic situation; time lock?; inciting incident; crisis; climax/TP1; raising the stakes; character-audience identification.

*Needs:* information; correct dramatic arrangement of story elements.

*Dangers:* lack of clarity and/or direction; insufficient identification with protagonist; unclear who protagonist is; character motivation vague.

### Act II
*Purpose:* develop story via conflict and confrontation; build motivation line from dramatic need/goal; move character through point of no return; orchestrate character transformation and growth; advance story via upward progression towards Act climax; maintain momentum.

*Elements:* build from strong TP1 and clear, strong set-up; dramatic need/goal/external motivation; focus points; half-way point; script mechanics (dilemma, obstacles, complications, set-backs – time lock?); sequences; rising action; suspense; scene causality; major crisis; TP2/moment of truth; development of subplots.

*Needs:* momentum; focus; powerful causality.

*Dangers:* a very long section (for audience and writer); often unstructured or understructured; may not have essential incidents/scenes; a too-linear plot line (not enough complications, set-backs, etc.); weak or false point of no return; incidents not integrally and logically linked to central 'problem' and characters (i.e. lack of focus, weak causality).

### Act III
*Purpose:* resolve story; heighten tension to climax; integrate theme, unify story; final transformation and growth of protagonist; bring story to satisfying close.

*Elements:* build powerfully from TP2/moment of truth; payoffs; key confrontational scene (protagonist vs. antagonist); increased pacing.

*Needs:* pay off all story elements (including tying-up minor loose ends).

*Dangers:* momentum lost or weak; payoffs neglected; climax unsatisfactory or disconnected from preceding build-up.

## Plots and subplots

Examine your subplots, especially the main subplot (the one that will most affect your main plot – and your protagonist).

1 For each subplot, ask: does it perform at least one or more of the eight functions on page 65.

2 How do these eight points help me when rewriting?

• Most new writers' subplots don't inform the main story as they haven't worked it out on a thematic level yet

• Crucially, when rewriting, most new writers are not prepared to drop a subplot if it does not inform the main story or perform any of these eight functions. 'Kill your babies' is the core of rewriting

• If the subplots *do* inform and/or perform, do they do it effectively? Are there minor adjustments which would make them more dramatically effective?

3 Know the extremes you can push your protagonist to. Find them, push them further; find their most dramatic elements and place them at your Act III climax.

## Climaxes

1 Look at the three end-of-Act climaxes. A climax is a precise moment and a turning point in a story. However, your screenplay is a composite of several stories (subplots). Hence each climax needs to be a turning point within the broader story sweep.

2 Are the subplot climaxes effective, increasing, believable? Look at each climactic sequence and examine it.

3 The end of Act II climactic sequence is often problematic. The protagonist should be as far away as possible from the goal, revelation or realisation of the Act III climax. Logically, they should have abandoned the quest by now (page 133 – Moment of Truth). Examine that climactic sequence and its functions. The protagonist:

• denies responsibility for their actions
• abandons the quest (considers it again)
• and faces their moment of truth.

If it doesn't do any of these, what's the remedy? You could:

• introduce another character (hence another subplot)
• show confrontation (in present linear time or flashback)
• show evidence of some revelation, e.g. tape, diary notes (and plant earlier the expectation that this evidence exists – another subplot)

- show action to reveal the protagonist's state of mind
- use flashback as parallel action and structure your script to set up the two stories in parallel time, so that the first leads to the second, and hence confrontation (see above).

4 Finally, ask yourself the following:

- Do your climaxes build, from the least significant to the most significant at the end?
- Each climactic sequence should run: plant the possibility of a climax; allow the audience to ruminate on it; present the climax itself.
- Climactic sequence structuring is steered by two factors; your choice of what information is revealed and when you reveal it.
- After a significant dramatic climax you need a pause, and that moment or scene should be in keeping with the rhythm and pacing of the overall script.

## Openings and endings

Your choices of where and how you open and end the script are crucial; they tell your audience what *you* think is significant in your screenplay.

## Scenes and sequences

Openings:

- Are characters, conveyed clearly, effectively, interestingly, well?
- Is the visual setting interesting?
- Are sound and the pacing of dialogue used effectively?
- Is there suspense?
- Has the plot been set up?
- Is there any conflict?
- Does anything happen?
- Do you know the protagonist, what they want, their motivation?
- Does the writer bring an individual P.O.V., an individual idea?
- Is the world coherent? is it different?
- Do you want to turn the pages?

# Scenes

## Work out the aims of each scene

Ask yourself: Why do I need this scene? What is its purpose? What contribution does it make to the overall storyline and final climax? How does it contribute to the action storyline and character motivation storyline? The worst answer is 'because it follows the previous one'. Each scene should have a function in itself.

So ask yourself: What is each character *doing* in this scene (action) both at the start and at the end? Remember: Arrive Late – Depart Early. Cut the intro and departure; you only need the middle of most scenes.

## Focusing

Who is the scene about? What is the scene about? What does each character need or want to happen? Why can't the characters achieve this and how best can I express it on the screen? Move away from *your* dramatic needs and towards *theirs*.

What's the character's attitude in this scene? What is their emotional response both to what they have to do and what happens in this scene? Look to subtext in what they say and do: they may mask or contradict each other. Are the audience getting the levels of meaning *you* want?

Remember, a scene consists of: a character's action meeting an obstacle, opposition or disruption, giving rise to tension which is either resolved or heightened; the information is *delivered*, then they *exit*. See the scene construction flowchart Figure 9.1. (page 169)

## The scene ending

Is the scene ending surprising enough or is it predictable? Try applying William Goldman's 'a surprise on every page' to every scene. Know the ending and make everything build towards it, but don't take the obvious, predictable route.

## Nature of the scene

Does the scene depend on dialogue or on action or a mix of both? Is there dialogue deadlock? (see Fourth rewrite).

## Sequences

(See page 159). Remember, the three-Act structure is a template; the writer's craft comes in disguising this artifice without the audience realizing it's there. So for each sequence you should know:

- What do all the characters *want* in each block? (Not just your protagonist.) Why do they want it? What's their state of mind?
- What is actually happening in *each sequence* of the stories and subplots, and how do they underline or reinforce the main plot storyline?
- What's the *emotional engagement* of each sequence? What is it in each one you want your audience to relate to?

Decide on the above, then ask:

- What is the actual dramatic structure of this sequence? How and where do all the subplots fit in?

# Third rewrite: characters

Always try to trip yourself up: look for the places where you've done something which was convenient rather than true.

*Clive Barker,*
writer/director

## Changing characters

Two key things to address:

- do I *need* all my characters?
- are they distinctive?

### Common problems

- there are too many characters
- you've invented a character just to help the story along.

Ask yourself if you really need them all, if not, drop them or have their function done by another character. Look at the length and format of your script: are there too many characters for that format to support? (page 69). Too many, and you will lose focus.

Remember, most scripts hinge around three key players (the rule of three again): protagonist, opposition, reflection/mirror, with sometimes a romance character (who may also be one of the above).

The characters have to be clear from what they *do*. Learn to pare down.

*Norma Heyman,*
producer

## Main characters

The first time they enter the script, their presence must be neatly summarized – powerfully, immediately: go for *dominant impressions*. For your protagonist it is worth writing two or three sentences of information (age, attitudes, background) so the reader has a greater sense of the person in the script. Choose your words carefully. You need to get a *feeling* across.

With main characters, ask yourself if this character possesses a strong through-line: a spine linking their actions to their goals via their motivation (page 184).

## The transformational arc

Look for this arc in all your main characters (especially the protagonist). See page 95.

- Which characters have one: the protagonist, other main characters, on-going minor characters? Are they all developed to their fullest extent?
- What changes do they go through? Where do they make those changes?
- Have I established from the very beginning the values and emotions that exist in that world?
- At your screenplay crisis points, do the emotions pitch and waver? Are the characters' values challenged, especially the protagonist's?
- How have the characters changed by the end? What value systems and emotional responses have been altered?

Distinctive attributes you can use to make a character unique include:

- Attitude (crucial): distinctive and unique ones make for interesting unpredictability. Also, how does that attitude work in terms of the other characters in the script?
- Characteristics: the way they look, talk and move on the screen

- Surprise: look for the unpredictable action (not one that comes from attitude). At a key moment in the script, get them to do something completely unpredictable
- Motivational uncertainty: can you generate any enigma around why this character is doing what they're doing in the script? Establish and maintain that uncertainty for the path of the story. (If another character doesn't understand why the protagonist did a certain action, it signals to your audience that we *will* understand it by the end)
- Originality: add it by making your character: the opposite of audience expectations or of their character type; give them a distinctive attitude or characteristic or occasional unpredictable actions; you might also like to make them a 'fish-out-of-water'; give them motivational uncertainty
- Minor characters: although on screen for only a short while, the audience must know everything they need to know about them to work believably. Create your cameos believably (without disrupting the script's overall tone) through dress style (usually related to their job), through physical presence and body language and also through the way they talk
- Stereotypes: how do you avoid cliché in a character? Try to ensure their story contains unexpected outcomes. (Comedies rest on stereotypes and their contradictions.) There is no problem if your character starts out a stereotype (quick audience identification is an advantage); but *stay* there and boredom soon sets in. Do something unpredictable with your stereotype – enough to make the audience stay with it.

# Fourth rewrite: dialogue

Dialogue comes because I know what I want my characters to say. I envision the scene – and the dialogue comes out of that. Then I rewrite it. Then I cut it. Then I refine it until I get the scene as precise as I can get it.

*Paddy Chayefsky*

This is always a difficult rewrite. Writers don't like cutting their dialogue once it's written. However, the best dialogue is rewritten dialogue which is *cut, compressed* and *focused*.

## 'Dialogue deadlock'

Classic problems you may encounter include:

- Blocking: the exchanges block each other and don't allow anything to develop. For example: 'Are you ill?' 'No'. This is wrong, as it blocks any further development. Try it like this 'Are you ill?' 'Mmm, feeling queasy'. Now you can continue the exchange.
- The dialogue may ramble, lack direction, get nowhere or be too 'talky' (especially in scenes lasting five or six pages) or refer to something happening outside the scene. Get them to say the things that need to be said, but keep it relevant to what's going on inside the scene and in that location.
- The scene may be too flat; the words may do their job, but the result may be unemotional; with no spark, as if the scene died in the writing. Try swapping styles: conceive the scene in a radically different style. Heavy drama? Rewrite as comedy. A purely dialogue scene? Try it as visual slapstick. Try it anyway. Find ways to bring a scene back to life. Do whatever tricks you must, whatever works best for you, to bring the scene back to life.
- Most major speeches in screenplays are built around the two concepts of taglines: the rule of three and contrasts (page 56). Do yours echo these ideas?
- In dialogue and scene rewriting there are a number of classic strategies you can use to try to make the scene come to life. One is to change the focus and/or attitudes of one or two of the characters. Another is to ask yourself: can I do this *visually*?

Don't think of a scene as 'people talking', think: 'how can I put this onto the screen or page *without* talking?' Think visual and use the medium to its absolute limits.

## Subtext

Examine your scenes, their dialogue and action, in the light of your new rewrite knowledge. Is there any subtext there at all? Does it fulfil any of the functions outlined on pages 179–81? If not, change it – either the dialogue, action or subtext.

# Fifth rewrite: style

## Pacing

(See page 192) Pacing: overall; your sequences (length); scenes; within scenes. First decide on the overall feel of your screenplay – this decision determines the pacing of your sequences.

Next, determine the dramatic pace within the scene itself. Always look for the most dramatic way of using what you've got. If you're in danger of losing your audience, throw in something to keep them interested or set up something for the next or a later scene. How do you determine the dramatic pace?

## Use of tone

Look at the use of tone expressed in:

- the scale of dramatic action: are you employing the right lengths for the moments (love scene, chase sequence, climax, etc.)?
- lengths of scenes and sequences: do the longer scenes all occur at one point in your script, slowing the pace?
- characterization: do all your characters belong in the same screenplay?
- *mise-en scène*: look at the settings, locations, weather, costumes, choice of day or night – do they make a whole and add to the dramatic tension of the moment?
- dialogue: review it; does it fit consistently with the storyline and the genre?
- images (page 200): work out the visual references, what they symbolize and what they tell the audience; look at the symbolic meanings of location and landscape (for example in Merchant Ivory films)
- soundtrack (including the use of v.o.) – does it contribute to the mood? Don't specify the exact music track you want, but say, for example 'ethereal pop song that creates a mood of...'; describe the atmosphere without dictating the musical language.

## Transitions

Every scene must end and lead into the next one. Apply those tools of similarity or contrast to each scene juxtaposition. (See page 194.)

Decide what the last line of your scene is: visual description or dialogue? Moving or static? Is the transition one of continuity, jump-cutting or overlapping? If it's dialogue, can you change it to a reaction shot?

The next scene's opening: visuals are always noticed first in any new scene – your choice is crucial. How does that first visual relate to the last visual of the previous scene? What does it establish about this new scene? Normal conventions are: if you end on a moving image then you start on a moving image; if you end on a static shot then start on a static shot.

If you have a big transitional jump (in time and/or space) try:

- inserting an extra bridging scene that establishes the next scene
- using DISSOLVE TO: for the next scene instead of CUT TO:
- using FADE TO BLACK then FADE UP: into the next scene.

If you've got a dialogue-driven scene or sequence and need to make a big jump, try overlapping your dialogue from one scene into the other, denoted in the following scene as:

JOHN (v.o.)   or   JOHN (over)

It is important that the audience should not be aware of the jarring nature of these transitions.

### Reliefs and pauses

Don't forget those pause scenes or moments following highly climactic or emotional incidents – let your audience breathe and assimilate.

For reliefs *within* scenes, the general rule is: high drama scenes can only stand one moment of light relief (unless the scene or screenplay's purpose is light relief).

When considering reliefs and pauses in pacing, look for the opposites and use them.

## Emotion on the page

Emotion is at the core of a story's believability, and expressing emotion on the page is difficult to discuss: one can only watch, read scripts and experience it to see how emotions work on the screen and are expressed on the page.

What is important in this rewrite is: *you must know the emotion you are aiming for* – within each scene, each sequence, and the overall emotional tone of the screenplay. The wrong level in a scene or climax can throw a script off-focus (if you *do* spring surprises, set them up first). Again, look to the post-emotional climaxes. Pause moments, allowing your audience to absorb the emotion, are crucial to emotional writing.

Even though each of your characters may speak in their own voice, the scene's emotional level *should* be the same for all, with one character (the protagonist) who goes beyond the emotional range to focus that emotion on. To discover the real emotional pitch of this character, ask yourself: how do they engage with the world, the way they express their own emotions? Also, keep the language consistent with the emotional pitch so that you milk the most emotional power from that moment.

In your script, if strong relationships have been set up, the strong emotional climax should be capable of being shown with looks and reactions rather than forceful emotional dialogue (especially by the end). Credible characters + credible desires + credible situations + credible relationships create credible emotion.

The important thing in this rewrite stage is to look for the pitch of the emotion, focus it, and then tighten it.

## Engaging your audience's emotion

The basic underlying principle is that the words you use on the page must reflect the type of emotions you want to reflect on the screen and push the right emotional button/s in your audience. A comedy script? Describe the action in a funny way. A tensely dramatic scene? Describe things spartanly. And so on…

Remember: don't put anything on the page that is not on the screen.

# Sixth rewrite: polishing

By this stage, you know your script works. With this rewrite you go through every single line with a fine-toothed comb, nit-picking over specific words of dialogue, description or action, asking all the time: 'is this the best word or gesture I can use here?'

There are no firm rules about how many rewrites you need to do; you should do as many as you feel is needed to make your script work (in America, nine or more is normal before sending it out). The important thing is: with each rewrite you address specifics, and each successive rewrite should make your script easier, more fluid and more enjoyable and engaging to read. Get used to doing rewrites; they are the mainstay of the production process.

The older I got, the more scripts I sold, the more I came to realise there's always something in criticism. You're always going to improve a script.

*Ian La Frenais*,
comedy writer/producer:
*The Commitments, Still Crazy, The Likely Lads, Auf Wiedersehen Pet*

In the original version of *American Beauty*, the story carried on beyond the final edited version. We filmed how Lester's wife went on to marry Buddy, we showed the daughter incarcerated in prison and the boyfriend in another cell. I was in the editing suite and Alan Ball [the screenwriter] said 'I think we may have cut too much', and I said 'Actually, I don't think I've cut enough'.

*Sam Mendes*, director

Now you've got this far, you should be pretty confident about your script. You can literally hold it like a crystal in the palm of your hand, examine each facet and say 'it works'. You'll also probably feel a temporary 'post-natal' depression (writing a script really is like giving birth!). Don't dwell on it, because you haven't finished yet...

Cutting is not a bad thing. When you are cutting good stuff – and for me that means your great jokes – it means you are on the right track.

*Graham Lineham*, creator and co-writer:
*Father Ted, The IT Crowd*

# 14

## the 'finished' item

**In this chapter you will learn:**
- about the process of getting feedback (a difficult step)
- how to choose a great title and know how to present your screenplay correctly.

# Getting feedback

Now you need to get feedback. Ask a wide variety of people to read your screenplay. Not your mother or favourite relative (they will be biased) but someone whose writing advice you respect; a member of a writers' group (if you belong to one) or someone who might not even like you very much. If that person likes your script, it probably really does work – and it might just work on the screen. Ask them to make notes of constructive criticism. When finished, read their notes, listen to their comments and if you find them perceptive and helpful, rewrite again incorporating some of their suggestions.

Try making a recording with actors (access your local amateur dramatic society): sit them around a table with your tape recorder. Give them the script and record a straight sight-reading (no rehearsals) – and don't direct them. At the end, ask them questions: not just 'did you like it?' but things from the checklist (pages 214–15). If they were unclear about certain things, ask them if they'd be prepared to improvise that scene or situation. If so, record it. Make notes.

An interesting service worth exploring is from www.iscript.com. Iscript does a reading and puts your screeenplay onto an audio file for iPods, MP3 players or CDs. Thus you can 'offer your script in a format that has never been available before' (it says on their website). At least it is a new and novel approach, a 'hook', if you like.

Now get a distance: next day (or week), play back the original reading. Is what is coming across aurally what you wanted to transmit visually? Are you creating the drama in the mind of the audience, the movie in the mind of the reader? Does the dialogue sound like newly minted thought, as if that character were speaking it for the first time? Does it sound like words spoken or words read off a page? Does it flow? Does it sound natural? Go through your notes; rewrite again if necessary.

Eventually you'll reach a point where you know any further rewrites will only take you further away from the original intentions of your script. Stop there. Decide on your final title.

# Titles

Think of a great title: something that stands out, something the audience can hold on to.

*Julian Krainin,*
Krainin Productions

Re-read pages 60–1. If you are happy with your working title, that it imparts the essence of what's in your script, keep it. If not, brainstorm other possibilities with more impact or hook. Tip: when handing out your script for critiquing, try doing so without a title; ask them to suggest one after it has been read. If the vision you had in your mind has translated onto the page and transmitted to the audience, they may come up with a good, hopefully better, one.

Now start printing it off: you can now officially call this your first draft.

# Presentation

This is the total 'look' of your screenplay as it lands on the desk of the Reader or producer. Your job is to make it look professional: properly typed, no spelling mistakes, properly covered and bound. Assume the recipient has received your script on a bad day and that they'll look for the slightest reason to reject it. Script Readers already have to read over 50 scripts a week, so whittling down the unsuitable is ruthless. Don't give them a reason. Presentation is important, and here rigid rules apply.

### Covers and binding

The covers (front and back) should be plain thin card, no gaudy colours (be conservative), no pictures, photos or graphics. The binding is by two (or three) metal paper-fasteners (or 'brads') – see left – through punched holes in the left-hand margin of the script. Some screenplays use comb or spiral-binding and clear PVC covers (acceptable in the UK but not really in the US).

## The title page

Now type your front page. Look at page 235. What strikes you about it? It is plain, simple, clean and bare, with no unnecessary information. No year of copyright, graphics, cast lists, set lists – it's not your job. The title page should contain the title, author's name, and sometimes a contact name and telephone number (your own or your agent's, if you have one) in the bottom right or left-hand corner. Nothing more. There's no need to add 'an original screenplay by' under the title. If it's based on a life-story or an adapted script, you state it thus:

<u>Black Beauty</u>

by Caroline Thompson

Adapted from Anna Sewell's novel of the same name

Never use taglines on the title page. If you need to use them, they go on a separate sheet immediately after the title page, before page one where the screenplay starts. A good title, by-line (author) and perhaps a contact point is all you should need.

## Script length

Remember, you are a first-time writer; your script must be the right length. For feature films, especially for Hollywood, this means a maximum of 120 pages. Some say they now prefer a maximum between 105 and 115 pages. Indeed, Blake Snyder's 'Beat-Sheet' template (see Chapter 08) assumes a script length of 110 pages. Comedy and horror genres tend not to go beyond 95 pages. And a 90-page script will get read quicker and before a 120-page one.

In television, it is even more important: know the page length (how long one page plays on the screen) for the type of series you are writing for (commercial or non-commercial TV). Don't forget the ad breaks if it's for commercial TV – never send a script with breaks to a non-commercial company (e.g. the BBC). Remember, commercial TV scripts run shorter (to accommodate the ads), hence a 60-minute drama would be about 47 or 52 minutes.

## The covering letter

Everything you write – especially your letter of enquiry, covering letter and title page – will be judged as part of your ability as a screenwriter. Be professional, brief and to the point – no 'I wrote this especially for . . .' 'This is a sure-fire blockbuster', 'This is my *American Beauty*' or 'The reason I wrote this was . . .'; say more by saying less. Your script should sell itself. Increasingly, industry practise is: you don't send out a complete script at all unless the recipient (agent, producer, whoever) has specifically asked for it. What you do is send a short letter of enquiry. This should contain three essential elements:

LESBIAN VAMPIRE KILLERS

by

Phil Hupfield
and
Stewart Williams

**figure 14.2** the title page

- a brief sentence or two about yourself; that you've written a (feature/TV drama/sitcom) script; its title and the genre it's in (see Chapter 04 – the one-liner).
- the paper Pitch: sell it in about three to five lines. (Remember your Story Concept – Chapter 4: It's about … who wants to … etc … and ends up …). Make sure your ending hooks them, makes them want to see the full version.
- the reason why you are sending them this letter (to an agent – I'm seeking representation; to a producer – is this a project that might interest you?)

If you want to include a *brief* short paragraph on your aims and career ambitions as a writer, that's acceptable. Ideally, the only time your presence need be noticed is when the Reader or producer says: 'Hey, it's great. Who wrote this?'

When mailing any script out, use a padded envelope (plain ones easily get torn in the mail and your script could end up on somebody's desk looking very ragged), enclose a stamped self-addressed envelope (plain is fine here) and move onto your next script. And don't forget to include your contact details.

And why is this all so proscriptive? It's all to do with your perceived professionalism and with marketing – your screenplay and yourself.

> The key is to get your script into as many hands as possible and not take rejection. Be dogged about submitting your material, until someone who senses your ability likes it.
>
> *Lew Hunter,*
> Professor at the Screenwriting
> School, UCLA; screenwriter:
> *Desperate Lives, Fallen Angel*

Two places to visit that you may find very useful:

oscars.org/nicholl/format.html [Read script foibles: how not to do it]

scriptsupplies.com [Everything from brads and books to mailers and washers]

**assembling your portfolio**

**In this chapter you will learn:**
• how to get your ammunition and armoury together: your taglines, one-page synopsis and your new treatment – everything you need to pitch your script to the industry.

When you finish writing a script you cease to be a screenwriter and become a business-person; you then embark on a series of strategies to market and sell your work – and yourself.

*Emma Darrell,*
agent

Before you read further, look at the flow-chart on the opposite page; it refers to the information covered in the next six chapters.

So, having completed your first script, it's only natural to want to start sending it to people, especially agents and producers. By all means do so if you wish, but my advice is, don't start sending any scripts out to the industry until you have at least two completed ones you are happy with, and a third nearing completion. These should show the breadth, depth and variety of your writing styles, subjects and themes. Take a tip from Shakespeare: try writing one tragedy, one comedy and one history.

It's a mistake to think that what you write and send to people will be accepted as it is. Production companies and broadcasters tend to view first-time scripts as writers' calling cards.

*Charles Elton,*
producer: *The Railway Children,*
*Dancing Queen, A Masculine Ending*

When you are ready to begin sending out your script(s) you will need four things:

- Your 'calling card' script: the one to hook them and make them ask 'have you got any more?'
- Another script (or two) to follow through: good agents and good producers look for the potential to develop a possible long-term career relationship (Chapter 19), so prove your calling card is not a one-off.
- A very thick skin; you will be rejected – a lot. Get used to it. *Reject Rejection.* Remember, they are rejecting bits of paper, not you.
- Persistence – bags of it.
  (Persistence and rejection will be covered more in Chapter 20.)

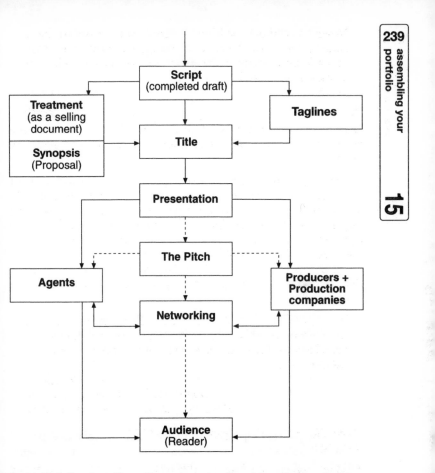

**figure 15.1** flowchart: The selling process (continued from the flowchart in Chapter 03)

There are two struggles: the struggle to write something good and the struggle to get it read. You have to attack both with single-minded persistence.

*Christopher McQuarrie,*
screenwriter: *The Usual Suspects,*
*The Way Of The Gun*

Tip: If you receive back one of your scripts in the morning post, make sure that script goes out to someone else by the afternoon collection – but make sure it's in good condition: no dog-ears, coffee cup rings or pencilled margin annotations.

Prior to sending it out, make that all-important phone call to agents to ask if they welcome unsolicited manuscripts (page 252), and to producers to ask them if they're looking for projects and, if so, what type (you should have an idea already – page 268).

When sending your script (and *never* send the original, *always* a photocopy), also enclose:

- a short covering letter (page 234)
- a short, *relevant* CV
- a stamped, self-addressed envelope big enough to return your script.

And don't worry about feeling insecure; all writers feel like that – it comes with the territory.

## Taglines

> Now try creating a new tagline for your project based on what you now know about the script. Re-read pages 56–8. If the slogan is good, you should use it in your pitch or script presentation, either as a cross-heading on the proposal, or as a tagline on a separate sheet after the title page. When pitching, they may well ask you 'What's the tagline?' – have it prepared.

Remember, a tagline has one main function: to make people want to watch. At a very basic level, it's about managing (manipulating) your audience's responses.

## The one-page synopsis (proposal)

All media people's time is limited. They are continually bombarded with ideas every waking moment – producers by writers or agents, commissioning heads by producers. Hence the practice of asking to be sent a *synopsis* (or *one-pager* or *proposal*).

This is a *one-page* prose *selling document* intended to hook your audience with the originality of your project idea, and make them want to see the treatment or (preferably) your first draft script. It has to contain enough of the story to draw them in. A synopsis should not be confused with the writer's one-page synopsis.

The important things about this synopsis are:

- it should fit onto a single side of A4 paper
- the fewer words and the more white space the better.

A synopsis has one goal only: to create interest in the story – but to do this it doesn't have to tell the whole story.

A one-page proposal has to:

- tell the basic idea of the story: let the reader imagine the project; where you start from, what the journey is, the setting, location, mood and period, an idea of genre; if *absolutely* necessary indicate the *kind* of actor who might play the lead
- tell them who will watch, who the target audience will be
- tell them (for television) where it will fit into the schedules
- contain 'the question': will Billy Elliot achieve his dream? does Tom Ripley get away with his crimes? will Annakin Skywalker and Princess Amadalla finally get together?
- tell the reader if any 'elements' (actor, director, executive producer, etc.) are 'attached', i.e. interested in the project.

The test of a good synopsis is:

1 Can the producer/agent easily pitch it to others? (again, remember your one-liner and story concept)

2 From the first quick read, can anyone – even an idiot – understand it instantly and know what it is about? (i.e. without needing further, detailed explanations)

3 Does it honestly give the Reader/producer an accurate picture of the story?

A good example of a synopsis is the one used to attract backers for *Strictly Ballroom* (page 242). Note its energetic use of short descriptive phrases, visual language, active verbs, vividly imparting a sense of energy and excitement about the project. Note too that it encapsulates the project on one sheet with plenty of white space.

You might find these websites useful: www.screenscripts.com or try www.imdb.com or trawl through the many awaiting you in Chapter 22.

---

Now write your synopsis.

# SYNOPSIS

Borrowing from the classic Hollywood dance films of the nineteen-forties, STRICTLY BALLROOM is a romantic comedy in the style of PRETTY WOMAN and DIRTY DANCING.

Set in the glamorous world of ballroom dancing, it is the story of a young man's struggle against the system.

When twenty-one year old ballroom champion, Scott Hastings, commits the cardinal sin of dancing his own steps and not those laid down by the all powerful Federation, retribution is swift. He is dumped by his partner Liz, his hopes of winning the coveted Pan-Pacific Grand Prix are dashed.

All seems lost when out of the shadows emerges Fran; a beginner and the ugly duckling of the studio. Through sheer persistence she convinces Scott to give her a chance, and an unlikely partnership is born.

Scott and Fran's first public appearance sends shock waves of excitement through the dance world. The Federation must stop them at all costs.

Scott's Achilles' Heel is his father, Doug. The night before the Pan-Pacifics, corrupt Federation President, Barry Fife, reveals to Scott the terrible secret of Doug's past. Scot is trapped. In order to save his father, he must turn his back on Fran.

On the day of the Pan-Pacifics, minutes before Scott and his ex-partner are to take the floor, the truth is revealed – Barry Fife has lied; Scott is free to follow his heart...

Scott and Fran burst onto the floor; the response from the crowd is "unearthly", but, Barry Fife will not allow it – the music is stopped.

Defiantly, twelve thousand spectators clash their hands together. Scott and Fran dance to their rhythm; the Federation are destroyed; and the floor is flooded in a sea of celebration.

**figure 15.2** the synopsis document for *Strictly Ballroom*
Source: © M&A Film Corporation Pty. Ltd.

# The treatment as a selling document

> A treatment may not get a project made, but if it's good and interesting it will at least get you an interview with the powers that be.
>
> *Allon Reich,*
> DNA Films

We've already looked at the treatment as a vehicle for focusing your story ideas (pages 206–8). Re-read that section; everything discussed there still holds true.

Now let's examine the treatment as it is mostly used: as a selling document sent by writers to producers (or by producers to commissioning heads) so they may decide if they want to commission the project, with you writing the screenplay (or see the already written script – increasingly executives expect to see completed first draft scripts first before they commission).

As with the earlier piece on treatments, the rules remain: single-spaced typed on one side of A4 paper, present tense, short paragraphs, crispness and pace, visual appeal, event-driven, outlining the main characters and imparting the essence of your project. The only differences are that, as a selling document, it is unwise to let this treatment go over twelve to fifteen pages for feature length or eight to ten pages for an hour-long drama. Creating impact in your first two paragraphs is also very important, as is your presentation (neatly printed and pleasing to the eye, no spelling mistakes, only very occasionally with photographs and interesting graphics, although these should not overwhelm the text – again, there are no rules). Lastly, if you want to put a list of characters and locations, do so, but put these on a separate sheet at the end as a caveat; at the front they have no meaning.

So make it look:

- professional (Style)
- interesting and different (Substance).

Have a look back at the list of books on treatments at the end of Chapter 11.

---

**Now write your treatment.**

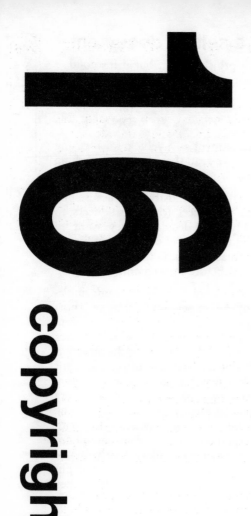

# 16

## copyright

**In this chapter you will learn:**
- what to do now that you've got a completed script and you want to start sending it out to the industry – copyright it first.

# A brief and painless guide to knowing your rights

Prior to sending your script to the industry, you may want to register its copyright i.e. to officially register your claim as being the rightful author of that said original work. Probably the question I am most frequently asked is: 'I've got this idea for a film/TV series/treatment – how can I copyright it and protect it from being stolen?' The facts are: you cannot copyright an *idea*. An idea is just that: an idea. You *can* copyright work (a synopsis, proposal, treatment or script), which is defined as the material form in which an idea is expressed. And the more fully-realized that expression of your idea is on paper, the more solid your copyright is (for example, it's better to copyright a treatment than, say, a synopsis).

Technically, according to law, the very fact that the idea is now expressed on paper in black and white means that it is copyrighted. However, effectively it is meaningless and only a small part of the scenario. Also, a work marked © by the owner's name and a date does not guarantee protection, but it does provide evidence both of the date of the work's creation and the claimed ownership of copyright.

Copyright is precisely what its name suggests. It does not offer protection against another individual coming up with the same idea separately and independently. (There are only eight basic stories, there is nothing new under the sun, and remember, talk is cheap – so don't chatter about your ideas until you've put them down on paper and done something about it. The more you talk, the more you invite trouble.)

The more you become involved in the media industry, the more gossip you will hear concerning ideas, formats, even whole scripts allegedly stolen and later screened with someone else claiming authorship. But in truth copyright theft forms a very tiny part of the industry. In practice, it is easy to steal something like a treatment simply by abandoning the original copyright holder's existing text, grammar or language, and rewriting it in your own style.

A common industry practice today, when a company acknowledges receipt of your script, or subsequently when they send you a rejection, is to include the following rider (or similar) in their covering letter:

'(This company) receives a very large number of proposals, many of which are similar to or the same as each other. For this reason, I am sure you will appreciate that even if, in the future, we produce or commission a (film/programme/project) which you believe is the same or similar to your suggestion, but which has come, coincidentally, from another source, we cannot compensate you.

I am returning your (submission/proposal) with this letter. I have not circulated it to anyone else.'

This action might just be to cover the company over things like moral rights and intellectual property claims, but to the untrained observer it looks like an attempt to have one's cake and eat it. In truth there is little you as an individual can do.

## Release forms

Another common industry development is the release form, whereby the receiving party gets the submitting writer to sign a form or indemnity waiver before the receiver even begins to read the submission. This short document (between one to three pages) will contain clauses like the following:

'Although we have not read the work we recognize the possibility that it may be similar to and/or competitive with material which we (or one of our subsidiaries or affiliates) is contemplating, developing and/or considering for production. Accordingly, in order to avoid any potential problems:

1 You recognize that the work may contain similar concepts and material which we have or are developing.

2 You agree that in consideration for our reviewing and discussing the work with you, you may not at any time assert or attempt to assert any claim against us (or any of our agents or employees) with respect to our use of similar material in any project or series, which we may develop, produce, distribute, license or sell to a third party.'

And if you don't sign the release form your manuscript will be returned to you unread and your masterpiece undiscovered. Catch 22. The final decision on signing obviously rests with you and how important it is for you to get your work read and circulated. If you do sign, just go in with your eyes open, because you could still end up with your ideas being taken, only now you've got no leg to stand on. However, your first task is to get someone – anyone – to read your submission at all.

Release forms are generally not to the writer's advantage. But writers, especially new ones, are paranoid about having their ideas stolen. Put your paranoia aside. Life is risk!

*Jeff Polstein,*
Head of Story Department,
ICM (US)

Some American writers are now submitting their original manuscripts on red paper. Why? Because red paper cannot be photocopied!

## So what do I do?

Probably the most widely used and cheapest method is to mail your script back to yourself in a sealed (do not use sealing tape) *registered* envelope (not recorded delivery) and keep it stored away in a safe place, unopened. It's a method the teenage John Lennon used when home-recording his own songs. The key points are: the envelope is clearly date-stamped over the seal and remains sealed – the theory being that if matters came to court, you could produce the envelope and have it opened by and inspected in front of legal representatives. So if it's good enough for John Lennon, it's good enough for me. Note: if using this method, mail the hard (paper) copy – computer disks may tend to corrupt.

For added protection you might wish to register your script with a recognized third party – lawyer or bank, for example – but, inevitably, costs are involved. You could also register it with one of the many, and growing, Copyright Registration Schemes. Registration schemes are now run by a number of industry bodies (BECTU, PACT, Raindance, Screenwriters' Workshop, and the Writers Guild of America), independent set-ups and some regional arts boards/Media Development Agencies (these are accessible via the BFI). Again, they will charge something, but they may offer reduced rates to members. Contact details are at the end of this chapter and in Taking it further.

While registration does not guarantee that your ideas won't get stolen, it does at least mean your work is dated and registered with a recognized independent entity. It may give you a sense of security, and make you both feel more able to openly discuss that work with others.

Similar registration schemes are multiplying, possibly a symptom of a growing fear (or incidence?) of industry plagiarism. All furnish you with a signed and dated registration document, but they do charge. The decision is yours.

One thing you could do on your submissions is to type on the front page (and on every page if you feel it really necessary) the words: 'Commercial In Confidence', together with the legend ©, followed by your name and the month and year it was written. Again, it may not guarantee against plagiarism, but at least it dates your manuscript and formally notifies claimed ownership. It gives clear signals to the receiver, both that you are aware of your legal position and that you are completely paranoid about ideas theft. But it might give you some peace of mind.

All screenwriting is a risky business; be aware that similar ideas are often in circulation at the same time. But you have to distribute your project widely to find the right person to get it on screen, and nothing is gained by leaving a script on the shelf gathering dust. The choice is yours.

## Some useful publications and contacts

**UK**

*Quick Guide to Copyright and Moral Rights* (booklet) Available from the Society of Authors (www.societyofauthors.org) Free to members, £2 post-free to UK non-members.

[Also visit: ww.societyofauthors.org/publications/quick_guide_permissions/]

Cavendish & Pool: *Handbook of Copyright in British Publishing Practise* (Cassell, but dates from 1993)

Helen Shay: *Writers' Guide to Copyright and Law* (How To books) [You can also get some free downloads from her www.incwriters.co.uk/freedownloads.htm]

**US**

For all US copyright matters, refer to:

Library of Congress Copyright Office (www.copyright.gov) or The Public Information Office (Tel: 1-202 707 3000).

Stephen Breimer: *Screenwriter's Legal Guide* (Allworth Press)

Ted Crawford & Kay Murray: *The Writer's Legal Guide: an Authors Guild Desk Reference* (Allworth Press)

Brooke A. Wharton: *The Writer Got Screwed, but didn't have to* (Harper Collins)

## Some script registration schemes

You will find a great many script registration schemes listed these days. You could pick at random URLs from Chapter 22 of this book (Screenwriting and the Internet) and many screenwriters' websites may well have some sort of scheme. The ones I list here are probably the more well-known ones or have been endorsed by a well-respected writers' organization:

**UK**

copyrightservice.co.uk [UK Copyright Office]

thescriptvault.co.uk [Endorsed by the Writers' Guild of Great Britain]

wcauk.com [Writers' Copyright Association; linked with the WGGB; worldwide links and info for UK, Europe, USA, Canada and Australia]

**USA**

goasa.com [American Screenwriters Association; click on Writers Resource tab, then Bookstore]

scripped.com [Click on Scripped Vault]

wgaeast.org/script_reg [Writers Guild of America, New York: annual registration $10 members/$22 non-members]

wgaregistry.org [Writers Guild of America, west coast]

writesafe.com [Secure registration from trusted organization]

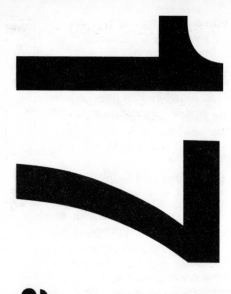

# 7

# agents

**In this chapter you will learn:**
- about the murky and mysterious world of the agent and how to go about getting one.

# What they do, how to get – and keep – one

> Having a good agent is very important, an agent who understands what your goals are, and looks at career in terms of 30 or 40 years. It's important to have someone there to remind you, when you forget, what your career goals are and what the big picture is. You will be ill-served by an agent only interested in the immediate 'what's hot' one-off quick-hit.
>
> *Paul Attanasio*

## What is an agent?

Essentially an agent is a writer's eyes and ears, their business manager and shop window. He or she (many agents are women) handles everything for you, supposedly leaving you free to write. For a percentage (usually 10 per cent and upwards) an agent will negotiate contracts, wine, dine and schmooze contacts, keep an ear to the ground for future work, (theoretically) generate new work, even suggest changes in your script to make it more marketable. You the writer are the commodity, and the agent is there to get the best deal without losing the contract. It has been suggested that a writer must earn at least £15,000 per annum before the agent will cover their overheads and start to see a return on their investment.

## Do I need an agent?

If you don't have one, you are operating with a handicap. In the marketplace of screenwriting, having an agent is the equivalent of having a merit badge saying: 'This writer can deliver the goods'. It is a sign that some other independent, respected person believes you have talent. If the agent says you can turn in scripts, and to a deadline, it helps a producer trust their own judgement (and blame someone if the project fails). Putting it bluntly: many people with the power in this industry have a reluctance to commit themselves to new untried talent – it's the inherent insecurity of the business. So, if a producer receives a script from an agent it means that at least *they* think you can write. Consequently, that script will be read by the producer rather than the Reader, or at least given some precedence. Basically, having an agent is a rubber stamp of confidence – a reinforcer. Hollywood generally only accepts scripts submitted via agents.

Of course, you could always handle your own contract negotiations, but do it with a good (preferably media specialist) lawyer at your side.

## How do I get an agent?

As much a Catch 22 as an actor trying for an Equity card. Even assuming an agent likes your script, if there is no guarantee of work (i.e. a percentage) it is not that likely you will get taken on. Then again, actually getting work is ten times more difficult without an agent.

Conversely, if a production company or director is interested in your script and talking money, just watch the agents flock around and invite you in for a chat.

> One responds instinctively to good writing, you get that feeling in your stomach and know you're in the presence of something quite special.
>
> *Mel Kenyon*, agent

## Where do I start?

*The Writer's Handbook* (Taking it further) has a section listing agents, contact names, numbers, their catalogues, percentages and attitudes to unsolicited manuscripts. This is your bible. You can also hit the Internet.

Make a list of agents you feel might be interested in your type of work and who accept unsolicited manuscripts. Then send a preliminary letter (it's quicker to read) briefly (in two or three sentences) outlining your script and career ambitions. Better still, pick up the phone (*never* be afraid to do this). You probably won't speak to the agent personally, but at least you might get to their secretary (a *very* important conduit) and ask whether they would mind your submitting something. They can only say no. If they do, go to the next name on your list. They may tell you they are not taking on new names at present, so ask them when they might be trawling again (some agents have an annual or bi-annual clear out which is where your opening may come).

If they do ask you to submit a full script, I would be very surprised. Today's standard industry protocol for approaching agents (and producers, and anyone else in the industry who can advance your work) is to send them a short introductory letter with the three main bullet-points I outlined at the end of Chapter 14 – covering letter. They may also ask you to submit a synopsis and/or treatment and a short CV (make it relevant). Whatever they ask for, you provide.

Know your agencies first – their international contacts (Europe? US?), specialized fields – and target your script. You may find the larger agencies with new young blood (i.e. an ex-tea boy who wants to be a budding agent and is looking to build up a roster) more approachable. But increasingly, as larger agencies expand into more areas of revenue generation like packaging entire movie deals with their own talent at all levels (it's called multi-tasking), the smaller agents are coming more into their own for new writers. Also some agents charge a small reading fee. Be professional: at all times be business-like, to the point and, above all, courteous. And don't forget that SAE.

## Responses

Remember, everything in this business is based on a purely subjective response, and that goes doubly for agents: your script may be slaughtered by one, criticizing character A's outdated and stereotyped attitudes, whereas another might praise character A's wonderfully old-fashioned views. So don't give up. Rejection is part of this industry and your learning curve, and if you can't take rejection or criticism, you are not the kind of writer media people are looking for.

## Follow through

If you manage to send your 'calling card' script to an agent and (heavens!) they don't dislike it (they rarely say they totally love something), they may ask you if you have anything else. Remember: *you must have that back-up*. You send in your second script (the one more likely to convince them), together with about five or six further script ideas in synopsis. So having that portfolio of scripts is essential (page 238).

It is inadvisable approaching an agent until you have your portfolio together. There's little point in an agent taking on a writer with just one script or one idea – where's the potential for developing that writer's work and career? Agents want writers who are marketable, not just a script that *may* be sellable.

And don't fret if, after sending in your calling card script, you hear nothing. Agents are seemingly perpetually busy, so expect to wait up to three months for a response. Perhaps give them a reminder call after four to six weeks.

If they call you in for a meeting they will want to discuss your career goals. Do *you* know what they are?

## Final points

If taken on by an agent, there is usually no signing of contracts; it's a loose arrangement, made either verbally or by an exchange of letters, after an initial meeting. However, once you've got an agent, it is not a meal ticket. Don't expect them to get work for you. They may be able to point you in certain directions, but you must go out into the industry and network, hear where the breaks are and who's looking for what.

Remember, getting an agent is not an end in itself, it is a beginning – the beginning of your career as a writer, and keeping one depends on how that professional relationship progresses. They can drop you from their books just as quickly if you are unsellable (you're only as good as your last script), or if you prove 'difficult to work with'.

I would advise against the 'my agent, my best friend' attitude. The bottom line is business, and ultimately you must feel able and happy to trust your agent's business and literary judgement.

Try to remember that the agent works for the writer, not vice versa. Look at the split of the percentages: who gets the 90%? In a very real sense you 'employ' the agent – but just who needs whom more is debatable.

You don't have to have an agent in order to write.

*David Thompson,*
Head of BBC Films

… but it sure helps. I can't think of any full-time working writer who doesn't have an agent – and a good one.

*David Koepp,*
screenwriter: *Panic Room, Spider-Man,*
*Mission: Impossible, Carlito's Way*

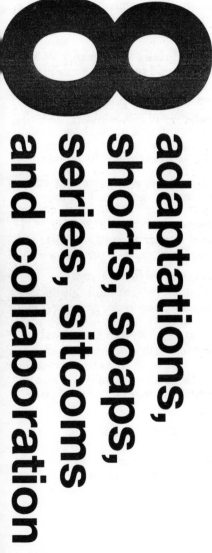

# 18

# adaptations, shorts, soaps, series, sitcoms and collaboration

In this chapter you will learn:
- about some specialist areas of screenwriting
- about adapting someone else's work, writing short films (a useful way to get noticed) and writing sitcoms
- some tips about collaborating with other writers.

adaptations, shorts, soaps,
series, sitcoms and
collaboration

18

# Adapting for the screen

Adaptation is the process of changing or transforming material from one medium (novel, stage play, short story, real-life story, etc.) into another medium (i.e. film or TV). Although over 60 per cent of all produced screenplays are adaptations (mostly from novels), the vast majority of first-produced screenplays are original. Why? Because most adapted screenplays are done on commission by already established writers; and before a writer can begin any serious adaptation, the commissioner (usually a producer) must first obtain the screen adaption Rights to the source material, and that costs money – often lots.

Writing screen adaptations is not really the territory of this introductory book. It is a specialist skill for which you will find many specialist publications on the existing market. Understand that each medium has its own underlying principles of action and conflict, its own unique limitations and liberties. In adapting for film you are searching for those basic strong elements that can be dramatized and will play on the screen. If considering adapting something as an exercise, ask yourself:

- Can I reduce the material to a simple strong storyline and a two-hour slot? (A novel has many pages to tell a story; you have only 120).
- Does it have an *intention* which seeks a *goal* which can be made dramatic, and expressed visually on the screen? Are the needs strong and clear enough and do they drive to a final climax?

So: *find the spine*, that central storyline that fulfils all the key screen requirements and can be described in one sentence, your story concept (page 44). Then ruthlessly decide what fits with the spine and what doesn't. Next, creatively decide what to keep and what to dump (select, compress, cut, rearrange, transform; clarity is essential). Then reduce that work to its basic essential story elements. Next, find the beginning, middle and end of your potential script story. Finally, distil out the *spirit* of the story.

This spirit is your jumping-off point, and what demands loyalty. Screen adaptation is creating a new type of reality, so obey the underlying principles for that form. It doesn't mean throwing the book away entirely. Clarity is essential: know what you seek and what the screenplay's ultimate shape will be.

Being faithful to the book isn't the same as repeating every word.

*Andrew Davies,*
Adaptor: *Pride And Prejudice,*
*The Old Devils, Tipping The Velvet*

For example, in the film version of *The Talented Mr. Ripley* there are clear indications that Tom will finally get caught, but in the novel's ending, the opposite happened; in the original graphic novel of *Road To Perdition* Michael Jr. grew up to become a priest, but the film ends while he is still a child (although the voice-overs are spoken as the adult); and I'm still searching my Jane Austen (*Pride And Prejudice*) to find the part where Mr. Darcy exits the water in wet, clinging jodhpurs. Yet all these screen versions still 'work' believably in their own terms. Ask yourself *why* these decisions were made.

Remember, to the media industry, a book is a property to be purchased – and with the Rights comes the licence to do anything necessary to make it work on screen.

One final tip: adapting your own novel rarely works – you are too close to your precious source material!

---

They say 'Good books make bad movies, bad books make good movies' (e.g.: *Bonfire Of The Vanities, American Psycho* and *The Bridges Of Madison County*). Do you agree? List three of each type. Can you think of exceptions? List them.

---

Two recommended books on adaptation:

Gabriel Miller: *Screening the Novel*
Linda Seger: *The Art of Adaptation: Turning Fact and Fiction into Film*

… and a website article you should read; Michael Hauge's Rules for Adaptation: screenplaymastery.com/Rules.htm

# Writing short films

We all started in shorts, it's where you can show your talent without spending a billion dollars. You can take your piece of passion and get it on the screen, someone somewhere sees it and you springboard into your career.

*Paul Haggis*, screenwriter: *Crash, Quantum Of Solace, Million Dollar Baby, In The Valley Of Elah*

Short films (generally anything between 5 and 30 minutes) are often a good way for new writers to enter the industry. Many are made by film schools, but increasingly independent low-budget/no-budget/'guerilla' enterprises are emerging. Some TV channels are increasingly supportive of the short (for TV transmission, the maximum length is 11 minutes).

Writing a short is a different skill from writing longer form drama – possibly the most challenging and difficult of all screenwriting forms to do well. Here are some broad considerations:

- One thing all successful shorts share is: the idea and its expression 'fits its space'. It's not a longer story forcibly squashed to fit the allotted time or a sketch idea artificially stretched; nor is it a promo for some future envisaged feature – a good tactic if you can pull it off.
- The tenets of screenwriting (every line justifying its existence) are even more important in a short: you only have approximately 15 pages. Economy of form and expression are everything. So try dropping straight into the life or world of your protagonist immediately; take a particular incident in that character's life which, when dramatized, illuminates their wider existence and history.
- Think twice about 'twist in the tail' stories. Readers are cynical enough to predict endings and generally get them right.
- Humour seems to work well in the short, as long as you are not using it as a sketch substitute.

Despite their denials, industry executives still see shorts as a director's medium, a calling card demonstrating their ability to go on to make their first feature. So link up with new directors and producers; view the project as *your* calling card.

I suspect that the future of Shorts is on the internet, that's where the market is. You post up your masterpiece on YouTube.com and get discovered (simple as that!). Just don't expect to make any money out of it – yet. And don't forget the growing market in creating 'content' for the mobile/cellphone portals. Short, punchy microdrama-stabs, barely a minute or three long. (The same goes for the three-minute interactive mini-drama content emerging on myspace and bebo now – see Chapter 22 Screenwriting and the Internet).

Some useful websites worth visiting:

atom.com [Got short comedy videos? Post 'em up here]
britshorts.com
encounters-festival.org.uk [Bristol Short Film Festival, UK]

fortheloveofit.com [Hopefully this site will be back up soon]

funlittlemovies.com [The mobile/cellphones channel making micro-dramas]

hollyshorts.com

lashortsfest.com [Los Angeles annual shorts festival; very informative site]

mamut.net/filmfestivals/newsdet1.htm [Shorts festival news]

moviepoet.com [Home of the New Jersey Writers Group; shorts-focused]

shortfilmbigshot.com

shortscriptsonline.com

sohoshorts.com [Home to London's annual Rushes short film fest]

studentfilms.com

TheSmalls.com

triggerstreet.com [Kevin Spacey's initiative]

...and don't forget to check out:

- myspace.com (go to myspace.com/tyscreenwriting and explore my Friends list. There you will find...futureshorts, a worldwide network of groups; lashortsfest; shortfilmbigshot and many more)
- the various groups on facebook.com and yahoo; there's gold-dust to be discovered in these groups sections.

...and some books:

Jim Piper: *Making Short Films* (Allworth Press)

Shooting People: *Get your Short film Funded, Made and Seen* [Available from shootingpeople.org]

Clifford Thurlow: *Making Short Films: the Complete Guide from Script to Screen* (Berg) [Available from cliffordthurlow.com]

# Soaps, series and sitcoms

Lose your prejudices about writing for TV soap operas and series being downmarket 'hack' work. They are a regular and proven entry point for many new writers and a very good training ground in the writing discipline. Be professional: be adaptable.

Soap at its best is dramatised gossip in a kind of never-ending middle act.

*Adrian Mourby,*
author/writer-producer/former
editor of *The Archers*

**260**

adaptations, shorts, soaps,
series, sitcoms and
collaboration

**18**

Part of any TV script editor's job remit is looking for new writing talent, for which they are ever hungry. Each series will have its own 'Bible' – a hefty document containing full details of the series characters, story backgrounds, its ethos and approach, and other production information. However, obtaining one is difficult and you may not see one until offered a chance to write for the show. More established series (*EastEnders*, *Hollyoaks*, *The Bill*) will have writer's intern schemes where novice writers shadow established ones through the production process.

How do you get on these schemes? Target the programme, watch as many episodes as possible and get the rhythm of the show inside you. Speak to the script editor and/or send them a speculative script you've written. What they *don't* want is a spec. (speculative) episode of that series using the same characters. They want something in the same genre or background as that series. Mostly, they want evidence that you can write, potential they can nurture.

If they are impressed, you'll be invited in for a chat (see Chapter 19). Always have five or six one-page story outlines ready. Upon meeting you, they want to feel you know the series well, its structure, and can (or can be trained to) deliver to deadlines. *Never* criticize the show destructively (you are criticizing these people's reasons to exist!). Be enthusiastic and receptive; listen and learn.

Be prepared to have your initial outlines rejected – don't take it personally. Be persistent: with every batch rejected send them another, better batch; eventually one will hit a target.

A typical soap/series commissioning cycle might run:

| | |
|---|---|
| February: | writers meeting – agree storylines |
| Late February: | story draft delivered |
| April: | story modified by producers |
| May: | first draft commissioned |
| Mid-July: | second draft with the production designers |
| Late July: | final draft |
| Early September: | episode recorded |
| Mid-October: | episode transmitted |

Many soaps and series have annual or bi-annual open trawls for new writers – find out when the next one is, and have a good script ready.

# Sitcoms

> The comedy moments we remember most and cherish the most are almost always visual.
>
> *John Cleese,* writer/actor:
> A Fish Called Wanda, Fawlty Towers, Monty Python's
> *Flying Circus*

Sitcoms are, again, a specialist area with their own separate books. As with 30-minute soaps, two-act Structure applies (see Chapter 08). Remember, sitcoms have *two* components: situation and comedy. It's the characters responding to a situation that makes it funny. Audiences respond to memorable characters – so create them! Comedy dialogue is the difference between saying funny things and saying things funny. People want the latter.

Producers say they like to see at least three 'laughs' per page, but natural ones. Also note the cyclical nature of sitcoms: at the end of the episode the characters may have travelled a journey but their basic predicament is exactly the same as it was at the start. And note how sitcoms often make an advantage of their restrictive environment: here are characters who desperately want to break out of or change their life situation but, through force of circumstances or relationships, end up unable to (*Steptoe and Son, Hancock, Cheers, Frasier, Will & Grace*). Indeed, when a sitcom attempts to venture outside of its normal, familiar territory it is often less successful.

And *don't* write something you think someone else will find funny; write what makes *you* laugh.

When submitting something, producers want to see:

* a completed episode – preferably the first (pilot) episode
* half-page story outlines for each of the next six to seven episodes (at least)
* a one- or two-page series format digest, including six to eight lines on each of the main characters.

A couple of observations:

* It has to be said that, as with the more cutting-edge dramas these days, the more edgy types of comedy where the characters say the unsayable, however outrageous or 'offensive' that might be (*Family Guy, South Park, American Dad, Arrested Development*), are more likely to be found on the privately subscription-funded channels and/or on cable (HBO may be owned by Warners but it has its own unique subscription networks) or on one of the more maverick

262

adaptations, shorts, soaps,
series, sitcoms and
collaboration

18

subsidiaries or areas of a national channel (e.g. Fox Network). And they are mostly animated.

- More recently we've seen the emergence of 'the comedy of embarrassment' (*Curb Your Enthusiasm, The Office, Extras*). The keynote is the cringe factor: those traits of character and awkward situations that we all recognize in ourselves and our lives, that make us relate to (and ultimately empathize with) these characters we see on the screen. All I will say is: why try to compete with Larry David, Ricky Gervaise and Stephen Merchant? They have perfected this approach to comedy, and while you're sitting there thinking about a possible script idea, they are no doubt already working up their next three projects.

Find your own unique voice, your own style, what *you* find funny. (Even Jerry Seinfeld made comedy out of... well, nothing!).

Useful comedy websites:

http://groups.yahoo.com/group/SitsVac
www.bbc.co.uk/writersroom
www.britcoms.com                    [UK comedy programmes]
FunnyorDie.com                    [Will Ferrell's site for old and new
                                              comedy talent]
www.robinkelly.btinternet.co.uk   [Has a useful sitcom section]
www.sitcomtrials.co.uk
                    [Regular performances of new writers' works]

and a couple of books:

*Teach Yourself Comedy Writing* by Jenny Roche (Teach Yourself Books)

*What Are You Laughing At? How to Write Funny Screenplays, Stories and More* by Brad Schreiber and Christopher Vogler (Michael Wiese Productions).

## ... On collaboration

Find someone to write with. Writing with a partner is paid socializing. Writing on your own is work.

*Ricky Gervaise,* co-creator/co-writer:
*The Office, Extras*

In previous editions of this book, when covering writers collaborating, I advised: before you start, set out some ground rules, i.e. who does what in this relationship (know your mutual writing strengths and weaknesses), the order of credits (usually

**263**

adaptations, shorts, soaps,
series, sitcoms and
collaboration

**18**

done alphabetically) and the payments split – as this will save many arguments later.

Of course, in those days, I was referring to the traditional face-to-face type of writing partnership. Since then, we have had some revolutionary pieces of software which enable you to collaborate with other writers online across the globe. And it's all free!

## Collaboration online

These programmes connect with an online community where you can develop a script with other collaborators and writers. You sign-in, download the software, post your work up and wait. To put it like that is simplistic, you need to visit the websites to appreciate these revolutionary bits of kit. So visit:

Celtx.com
PlotBot.com
Protagonize.com
Scripped.com
ScriptBuddy.com
WordCircle.org
Zhura.com

Visit them all, as they each have their own unique approach. However, the one that really enthuses me is Celtx.com. It is a free, open-source Canadian programme that connects with an online community (Project Central: ps.celtx.com) where you can develop your script with other writers and collaborators, and eventually showcase it.

Unlike the other software, it's stand-alone, you don't need to be online to use it. It also has built-in storyboarding, casting and scheduling features, all of which can be shared online if you wish to build interest in your project – it boasts over 250,000 active users.

There's another neat feature, whereby you can assign scenes to a date in your shooting schedule calendar. The programme then gathers together all the information about all the associated characters, props and locations and creates a call-sheet. And it's all free!

You can also access the download (for PC, Mac or Linux) from:

www.netribution.co.uk/content/view/1503/182/

...you might also try the following Yahoo group:

http://groups.yahoo.com/group/WritingBuddies

# 19 the industry: how it works and your place in it

**In this chapter you will learn:**

- about the industry, and where you stand in it
- how to target your markets
- how to take meetings with, and pitch to, producers
- about that blissful state of immobility called 'in development'. Be afraid ... be very afraid!

If you don't conduct your relationship with the industry, it will conduct you.

*Paula Milne*

# Breaking in

They say it's not what you know but who you know. That certainly goes for the media industry – much of it is down to knowing the right people, which means networking and contacts: selling yourself as well as your scripts – it's your marketing strategy. Luck also plays a significant part – having the right script in the right hands at the right time. So, how do you get that first break?

- Use your initiative. Is there a conference or seminar being organized where the speaker is an established writer or industry executive? Attend it.
- Attend an extensive weekend or week-long writing course (Chapter 20). Fellow attendees are aspiring and established writers and key industry professionals. Many writers get their first break (particularly into TV soaps or series) through meeting someone at a course.
- Some TV networks and film schools run occasional courses or schemes, mostly free. Entry is by script submission. Find out when the next one is.
- Regular competitions and scholarships are publicized via the monthly writers' magazines.
- Join a Writers' Group (local libraries have lists). Attend, network, suggest a seminar with an industry player. Volunteer to organize or help in its organization; don't be scared, it's not as daunting as it seems. Many executives (especially writers) are prepared to do it for expenses or a bottle of wine – diaries permitting.
- Join one of the industry bodies (SW, NPA, PACT, Raindance, etc. – see Taking it further), meet fellow emerging talent, especially producers and directors. You stand a better chance of breaking through if part of a package (with other elements: producers, director or 'name' actor). It also boosts your confidence.
- If your local theatre has a writers' group, join it. I know you want to write for the screen, but there are more openings here. Also, when executives look for new writers, often their first thoughts turn to the theatre (even though it is a totally separate skill!) If you get something (however insubstantial)

performed, it establishes an all-important track record – as does a radio play.
• Some independent production companies and TV series (*EastEnders*, *The Bill*) run intern schemes (Chapter 18).

When interfacing with the industry, at whatever level, at all times be pleasant, courteous, confident, professional; not pushy, overpowering, over-confident or loud-mouthed. Learn to listen and take advice. Networking is another skill in your box of tricks. However, remember: you can have as many contacts as you like, but if you don't deliver a good script, it will embarrass people.

## The industry: your place in it

There are more stars on the Hollywood Walk of Fame for dogs, cats and horses than there are for writers.

*Brian Helgeland,*
screenwriter: *L.A. Confidential, A Knight's Tale,*
*Conspiracy Theory*

Power? Writers have got fuck-all power, unless they're rich or famous.

American TV executive
(who requested anonymity)

In the industry hierarchy, writers have traditionally been near the bottom and the worst paid. The maxim runs: if a film's a success, the director gets the praise; if it flops, they all blame the writer. However, the importance of a good script is becoming increasingly acknowledged; those who can deliver are getting highly paid, heavily feted and respected (so long as they continue to deliver).

It no longer matters what a film is about … it's 'who's in it?'

*Robert Altman*, director

Here's an industry fact: at the turn of this century, over 40 per cent of the US film-going audience were over the age of forty. Perhaps this explains why Hollywood – with its obsessive targeting of the 17–24 age group, and the ascending power of agents to package everything i n a production – has for some years been steadily losing the plot, while ever more media-savvy audiences increasingly embrace the independent sector and innovation.

When I first sent round the original script of *My Big Fat Greek Wedding*, people loved it but the studio bosses said 'Can you make it Jewish?' or 'Could you rewrite it as Hispanic?' I said 'No, it's Greek, it's what I know, it stays Greek'. The studios said goodbye, so I just turned it into a one-woman stage show ... and then Mr and Mrs Hanks visited the show ...

*Nia Vardalos,*
actress, screenwriter

To achieve any level of greatness you have to be willing to say 'yes' no matter who says 'no', and 'no' no matter who says 'yes'.

*Sharon Stone,*
actress, producer

# Targeting the market

You need to know as much about the industry and how it works as you do about screenwriting itself. You need to acquaint yourself with the names (especially of producers and production companies): who's doing what, who's looking for what, commissioning trends, writing initiatives, budgets and box office.

Immerse yourself in the 'trades' (the weekly trade papers) for films – *Variety*, *Screen International* or *The Hollywood Reporter*; for UK television – *Broadcast* (see Taking it further for details). Read them thoroughly, and regularly – ideally subscribe to a couple. Similarly, take as much interest in the end credits of a film or TV programme as you do in the production itself. Be like me: one of those people who irritate the theatre owners by sitting there until the end of the last credit.

In all cases note the names, create a filing card system for yourself: one each for producers, agents, comedy, etc. The key people to look for are: in film – script development executives, heads of development (HoDs), producers and directors; in TV – script editors, producers, directors and commissioning editors. Build up a database, cross-referencing names with productions, projects, their track records, tastes and preferences, their attitudes towards new writers, of industry people you may meet (note where and when met, what was discussed, opinions exchanged, general impressions, etc.) As the database grows these names will become second nature.

When sending your scripts out to the industry you shoot with a sniper not a blunderbuss: target your market – and this database is your market. Information is power.

# Producers and how to survive them

A key factor in *Four Weddings And A Funeral* ending up a strong film was: I had a producer and director who shared my vision regarding how this film should be, and we all remained loyal to that shared vision.

*Richard Curtis*

The key figure in any production – the one with the ultimate responsibility for a project – is the producer. Good producers get things made; bad ones waste your energy, talent and time. Good producers generate the 'heat' (enthusiasm and commitment) necessary to get a lot of different people with different talents to come together into making a movie or TV production, and then sell it. Crucially, producers also find the money – the single most important fact of life for them. Their aim is to get the best production made for the lowest cost. Get used to the idea that film and TV making is the art of the possible: what the budget and time allow. Sometimes producers take a more hands-on creative role in the project.

Today the producers with talent, energy and vision predominantly work in the independent production sector. Target the people and companies whose work you admire. Know their past track record: are their productions similar in feel to your script? Phone and ask the switchboard if they accept unsolicited material. If yes, they'll probably suggest a specific name (HoD or script editor) to send it to. Mail off your package, but don't expect an instant reply. It may take up to three months for a response. After six to eight weeks try phoning the recipient or their secretary and politely enquire about your submission. (At least you've made another contact.)

Some companies may require you to sign a release form before submitting your script (see Chapter 16). The decision is yours. New writers are always paranoid. If you want your script read you have no choice; if you don't sign, nobody will discover your masterpiece.

Lastly, at the risk of banging the same drum again, you may wonder why so many rotten movies get released by Hollywood and the major studios. It's because decisions by the 'suits' are very often based on the financial structure of a deal and not on any creative merits of a project. So you need to feel confident that the producer you work with can put together an equitable deal package as well as understand the artistic dimensions of a script.

Acknowledge the mutual differences and priorities: the screenwriter's primary concern is getting the script right, the producer wants to find the money and get the thing made.

## Taking a meeting

I'm in my nineties now, and a couple of years ago I took a new project into one of the suits at the studio – young guy, mid–late twenties, he  was – and he sat me down and said 'So, Mr. Wilder, tell me: what have you done?' I looked back at him and I said 'No, kid, you tell me: what *you* done'.

*Billy Wilder,*
director: *Some Like It Hot,* etc. etc.

So a producer likes your script and you're invited in for a meeting or a 'chat'. This first meeting is usually a casual affair with both sides trying to sum up the other. You should be deciding if you want to work with this person, for they are certainly trying to decide if they can work with you. Just remember that fundamental principle: screen production is a collaborative medium.

Producers look for 'personal chemistry' when working with colleagues.

*Adrian Hodges*

If there's an obvious personality clash, or if they feel you're a writer who is totally inflexible or too precious about changing your words on the page (i.e. you aren't open to rewrites), they'll probably say 'thanks, but no thanks'. They are seeking to be reassured in this meeting: they want to have confidence in you as a writer who is not only good, but also reliable, can deliver the goods and to deadlines. Never be rude or sycophantic about their work. Be punctual, dress well (smart-casual at least), and be open, constructive and confident.

They won't usually discuss money at this meeting. They may want to discuss your submission in depth, they may want to talk about other ideas you have (have the synopses ready: see page

240), or they may well have a project or idea of their own they'd like you to flesh out and write the screenplay for. If there is agreement it is usually just verbal. Follow up this meeting with a short, appreciative letter; if anything was agreed in the meeting, state them here.

The producer may offer you an option agreement. Taking an option means for an agreed amount (from £1 to £500, but nearer the former), they own the full Rights on that script or synopsis to exploit for a set period (usually one year, renewable annually). This also obliges you to do rewrites from their 'notes'. Get used to it. If you don't do it, someone else will.

If you are offered a decent amount of money, consult the appropriate Writers Guild for the relevant rates (see Taking it further). If offered, say, one pound, ask yourself: can this person get the project made? Remember, you need that first screened credit. Besides, you'll get your first major payment when the project starts shooting. Subsequent script sales fees are based on how much your last script sold for (or your agent). A growing practice is the Buy-Out, where you sign away *all* rights in perpetuity for an up-front payment of two–three times the normal Guild rates. The decision is yours.

Good producers (with their hopefully shared vision) will help you realize the full potential in your project, and if the relationship proves fruitful, enjoyable, challenging or fun, it may develop into a mutually beneficial long-term partnership. Many producers like to build up trusting long-term working relationships with a stable of favourite writers they've discovered, can nurture and rely on.

> If you've been paid to write something, the ultimate sin is
> not late delivery, but non-delivery.
>
> *Colin Clements,*
> screenwriter/script executive

## The pitch and pitching

Many articles have been written about, and entire courses been built around, acquiring the skills of pitching. For the novice it can be quite a daunting prospect, but some basic thoughts are given here.

A pitch is a verbal presentation of your script or idea to anyone with the power to say 'Yes'. Although more often done by producers to commissioning HoDs, writers are increasingly pitching to producers. Traditionally, you have no longer than three minutes – nearer two – to get it all across. (In *The Player*, Griffin Mill tells a writer, 'tell it to me in 25 words – no more'). This is where your work on the story concept, one-liner and taglines pay off.

Formal pitching is now as common in the UK as it is in the US, but perhaps not quite as frenetic. There is also a lot of informal pitching: every time anyone – agent, producer, script editor, or director – asks you over a meal or drink, 'what's the project about?', your response is the pitch.

A pitch contains: the main characters, the journey they take, the ending, and who will want to watch it (i.e. the same people who went to see such-and-such a film).

> A good idea, badly presented, sounds like a bad idea.
> *Stephen Cannell,*
> writer/producer: *Rockford Files, Profit,*
> *Columbo, Dead Above Ground*

So, how can you make your pitch effective? Have a strategy before you go in to pitch:

- **Know your objectives:** to make a good impression on the pitchee (be professional: be punctual, dressed smart-casual, cheery; speak clearly, confidently, with regular eye contact); to show your passion and commitment to the idea; express that idea so clearly the pitchee understands it completely, and do it so enthusiastically, so dramatically *they* get fired up by it too – enough to convince them this is the project they *must* make; to depart with a clear idea of that person's intentions for your project; to leave the door open for you to return with more ideas, even if they rejected this project. Remember: passion is great but please don't be manic.
- **Know who you're pitching to:** be aware of their production track record. Do they have the power to make a decision? If not, how close are they to someone who can?
- **Prepare:** you have only three minutes so be able to express your story concept in three or four sentences; the first sentence should contain the title, the type of story it is and an overview that hooks them; then focus on the story, main character/s, major story moments. A great tagline is useful. Be prepared to give a longer explanation if interest is shown (you'll then have 10–15 minutes).
- **Practise:** on your friends, family, tape recorder, mirror. You're not trying to memorize it; just be clear on the basics of what you're trying to say.

- **Anticipate** questions and possible objections ('it's too similar to ... x', 'too different', 'how do the audience identify with the Protagonist?', etc.) and have *constructive* answers – even build them into your pitch. Be able to explain your creative choices succinctly.
- **Have ready** the appropriate back-up material (one-page proposal, preferably a full treatment) for the pitchee to sell to their boss.
- **Sell** one thing at a time (and have the appropriate synopses ready, if needed).
- Overall, make it feel like a wonderful experience for the listener (keep the cinema poster in your head).

The bottom line is: the commissioner wants to feel the confidence needed to invest in the person they are commissioning. Ultimately, it is the script that will do the selling – or not.

> Get the person you're pitching to to ask questions. Because if they ask questions, you've hooked them, you know they're interested.
>
> *Tony Marchant*

...and try these for more guidance (see also Chapter 22):

moviepitch.com [Robert 'Mr Pitch' Kosberg]

screenplaymastery.com/3MinutePitch.htm [Michael Hauge's excellent advice]

scriptblaster.com [A site devoted to pitching]

storylink.com [Click on the Pitch Perfect tab]

Book: Eileen Quinn and Judy Counihan: *The Pitch* (Faber & Faber) [A refreshingly UK perspective]

DVD: Laurie Scheer: *How to Pitch and Sell your Screenplay* (Big Screen Software)

## In development

Once your script is in development, you will be working with or to either a script editor (in TV) or a development executive/HoD (film). They work with you to get the fullest potential from the piece. But, of course, they also work for the producer and, as such, act as a conduit between you and 'upstairs', and for the producer's 'notes'. Again, it's down to the mutual working relationship between you and your editor. Generally, they are there to assist you, especially as you probably won't see the producer again after your initial meeting. Also, be aware of 'development hell', where your script goes into permanent development and never gets made.

You'll get rewritten even after you're dead.

*(Sunset Boulevard)*

Useful databases of UK producers and Commissioning Editors:

www.farnfilm.com/uktv.htm
www.pact.co.uk                    [see also Taking it further]
www.the knowledgeonline.com
www.mediaresourcecontacts.com

# 20

# your career as a writer

In this chapter you will learn:
- all about you: as a writer, as a person, as a professional – your networking and marketing strategy
- about how you deal with rejections (there'll be more than a few of those) and what's the low-down on all those fancy intensive writing seminars you read about.

# Know yourself – market yourself

> Most writers don't have the sort of nature that lends itself to self-promotion. Today's writers and agents are teaching writers how to be better self-promoters; and that's making a major decision in why some scripts sell.
>
> *Stephen Rebello,*
> screenwriter

Generally speaking, most successful writers treat what they do as a business: a job, with regular work patterns, goals and deadlines, and a professional attitude. Some will have two or three projects on the go at the same time. Of course, this does not negate your other reasons for writing, but you must know yourself and know *why* you are writing.

Remember screenwriting is a collaborative medium; you shouldn't get too precious over a particular line or scene or even entire script premise (again, learn to 'Kill Your Babies'). Some see writing as a route to some ultimate career goal like directing (especially) or producing. So why not go straight there and direct a short film by some other (possibly better) writer? Most writer-directors are directors first.

Marketing yourself is down to knowing your strengths and weaknesses, as a writer and as a person. It includes everything about the way you present yourself and your work to the industry (and that includes submitting it in the correct format – hence the importance of Chapter 2). It is also about networking: opening up lines of communication that will hopefully prove fruitful later. And don't be shocked if somebody calls you a 'media whore' – in this industry it's regarded as a compliment.

Few writers subscribe to or even read the trade magazines, believing they deal in information not of concern to them. They do. Remember: your database = information = power = advantage over other wannabees.

> The writer naturally concentrates on the creative work, spends hundreds of hours writing a script, but almost none on marketing themselves. But when you're out in the marketplace, you're not just selling a piece of work, you're selling yourself too. The way you come across and are perceived is often more likely to bring you work than what you write, assuming you write reasonably well in the first place.
>
> *Julian Friedmann,*
> literary agent

Moreover, learn adaptability. Don't get obsessive about only wanting to write features; be prepared to tackle soaps, series, whatever comes your way. You want to work regularly, don't you? But you need that first break, to build a track record and a good reputation.

## Reputation

In this industry, your reputation is everything. The media village is very small, everyone knows everyone else and so much is based on word of mouth; your name crops up in conversation, somebody else says 'I've heard he's a bit difficult to work with'; effectively it will kill you.

*Malcolm Gerrie,*
MD: WhizzKid Entertainment

These were the words said to me many years ago as parting advice by the man who gave me my first break in the biz. More recently, Malcolm was the producer Russell Crowe held up against a wall and exclaimed 'I'll make sure you never work in Hollywood'. Some say this incident cost him his Oscar that year; that's how this game works. Strange how my boss's words echo down the years.

Think about how others see you. Get a reputation as being a new, talented writer who's good to work with, the word will spread. Producers, agents and others will be eager to meet you. Get a 'difficult' reputation and your career is already dead.

Some writers can be incredibly temperamental if they don't like what's being done to their work and sometimes behave immaturely. I am not saying roll over and take it, far from it. You have to react in a calm, considered logical way and negotiate. If a producer suggests changes you find unacceptable, don't have it out there and then in some unproductive shouting match. Say 'I'll have to consider that' and return a few days later with some good reasons why you think it won't work and offer constructive alternatives. Try seeing things from their point of view, create a positive debate and argue from a position of knowledge and confidence. There is always a middle ground without compromising totally. And never assume that a writer-producer partnership is entirely controlled by the producer.

Lastly, beware also of getting a reputation for managing to sell lots of scripts or treatments but none of them ever being made or reaching the screen.

It is very important to protect your reputation. Your reputation is more than just the sum of what you write, it is how you inter-relate with other people in the industry – especially the key players: producers, directors, your agent – and how good a team player you are.

*Julian Friedmann,*
literary agent

## Rejection – and how to deal with it

I can identify with screenwriters' frustration. I wrote over a dozen scripts before finally getting one made.

*Michael Tolkin,*
screenwriter: *The Player, Changing Lanes, Deep Impact*

You are trying to enter one of the toughest and most cynical industries around. Hence you will face rejection – a lot. Get used to it. Bounce back. Grow asbestos skin. In Art Arthur's words: reject rejection. Just remember they are rejecting the bits of paper, not you.

When rejecting material, it's not necessarily due to the quality of the writing. There are so many other factors at play; even well written pieces are rejected because either we're not presently in the market for them, or there's no room in the production schedules or the budget's too high, a number of reasons.

*Jan Leventhal,*
Carlton-Central TV

You can send the same manuscript out to a dozen people and get twelve different responses. The only time to start worrying and taking another look at your screenplay is if they all reject it citing the same reasons. Perhaps they're trying to tell you something: about your script or about yourself.

Most rejection letters will be short, curt and vague: 'not what we're looking for at the moment'. Try phoning them and asking exactly what they *are* looking for. Better still, try writing to them, politely, asking if they might expand on precisely why the script was rejected – weaknesses and strengths. You probably won't get to see a copy of the Reader's coverage, but you could always try asking! At least you've opened up a constructive dialogue with the producer or company.

Ultimately, it's down to commitment: how committed are you – to your script, your writing, your career? And, to quote Michael Hauge, commitment is scary – just ask anyone who's due to get married tomorrow! This attitude may also help you tackle writer's block. Should it happen, ask yourself: how committed am I to this script, scene or whatever? How much fear am I prepared to face in order to see me through this script or scene?

It's very hard to continue to believe in yourself when, with all the work you've done, you have so much trouble getting it read or a response. But a good screenwriter will always rise to the top given time, if you stick with it. What works over time is just persistence.

*Tom Schulman*

The stronger the wind – the stronger the tree.

[Old Japanese saying]

# Writing courses and seminars

An emerging fringe industry: intensive weekend or week-long screenwriting seminars are often led by an American screenwriting 'guru' (pages 294–6). Whether attending will be of use to you, only you can judge. Each has something to offer. Some observations on the plus side:

- they are useful as a kind of painless revision to remind you of things you may have forgotten or don't fully understand
- you may pick up some practical tips or opinions that illuminate or revise your own views on screenwriting
- they can be *very* good for networking (page 265)
- they *are* very intensive: you will leave exhausted but also energized and fired-up to write – harness that enthusiasm and write.

On the minus side:

- they can be expensive: most novice writers are poor; your money might be better spent on buying original scripts, some 'how-to' books, renting videos or DVDs or buying a computer; if you are desperate to attend, speak to the organizers, offer to help them in exchange for a reduced fee (or freebie?) – they can only say 'no', but an entrepreneurial attitude in this business can only be positive

- they tend to concentrate exclusively on the Hollywood three-Act linear structure; think for yourself, draw up your own conclusions and interpretative templates
- be aware of the dangers of attending courses as a substitute for actually writing (serial course-goers exist). My advice? Write a script, take a course, then write another script, take another course, and so on.

So approach them with the right attitude:

- don't go expecting to be given the keys to screenwriting heaven or some quick-fix answer (beware those who claim to offer such); each tutor has their own unique 'take' and approach to things
- take from each course what you feel is useful to you, put the rest into storage for future possible relevance; make up your own mind and don't feel 'this is how it *must* be done' or you'll end up with indentikit scripts; *you* are the writer, with your own voice, so use these courses as tools to help expand your talents
- ask yourself if you will actually get any writing done on this course; at this introductory stage you might find it more beneficial to attend those (mostly residential) ones where you will at least exit with a full or part-completed script
- as a newcomer you may fear feeling out of your depth; don't – there will be others attending more novice than you – honest!
- after the course, follow up the contacts met and keep in touch; you never know when they will bear fruit
- whatever approach works best for you, do it.

A final word about correspondence courses: I am not an enthusiast.

> Carry on having a talent for your talent. Create an area for it. You know you possess it.

> *Alan Plater,*
> screenwriter: *The Last Of The Blonde Bombshells,*
> *A Very British Coup, The Beiderbecke Tapes,* etc.

Let's face it, the bottom line is this: it's all about knowing the right people. And since the growth of the Internet, getting in touch with them has become that much easier – they all have a web presence out there somewhere. So when you've finished this and the next chapter, start on Chapter 22: start networking, start looking for openings, and don't be timid.

**21**

**final comments**

**In this chapter you will learn:**
- what industry folk search for when they first receive a script
- ten things to do – and ten things not to do – if you want to succeed as a screenwriter
- a few well-chosen words of wisdom about life, writing, and everything.

Screenwriting is not an artform. It's a punishment from God.

*Fran Lebowitz*,
author

# What do Readers and producers look for in a script?

The honest answer is: I don't know, but when a good script comes across my desk, boy, you certainly know it. It literally sits up and bites you in the nose. It's something to do with my 'gut' response.

*Duncan Kenworthy*,
producer: *Four Weddings And A Funeral*,
*Notting Hill, Gulliver's Travels, Heartlands*

What's lacking in most screenplays today is resonance: they don't stick to you. You not only forget them after you've read them, you forget them while you're reading them. They feel like they're written to order, with one eye on the box office or a star name.

*Stephen Rebello*

They want what everybody else wants: A good story. And that's down to the basic art of storytelling – making people wonder what's going to happen next. Master that and you're nearly there.

Because they read many scripts each week, Readers look for reasons not to continue reading the submission: bad layout, poor presentation, no concept of structure or characterization, wasteful dialogue, etc. So unless you hook them early they will toss your script onto the 'to be returned' pile.

A Reader has in their head a kind of template which they lay against your screenplay. This allows them to automatically sense if your story fulfils the requirements of that form: character credibility, character consistency, character distinctiveness, action credibility, plot consistency, dialogue credibility, structure, thematic integration and passion.

What they *don't* want is:

- last week's or year's movie or production but slightly changed; they all want something new, exciting, innovative, moving – give it to them
- something you think is commercial; they want what moves and excites you, makes you rant or dash straight to your typewriter

- something that has been written to meet a clearly perceived trend. They come in waves: revived classics (*Sense and Sensibility, Little Women, Romeo And Juliet, O, Pride and Prejudice, Richard III*); TV remakes (*Scooby-Doo, The Addams Family, The Flintstones, Thunderbirds, The Avengers*); baseball movies; cop shows, legal and hospital dramas; women in jeopardy; disease of the week; gothic horror revivals; romantic comedies; teen horror; super-heroes; gross-out comedies, etc. Films especially take at least 18 months to reach the screen. A trend popular now will be way out of date by the time your script is read. Screenwriters start trends, not follow them

- stories which fail to excite them, hook them, make them passionate; they don't want stories that fail to engage them (on some level) within the first ten pages

- they *hate* bad spelling, bad punctuation, bad grammar, awkward over-written prose, incorrect/inconsistent margin placement; mostly, they hate language which advances the story by *telling* them everything and *showing* them nothing – it's a visual medium, so tell it visually

- they hate anything not the right length (that's rigid).

Remember: *seduce the Reader*.

> The way to learn is to read stories, watch movies and trust your instincts. The more movies you watch the more the rhythm of film gets inside you.
>
> *Caroline Thompson*

So screenwriting, to be successful, must connect with the mind and emotions of the audience. To do this, the writer must know how what you create on the screen and on the page affects the viewing and reading audience; you must understand and create audience identification with the characters, and you must seek to draw out the common elements of our universal experience as human beings, truths that people can recognize and grasp; give new life to old stories and mythic structures; by finding the conflict, then personalizing it, then increasing the stakes by putting your characters at risk, and go on raising the stakes; by drawing out, shaping and *integrating* your theme, *unifying* the whole story in a way that is internally valid and profoundly satisfying for an audience. The artifice is there *but the audience doesn't notice it*.

> Write a screenplay that is personal and integrated. By personal I mean simply that whatever genre it is, it must address its author's most personal concerns and

considerations. And by integrated I mean that each and every aspect of it – all that we see and hear – accomplishes simultaneously the tasks of advancing the story and expanding character and theme.

*Richard Walter,*
screenwriting tutor, UCLA

Employ any device you can to affect and entertain your Reader: imaginative and emotive terms of description, funny or quirky lines of dialogue or in 'the business', whatever – as long as it has a reason for being there and does a job. Just don't go over the top.

Look on your script as a dialogue between writer and audience, and from the page *create the movie in the mind of the Reader.* What excites, grips, stimulates or moves you, may well have that effect on the Reader.

But knowing your market is also essential. Immerse yourself in the industry: there's no point in sending off a story that someone else already has in development. Being derivative – writing scripts which have thematically already been done to death – will also be of little value to you.

## Ten things you must do if you want to be a screenwriter

1 See lots of movies and television (i.e. the arena you want to write in). See what the marketplace is generating. See the good films at least twice: once in the cinema, once on video. (Ideally, see them several times in the cinema: first as an enthusiast, then with your craft templates, then watch the audience reactions.) Look for the *why* and *how* they were so great or awful. Try writing your own reports and reviews about them.

2 Read screenplays – as many as possible, and in their original formats (see Chapter 22 and Taking it further).

3 Join a writers' group (recommended) for information, networking, moral support and positive feedback.

4 Become knowledgeable about the industry: subscribe to and read the Trade magazines. Get information about the industry: for the UK, for the US, for Europe, worldwide. Be an industry watcher – then a participant.

5 Don't listen to statistics: you want a statistic? Try this: 100 per cent of all screenwriters working today at one time weren't working.

6 Apply the seat of the pants to the seat of the chair *daily*, and *regularly*, even if it's for only an hour. Do a minimum of 30 minutes or set yourself a minimum daily word target. Make an appointment with yourself and write – or get written off.

7 Don't get it right, get it written and finish what you write. Don't lose time. Enjoy it! Worry about perfection during the rewrites.

8 Have persistence and commitment: if you don't have it, learn it. Reject rejection.

9 Believe in yourself and your talents: *you* are the commodity, not your script. If you don't believe in yourself, how do you expect anyone else to? You weren't born with an agent, and getting one isn't an instant ticket to fame and fortune.

10 Every six months or so, ask yourself: 'Am I enjoying this process?' If it becomes painful, find another game to play.

It's a collaborative process, sometimes you get pushed around. But it's a game and you don't have to play it.

*William Goldman*

To say any script is truly finished is a fallacy; things will change or be changed by others. Try to regard every script as work in progress until it finally gets shown on the screen.

## Ten guaranteed ways to fail as a scriptwriter

1 Don't write anything.
2 Write badly.
3 Show ignorance of the market.
4 Be rude.
5 Promise what you can't deliver.
6 Don't take criticism.
7 Show ignorance of the production process.
8 Fail to adapt.
9 Be a nuisance during the shoot.
10 Think it's easy.

## And finally...

As a writer, you are what the industry calls a 'creative'. The writer is learning all the time: from each successive script written, from meeting other people (especially fellow writers and industry professionals), from everything you do; learning – about life, about yourself. Every day is a day in the classroom.

Experienced screenwriters expect to spend up to six months of full-time work completing a feature script. So anyone with the stamina and dedication to finish a script (especially a feature), whatever the quality, deserves admiration. It takes a lot of effort and hard work. But the more you do it the swifter it becomes.

There are certain assumptions about the nature of cinema which should guide most screenwriters: one, cinema is visual; two, cinema is largely a storytelling medium; three, once you have committed to telling a story, you have to tell it vigorously, economically and directly. After those assumptions are taken for granted, everything is up for grabs.

*Larry Gross,*
screenwriter: *48 Hours, Geronimo, True Crime,*
*Prozac Nation, Streets of Fire*

So... **1** Write from the Heart.
   **2** Be Original.
   **3** Act Professional.

Write a great, original, moving screenplay with your own unique perspective, voice and passions. Throw a bomb into the industry: wake people up – wake up their senses, wake up their hearts. Emotionally affect your audience – change them forever.

So... **1** Write Meaningful–Specific.
   **2** Think Global.
   **3** Think Timeless.

The only thing that makes life possible is permanent, intolerable uncertainty; not knowing What Comes Next.

*Ursula Le Guin,*
author: *The Wizard of Earthsea, The Left Hand*
*of Darkness, The Dispossessed*

Every great writer was a new writer once – even Shakespeare.

*Alan Bleasdale,*
writer: *Boys From The Blackstuff, GBH,*
*Scully, The Monocled Mutineer*

. . . and finally, William Goldman's famous words about the industry:

Nobody knows anything!

Now stop reading, stop talking about it – Go Write!

# 22

## screenwriting and the Internet

**In this chapter you will learn:**
- about the extraordinary opportunities that have become available for the new screenwriter by the growth of the Internet.

Just as going online for the first time will change your life, the Internet has transformed life for the screenwriter, opening out sources of information and contacts worldwide. Unfortunately, the one thing it hasn't yet freed-up are the sources of finance to make your production in the first place.

There are oceans of screenwriting-related websites lurking out there just for you, with much cross-referencing; and the decisions you end up making are more about which sites are relevant to your specific search – and especially those which are not. Another problem with writing about the Internet is that things change so rapidly, by the time something reaches print, matters may have moved on, sites shut down, new ones created.

Hence, I have tried to list those sites with the most (or most relevant) further-links for you to explore. I've also included the sites I find most useful or personally bookmark. (See also Taking it further for more links to the industry.)

# How do I manage all this 'data'? – RSS

You should investigate RSS technology (Really Simple Syndication or Rich Site Summary). It allows you to keep up to speed with any latest postings or updates to the websites (and even specific subsections and pages) that *you* choose to bookmark. These regular updates are fed back to you, often in headline or summary form, allowing you to decide on which sites you visit, the stories you read and those you keep in your own personal archive. Using an RSS reader, you can view the content of these feeds, either online or on your desktop.

To download an RSS Reader programme (or 'Aggregator') – and it's usually free – visit: www.RssReader.com (another place to try is www.google.com/reader). Some modern computer browsers have the technology already built-in.

The benefits of RSS are two-fold: the 'aggregation' of content from multiple web sources into one place; and its ability to filter. Newsfeeds, blogs, podcasts, videos, trailers, movies, TV programmes – it's all out there for you to source. Just remember, *you* control the sites you want to feed from, and those feeds you wish to follow, read, and keep or not.

As this technology is developing so rapidly, if you take RSS to its logical conclusion, you could end up creating your own television channel. Think about it.

# Search engines

But let's get back to basics first. Your first port of call will be a Search Engine. There are many, but the most often used, and probably most comprehensive, is www.google.com – simple, straightforward, fast, listing in order of relevance. Just enter into the window something like *Barbarella* screenplay or *Gattaca* script, hit the search button and see what you get. It's hard to go wrong with Google.

(You will notice in most cases that follow I have not included the www. prefix to these sites. If your links fail, try adding it or the prefix http://www. to the site name you require.)

Some other useful screenwriting-focused engines you might try:

about.com             [Enter Screenwriting into the search box]
cooltoad.com
filmfinders.com          [Search engine, contacts and info]
filmtalk.org
hollywoodnetwork.com
       [US gateway to many writers/producers/comps etc. links]
hollywoodsnextsuccess.com
http://inkpot.com/movielinks/mscripts.html
              [The Flying Inkpot – many assorted links]
http://search.scriptsecrets.com
       [Recommended search engine and free movie download]
http://search.yahoo.com/search?p=screenwriting
                [Yahoo's targeted links/searches]
movies.yahoo.com     [Generic Yahoo portal for all movie stuff]
pilot-search.com
           [UK based, put screenwriting into the search box]
screenplayland.com
screenwritingawards.com
scriptiverse.com/main.html
shortscriptsonline.com
thescript.com/newsletter.html         [The Script Report]
wcauk.com
       [UK Writers' Copyright Association – many handy links]
writerswrite.com/screenwriting
         [Useful links here to producers and the industry]
2ksearch.com         [Insert Screenwriting into search box]

# Reference databases

www.imdb.com – the Internet Movie Database. Probably the most comprehensive database on all movies and TV. Easy to navigate, a fast search, with productions and artists cross-referenced by title, cast, crew, taglines, one-liners, plot summaries (view with or without spoilers), reviews etc., with useful subsections such as Film Festivals. They also have their database divided country by country, hence the latest UK-based information can be found at www.uk.imdb.com/recent/uk. More useful sites are:

allmovie.com                          [A general site for movie buffs]
blackwellpublishing.com/lehman/links.htm
boxofficeguru.com      [Constantly updated box office stats site]
britmovie.co.uk
            [Covers many British films, from ancient classics to
                                              present day]
cinema.com
dvshop.ca/dvcafe/Canada/canscreen.html
                        [Canadian movies, links, industry info]
guardian.co.uk/film
              [The Guardian newspaper – an important UK site]
hollywood.com      [Comprehensive US entertainment news site]
hollywoodnetwork.com
                [Contacts and info, good script competitions link]
hollywoodnetwork.com/hn/acting/index.html
                          [More than just links to actors...]
http://ca.dir.yahoo.com/Entertainment/Movies_and_Film/Filmm
aking/Screenwriting
          [A mountain of Canadian links for screenwriters here]
http://timelapse.com/tvlink.html
                    [Site for production professionals, good links]
mandy.com
    [Worldwide film/TV resources site; includes good noticeboard]
reelclassics.com                          [Classic movies database]
showbizdata.com
    [Development deals, stats, jobs, latest industry production info]

You might also try accessing some of the extensive US Universities movie databases. Try putting into your search engine box University California Berkeley, UCLA Film School, Columbia University or New York Film School, together with words like Movie or Archive, and see what you get.

## Screenwriting – specific websites

absolutewrite.com/screenwriting
bbc.co.uk/writersroom
    [I've yet to hear a bad word for this UK community]
bfi.org.uk
[British Film Institute – type Screenwriting into the search box]
or try:
bfi.org.uk/filmtvinfo/gateway/categories/scriptsscriptwriting/writing
    [More targeted]
breakingin.net    [An Excellent site]
dmoz.org/Arts/Writers_Resources/Screenwriting
    [Open Directory Project – a goldmine of links]
european-television.net    [European screenwriters contacts list]
Euroscript.co.uk
    [UK script development organization; see Taking it further for more details]
filmfestivals.com    [Film festivals info and much, much more]
filmliterarygroup.com    [Screenplay submissions]
focal.ch
    [Dormant initiative; still some handy European links]
goasa.com
    [American Screenwriters Association: numerous drop-down menus and links to explore; subscribe to their regular e-mail newsletter. I am a huge fan of this site]
hollywoodnetwork.com
    [Classes, contests directory, much more]
keepwriting.com
    [Links include script evaluation and a writing school]
moviebytes.com    [Contests, agencies, newsletter and more]
moviepitch.com
    [Robert 'Mr. Pitch' Kosberg's informative site]

moviepoet.com
[Chris Messineo's New Jersey Writers Workshop, short films]
moviescripts.com                                    [Useful links]
netribution.co.uk
      [Good links for courses, networking and community, UK]
rinkworks.com/movies
[Film reviews: 1910 to the present day – good Genre section]
screenplay.com
   [More than a portal to sell software, explore the drop-down
                                                        menus]
screenplaytreatment.com
                    [Links to *Creative Screenwriting* magazine]
screenwriter.com
[Home to Screenwriters Online; excellent guest master classes]
screenwritersutopia.com
screenwritersvault.com
   [Project database; monitor your script's progress in the biz]
screenwriting.com
               [Screenwriting Resource Center – recommended]
screenwritingschool.dk
                         [Denmark's screenwriting school]
screenwritingvisualization.com
scriptcrawler.net
[Essential for accessing scripts online and in different drafts]
sciptfactory.co.uk
            ['Europe's premier script development organization';
                                            strongly funded]
scriptfly.com                             [Good articles here]
scriptforsale.com                [Some tips and a competition]
scripthouse.de      [German films industry contacts? Try here]
scriptologist.com
            [A useful site with its own Yahoo group, see later]
storylink.com
            [A great community here for links and contacts]
themegahitmovies.com
            [Useful structural analyses of blockbuster movies]
thescreenwritersstore.com
            [Great UK resource for all things screenwriter related]

thescriptvault.com

[UK script deposit and registration, approved by Writers
Guild of GB also many other useful links and services]

thesource.com.au

[Australian site; includes the Spec Script Library]

thestage.co.uk/connect/howto/writefilm.php

[Wisdom from myself and picture]

ukscreen.com/board/writing

ukscriptdoctor.com

wgaeast.org

[Writers Guild of America – East; lots of links to follow
here; as with wga.org, their west-coast presence]

wordplayer.com                    [Some very useful articles and links]

writemovies.com                    [Lots of excellent links here]

writernet.co.uk            [UK based site, handy for networking]

writersbootcamp.com      [An intensive west coast US experience]

writersdigest.com

[US, Writer's Digest, huge site: click on Browse By Genre]

writersservices.com

writersstore.com

[Sign up to their monthly e-zine; books, DVDs, software,
articles – recommended]

writersweekly.com

[General freelance writers site – follow the links]

writerswrite.com/screenwriting

[Very good, very useful links here]

writersuniversity.com                          [Impressive site]

writingclasses.com

[Home of New York's respected Gotham Writers' Workshop]

zakka.dk/euroscreenwriters.ht  [Very useful European database]

10dayscreenplay.com            [Download a step-by-step guide]

## Filmmakers' sites with screenwriting links/pages

blackflix.com

[General info site on black filmmakers and film-making]

channel4.com/film

[UK Channel 4 TV – informative with many useful links]

cyberfilmschool.com　　　　[The home of Film Underground]
donedealpro.com　　　[Useful links to production companies]
europeanfilmacademy.org
　　　　　　　　[Seem more in giving out awards these days]
exposure.co.uk/eejit/index.html
　　　　　　　[Witty, informative, handy contacts links; home of *The
Complete Eejit's Guide to Filmmaking*]
farnfilm.com　　　　　　[Very useful links and resources page]
filmmaker.com　[Regularly updated film and screenwriting news]
filmmaking.net
　　　[UK-based indie community; great for links and contacts]
filmscape.co.uk　　　　　　　[Definitely worth exploring]
filmsite.org　　　　　[Lots to interest the screenwriter here]
filmthreat.com
　　　　　['Truth In Entertainment' – an independent voice in
Hollywood]
http://industrycentral.net
　　　　　　　[A wealth of links, you'll spend hours here]
lfs.org.uk　　　　　　　　　　[London Film School]
liveplanet.com
　　　　　[More than just Ben Affleck and Matt Damon's
plaything: more receptive to maverick talent than most;
script-wise, they know their stuff]
mrbrownmovies.com　　　　　　[Mr Brown's movie site]
netfilm.com　　　　　　　　[Indie film network]
nftsfilm-tv.ac.uk　　[UK's National Film and Television School]
nyfa.com and nyfa.com/London
　　　　　[New York Film Academy; and it's London base]
reelscene.com　[News and info for filmmakers by filmmakers]
rivalquest.com
　　　[Guerilla filmmakers resources site and film school links]
runningdogfilms.co.uk
　　　　　　　[Some useful links here – so follow them]
scriptsavvy.com　　　　　　　[Producers seeking scripts]
storylink.com
sundance.org
　　　　[Robert Redford's renowned annual initiative +festival;
it even has its own fringe events now; see also Taking it
further]

theknowledgeonline.com

[UK industry professionals talent database – huge]

thrae.com/nbmm

[No-budget film-making and animation site; some
honest hard truths expressed here]

timelapse.com/tvlink.html   [Lots of handy links to explore here]

triggerstreet.com

[Excellent community site launched by Kevin Spacey]

ucreative.ac.uk                    [University of the Creative Arts]

USfilmproduction.com

[West coast-based resources site: cast, crew, companies etc.]

writeangle.org                            [Some good links here]

www-cntv.usc.edu            [University of Southern California]

zoetrope.com

[Francis Ford Coppola's exceptional site, especially for
screenwriters; repeat visits are strongly recommended]

zoom.info                         [Info on people and companies]

4filmmaking.com

[UK Channel 4's online film school (see earlier); great links]

## Homepages

Mostly the pages of the various screenwriting 'gurus'; all have
something of interest:

beingCharlieKaufman.com  [You really should subscribe to this!]

beyondstructure.com                         [David S. Freeman]

blakesnyder.com                                    [Blake Snyder]

brainstormnet.com

[Jurgen Wolff's creative thinking website; lots of good links]

createyourscreenplay.com                       [Barry Pearson]

davetrottier.com                                   [David Trottier]

dovsimensfilmschool.com/resources.html&hollywood.com

[Dov's two-day seminars; superb links]

http://members.aol.com/morgands1/closeup/indices/mainmenu.
htm

[David Morgan's site: excellent conversations with
screenwriters and filmmakers]

http://mta.montana.edu/docs/people/tobias.html

[Ronald Tobias]

ibiblio.com/cdeemer/essays.htm          [Charles Deemer – again]
kathiefongyoneda.com                     [Kathie Fong Yoneda]
lawrencegray.com
          [English writer/filmmaker based in Hong Kong; also runs
               the HK Writers Group; lots of good advice and links]
lesliekallen.com                             [Richard Walter]
lewhunter.com                    [Lew Hunter's excellent site]
lindaseger.com                                 [Linda Seger]
martinday.co.uk          [A personal homesite with useful links]
mckeestory.com                                [Robert McKee]
moviepitch.com              [Robert Kosberg – 'Mr Pitch']
myspace.com/michaelchasewalker     [Michael Chase Walker]
myspace.com/TYscreenwriting
                    [Ray Frensham: the site for this very book]
rayfrensham.com
rayfrenshamworld.blogspot..com       [My personal blogspace]
robinkelly.btinternet.co.uk        [Robin Kelly's very useful site]
screenplaymastery.com        [Michael Hauge's exceptional site]
screenwritinggoldmine.com                  [Phillip Gladwin]
screenwritersutopia.com                      [Chris Wehner]
script-consultant.com                          [Sandy Eiges]
scriptsecrets.net                          [William Martell]
showbusinesslifecoach.com                      [Danny Stack]
storyandscriptdevelopment.com/how-to-write-scripts/index.htm
                                         [Sandy Eiges again]
sydfield.com          [Syd Field - the man who started it all]
tameyourinnercritic.com     [Another helpful Jurgen Wolff site]
themegahitmovies.com
          [Richard Michaels Stefanik's excellent site; also interesting
                    structural analyses of blockbuster movies]
thewritersjourney.com                [Christopher Vogler]
thewritersloft.com                           [Jerry Cleaver]
timetowrite.com                [Jurgen Wolff strikes again!]
TVwriter.com                                   [Larry Brody]
tyscreenwriting.blogspot.com   [this book's very own blogspace]
unjobs.org/authors/dwight-v-swain
                         [Dwight Swain and Joye Swain]
vikiking.com                                     [Viki King]

writing.org.uk          [Robin Kelly's useful UK community]
yourwritingcoach.com         [Jurgen Wolff's fascinating podcast]

# Screenplays online

## Free downloads

One of the greatest benefits of the Internet has been the growth of sites offering free access to screenplays, to view and/or download, most in their original formats (and some in their earlier drafts). All of these sites below have something to offer, but the two most often-used are Drew's Script-o-Rama (www.script-o-rama) and the Internet Script Database (www.iscriptdb.com) – the ones that really started it all.

angelfire.com/nj/PLAQUE2
          [Satan's Script-o-Rama: sci-fi, action, horror movies]
awesomefilm.com
          [Scripts and screenplays in alphabetical order]
cinefania.com/script   [Horror, sci-fi, fantasy and thriller scripts]
corky.net/scripts
          [INFlow's Script Directory; to view, not download]
dailyscript.com                    [Movie and TV scripts]
http://blake.prohosting.com/bamzone
          [Alphabetical listing, various genres]
http://geocities.com/Hollywood/9371
          [Nemonic Turf, 500+ film and TV scripts]
http://geocities.com/moviescriptsandscreenplays
          [Movie screenplays web ring]
http://geocities.com/movie_starzz/BenandMatt
     [Transcripts and screenplays of films starring Ben Affleck
          and Matt Damon]
http://geocities.com/thelunalounge
          [Extensive alphabetical listings and links]
http://members.tripod.com/~scriptring/index.html
          [Another Screenplays webring]
http://scriptsgalore.tripod.com         [Great search engine here]
horrorlair.com                    [Horror and suspense scripts]
iscriptdb.com          [Internet Script Database, essential]
joblo.com/moviescripts.php
          [JoBlo's Movie Scripts and script drafts]

kokos.cz/bradkoun/movies
                    [Various action, sci-fi and horror screenplays]
mooviees.com/all/scripts [Links to movie scripts and transcripts]
movie-page.com/movie_scripts.htm          [Lots to find here]
pumpkinsoft.de/screenplay451
                [Diverse collection of downloadable screenplays]
scifimoviepage.com/scripts/scripts.html
                        [Sci-fi, fantasy and horror scripts]
screenplays-online.de          [To read only, not download]
scriptcrawler.net                          [Excellent links]
script-fix.com/screenplays.htm   [Listing of online movie scripts]
scriptologist.com
      [Click on Screenplays; leads to a wealth of free script sites]
script-o-rama.com     [Drew's Script-o-Rama, equally essential]
sfy.ru                    [Sceenplays For You – hundreds of titles]
simplyscripts.com          [Very good search engine here]
textfiles.com/media/SCRIPTS     [Television and movie scripts]

## To buy

Despite the deluge of free downloads, buying screenplays in
script form is still an option to consider. Average prices are $15
each (maximum about $20). Script City, one of the originators
in this business, is still a useful first port of call.

And the bargains are still out there – while updating these pages
I came across scripts for *Barbarella* and the 1966 *Batman*
movies at $2.45 each. (See also Taking it Further).

hollywoodbookcity.com          [Stacks of film and TV titles]
http://directory.google.com/Top/Arts/Movies
                        [Click on Scripts and go from there]
larryedmunds.com
   [Reliable bookstore; no scripts but Press Books and Press Kits]
screenwriter.com/scriptworld.html   [Lots and lots of titles here]
scriptcity.net                [A very comprehensive selection]
scriptfly.com/screenplays                  [Just loads of titles]
scriptshack.com
        [Check out their clearance titles – some bargains there]
thescreenwritersstore.com
   [London based, software, books, mags; and a CD of 900 movie
        and TV screenplays for £35, sounds like a bargain to me]

The days of screenplays published in book form but printed in stage-play formats, or as a product of someone sitting in front of a screen simply transcribing what they see in a finished cut, are (thankfully) diminishing now. Most paperbacks of screenplays these days are in their proper script format. Their USP (unique selling point) can be that the published version is a first, or early, draft of the script, including many (later deleted) scenes or with reprinted pages of corrected drafts; often there is a detailed essay by, or interview with, the writer or director revealing the decisions made in the production process and often why cuts or changes were made.

I would recommend seeking out Newmarket's *The Shooting Script* series (www.newmarket press.com).

## Auctions

A handy way to obtain screenplays. These days E-bay seems to have taken over the world: ebay.com, ebay.co.uk (eBay-dot-whatever country you happen to live in). You might also find some real bargains in their subsidiary site half.com. Another site worth a look is auctions.com. Indeed, you will still find many other sites if you explore the URLs listed below.

Just enter into the search box the title of the script you are seeking, add Screenplay or Script or Teleplay, hit the button and see what you get. Or, substitute the words Press Kit for your chosen project and you might be surprised. Sometime these kits have very detailed prose-story breakdowns (some even scene-by-scene) – the nearest thing to a Treatment you are likely to see.

As most bidding on any item occurs in the last 30 minutes, an army of sniper sites have emerged. Enter the maximum amount you are prepared to bid (make it an odd figure, like $16.73 – those extra cents might just win it), and they will automatically 'snipe' your selected item at the time you chose (I suggest about five seconds before the close of the auction).

Sites that I have found useful are:

auctionslotwatch.co.uk
        [Free; an umbrella site that covers many sites worldwide]
auctionsniper.com
    [E-bay only; charges 25 cents per successful snipe: no win, no fee]

auctiontamer.com

[Software downloads, mostly linked with other sites listed here]

bidnapper.com

[E-bay only; free 15-day trial; downloads if you wish]

lotsnipe.auctionstealer.com

[Free; click Affiliates and find links to worldwide sites]

Oh, and always check shipping/mailing costs, as these can vary wildly.

# Blogs and blogging

When the last version of this book came out in 2003 there were approximately 11,000 sites listed as 'movie blogs' (web-logs). Fast-forward five years and there are now over 17,200,000 (statistics supplied by www.themovieblog.com – one of the first and still one of the most informative and entertaining sites to visit).

Whether it's posted on a specific blogsite or on one of the many social networking sites – SNS – like myspace.com (see later), we are all at it – I know I am! But do try to keep them focused: we're not really interested in what you had for breakfast or your latest pet hamster.

So, where to start? Well, you could just put, say, the words Movie Blog into your search engine and begin your lifetime's career of pointless arguments. All I can do here is list the more established sites or those I've found to be most informative, entertaining or original.

blogsearchengine.com/category/movie-blogs

cdeemer2007.blogspot.com

[Charles Deemer's *The Writing Life*]

cinematical.com

dannystack.blogspot.com

filmjunk.com

filmschoolrejects.com

firstshowing.net

incontention.com

madscreenwriter.blogspot.com          [A Canadian institution]

moviesblog.mtv.com

mysterymanonfilm.blogspot.com                    [Recommended]
obsessedwithfilm.com
rowthree.com
screenrant.com
scriptmonster.wordpress.co.uk
                    [James Hartland's useful blog; lots of great links]
script-o-rama.com/blog/blog.html
                    [Another benefit from Drew's Script-o-rama]
shootingpeople.org          [Especially their discussion boards]
slashfilm.com
thedocumentaryblog.com
themovieblog.com                    [A particular favourite of mine]
timetowrite.blogs.com
tyscreenwriting.blogspot.com                    [it had to happen]
worldfilm.about.com/od/blogs/Movie_Blogs.htm

Sometimes I wonder why people should spend their time being constantly bombarded by the opinions of others when they should have opinions of their own…

…In which case, I heartily recommend John Campea's piece on themovieblog.com: '20 Tips for Starting your Own Movieblog'. (He recommends setting up a free blogging account at somewhere like blogger.com, wordpress.com or blogspot.com, by the way.)

## Groups, communities, forums, newsgroups, e-zines and newsletters

Newsgroups can be useful discussion forums if you have a specific problem or screenwriting issue you wish to raise.

First, go to google.com, click on the More tab, then Groups from the drop-down menu. Then enter in the search box something like Screenwriting or Screenwriters (or Treatments or Frensham or whatever you want) and suddenly you will get page after page of Groups listed, sub-broken down by Arts and Entertainment/Recreation etc., and also country by country. The choice is yours.

Most groups and threads (discussion strands) will be informative and supportive. Most of them will be monitored by a Moderator (as most things that go unmoderated on the net are prone to spam, unwanted ads and general abuse).

As an experiment, go to groups.google.com and put Screenwriters in the search box. It should take you to places like: misc.writing.screenplays.moderated or Orange County Screenwriting. Don't be afraid, just explore.

You might also find these communities and forums a useful place to start:

http://peoplejar.com/network/screenwriting
kamera.co.uk                         [Explore their film salon]
lefora.com                    [Forums made easy – it says here]
literatureandlatte.com       [Like a sophisticated chat-room!]
petesmoviepage.com              [Forum and chat links here]
screendaily.com        [Daily e-zine from Screen International]
stevens-arce.com/HollyScriptTalk.html
                       [Based in Puerto Rico but international]
uktheatre.net/viewpage.aspx?ID=200
                    [This community has its own facebook group]
writers.net/forum
                 [Some excellent forums and focused threads here]

…or create your own community/group on this site: network54.com

And don't forget to check out the sites already mentioned in this chapter, as they may well have their own communities or sub-links to a forum. To be fair, most e-zines and newletters have moved on to their own domains on a Social Networking Site or similar.

All search engines will have their own Groups – as will most SNSs like facebook or myspace (see later) – but Yahoo still has the biggest and most diverse selection. Go to groups.yahoo.com, put in Screenwriting or Screenwriters (or whatever) into the search box and you will be spoilt for choice.

Some Yahoo groups I have found particularly useful are [First put in the prefix http://groups/yahoo.com/group/ and then add the name of the group]:

Austinscreenwriters; bentubiquity (new filmmakers); eurofilmexchange; filminvestment; Hollywoodwriters; Kahlinlist (jobs and networking); movie report (latest US movie reviews); screenplay; screenplayers; screenplaysdownunder; screen-writers; screenwriting; scriptologist_blogs; scriptlogist_dot_com; ScriptReader (script readers exchanging experiences and advice); SitsVac (UK group for new comedy writers and performances);

Torontoscreenwriters; ukscriptwriting (friendly, supportive and informative); writemovies; WritingBuddies (lone writers seeking collaborators).

You may find a number of these groups have their own Blogspots (look for the link at the top of the group's homepage). Again, be aware of any unmoderated group, they usually end up collapsing under the weight of spam.

Finally, just remember that, like most things to do with the net, all of the above can be highly addictive and a great way to waste your time. Stay focused.

## Social networking sites

If you don't have a profile on an SNS, you're nobody – well, that's what we are led to believe. Trouble is, having a presence on a few of these sites is a near-essential in creating your own network of contacts and especially raising your profile in the wider world.

So, where do you start? There are so many of these sites out there and they expand exponentially: bebo, digg, facebook, faceparty, flikr, friendster, myspace, plaxo, teenspot, twitter, virb, wayn, yourblog... the list goes on (just put those three words SNS into Wikipedia and you'll see).

And migration between sites is fickle: at the very moment people might move from, say, myspace to facebook because the former isn't considered 'cool' anymore, another new site is already being created to supercede facebook! How many 'friends' do you really need in your social circle? (A network of 'contacts', on the other hand, is a different matter.)

However, what is emerging now is some of these sites' willingness to create and financially support 'content', i.e. specific dramas made for the web and their own site. For example:

**Bebo.com:** This site has started producing a series of three-minute dramas – on-going soaps for the Bebo generation – with an interactive element where viewers can decide exactly how the story develops: *Sophia's Diary* and *The Secret World Of Sam King*. Whether there is enough dramatic meat in this form to develop it substantially, or whether it's just an excuse for product placement, remains to be seen.

Bebo's approach is more akin to YouTube (see later). You can click on links to video, music, authors, bebo nation, backstage and groups (yes, they all have their own Groups subsections). But it is another site where a humble poster can now become one of the site's Content Producers.

As a place to start, you might try checking out bebo.com/tyscreenwriting, bebo.com/screenwritingnews and bebo.com/shootingpeople.

**MySpace.com:** At the time of writing, myspace is probably the most visually and aurally sophisticated of all the SNSs, and one of the easiest to navigate. The site has become an accepted window for a filmmaker, musician or writer to get their work out there and seen by a wider audience (and a way for the 'suits' to access new talent). Stars have been created. It's already an institution, whether or not it's hip anymore.

You will find a wealth of homepages here (prefix www.myspace.com/). Whether you're looking for a film festival (Austin? Toronto? Byron Bay? San Diego Asian Film Fest? Or try filmcalls) or browsing advice about your small film (gimmecredit, FutureShortsWorld, shortcutters, damshortfilmfestival, LAshortsfest), seeking out screenwriting competitions (themoviedeal) or just anything script-related, you're bound to find something here.

If the likes of respected filmmakers such as Mike Figgis and (it is said) Martin Scorsese have their own myspace homepages, then you need a profile here too.

**Tip:** the best advice is go to the page for this book www.myspace.com/tyscreenwriting and explore my Friends list, then explore the friends on their lists, and just click away asking to join those sites relevant for you. Soon you will build up a network of places and contacts yourself. And this business is all about networking. So start posting up your latest masterpiece.

You should also explore their Forums section (www.film.myspace.com) and myspacetv.com (channels, primetime, my videos, filmmakers, behind the scenes, and more). There's bound to be something of value for you here.

This is where you will also discover the site's own UGC (user-generated content): *Kate Modern* – an online drama created by a team of posters from the early days of myspace; and *FaintHeart* – the first full-length movie created entirely on the site (myspace.com/faintheartthemovie).

Finally, another advantage of this site is you can see when that page owner last logged in. So, if the date registered is three years ago you can be sure they've either closed down or moved to another site (in which case I suggest you google the name and follow any links).

**Facebook.com:** While this site may not be as audio or visually versatile as, say, MySpace (for the moment), one of its strengths is in its myriad of Groups.

Click on Groups, then in the Search Groups box enter your keyword/s. A mere selection of the facebook communities lurking out there includes:

Teach Yourself Screenwriting [of course!]; Bad Screenwriting Kills Braincells; Best Notes on Film-making and Storytelling in the World; British Screenwriters in LA; Future Screenwriting; Igglepiggle Appreciation Society; Ink Canada; InkTip; Is Film School even Worth It?; Loving Film; Making It in Hollywood; Media UK'ers; MovieScope Magazine; Outlandish Film Ideas; Screenplays; Screenwriters Club; Screenwriting; SCREEN WRITING; Screenwriting Mastery; ScriptXray; Shooting People; Talent Circle Film Network; WILDsound Film and Screenplay Festival; Writers on the Storm. (Have you had enough?)

...or just go straight to: http://groups.to/TeachYourself Screenwriting

**Flixster.com:** A site specifically geared to films. 'Share movie reviews and ratings with your friends' it says. Maybe I'm just getting old-and-crusty but I quickly tired of being mailed their latest list or poll or their never-ending quiz. I felt like I was wasting precious time here. Nonetheless, visit: flixster.com/user/tyscreenwriting.

## Next big thing...?

There are a number of sites vying for the NBT after facebook:

- twitter.com (More like a micro-blog and more for your inner circle of friends?) Try: www.twitter.com/tyscreenwriting
- virb.com (Currently more geared to blogging at the moment, it's bound to expand.) Also try: www.virb.com/tyscreenwriting

– ubik.com (Website geared to mobile/cellphones; it's all about technology convergence.) Nevertheless, try: tyscreenwriting. ubik.net

... Just covering my bases here, but who knows where it will end...

**YouTube.com**: These days, thanks to YouTube.com, we can all be stars in our own video broadcasts (indeed, as I type this, they are planning to launch a live streaming service; you can 'go live' to the world – from your webcam, from your i-phone). For every 'Foam! Lord Rupert has fun with a dishwasher' you will discover a gem like Hy Gardner's extended interview with Montgomery Clift from the 1960s or Kevin McCarthy's home video of Clift and Marlon Brando together.

But as with everything on the Internet, the results you get will depend on the keyword/s you enter in the search box. Try: Screenwriting, Screenwriters and Film School for starters. The possibilities are endless so stayed focused, tear yourself away from those endless clips of *Family Guy*, be clear about what you are seeking, and don't be afraid to occasionally think creatively 'outside the box'.

Some YouTube contributors are consistently informative and worth subscribing to. I would single out ShootingScreenwriter, TheDialogue, writersdocumentary, FirstLightVideoInc and tyscreenwriting – but you will soon create your own preferred list. Also, explore the Channels tab too: a place to begin is uk.youtube.com/BFIfilms and start to explore the British Film Institute's archives.

And, yes, even YouTube has its own Groups section (along with Blogs, Forums, Contests and so on). Go to Community, click on Groups, enter your chosen word into the search box, and a drop-down menu will list the relevant groups, for example: youtube.com/group/shootingpeopleorg.

Finally, let me recommend Reel Geezers on this site: two Hollywood octogenarians discussing various movies. But these two veterans happen to be Marcia Nasatir (producer: *Hamburger Hill, The Big Chill, Ironweed*) and Lorenzo Semple Jr. (creator and screenwriter of the 1960s *Batman* TV series and the 1966 movie, as well as *Three Days Of The Condor, Never Say Never Again* etc.). Pithy, opinionated, erudite, they wear their achievements lightly. Respect! [See also www.reelgeezers.com]

# Podcasts

Another way to waste your time or a source of infotainment? – you decide. You cannot deny the increasing popularity of Podcasts. So, how do you filter out the crap?

You might try www.digitalproductionbuzz.com/Podcast (Creative Planet), Filmmaking Central (filmmaking central.com), Indie Film Nation (indiefilmnation.blogspot.com), S-I-A Films video podcast (google it) and the entertaining Sam & Jim Go to Hollywood (samandjimgotohollywood.libsyn.com). You could also try the shootingpeople.org site, go to People, click on Podcasts, and listen away.

And if you are determined to create your own podcast, an alternative to YouTube can be found at these free services: Studio Odeo or Gcast (as recommended by John Campea of themovieblog.com).

# Script competitions

Competitions abound on the web. You could try googling the keywords and see where it takes you. Moreover, there is so much overlapping and cross-referencing on the net (so think laterally). These below just mention a few of the URLs not already covered in this chapter's earlier listings, such as screenwriting-related websites or SNSs (especially myspace). And if these sites do not run their own contests you will find plenty of links to other competitions and deadlines worldwide.

bluecatscreenplay.com             [See also myspace.com]
filmmakers.com/contests/directory
                             [A teriffic directory of links here]
goasa.com/competition.shtml
           [American Screenwriters Association's excellent site;
         competition run in conjunction with Gotham Writers'
                                        Workshop]
moviebytes.com                [Annual screenplay contest]
myspace.com/moviedeal
scriptapalooza.com
            [Regular comps for TV and features scripts]

scriptsavvy.net

# Networking, openings and opportunities

My first port of call for these things would be www.wordplayer.com. Just visit it and see for yourself.

I would also recommend you first check out www.shootingpeople.org (the international networking organization dedicated to the support and promotion of independent film-making). Currently UK based, with a branch in New York. Click on 'See what we're up to' then 'Shooters films' and explore.

Annual subscription is currently £30. For that (just for starters) you can get their daily e-mailed Network Bulletins: one each for Screenwriters (including a weekly Pitch Posting), UK Film-makers, NY Filmmakers, Animation, Documentary, Casting, Composers – basically, everything from who's looking for what, jobs, contacts, discussions, it's all here: industry events, networking – information. And you can contribute to the bulletins; they're a good way to find work (paid and unpaid). There is much to explore on this site. Some other recommended sites to visit:

bbc.co.uk/newtalent
[The BBC's regular trawl for new unsuspecting talent]
breakingin.net [Great portal to writers' sites]
hollywoodlitsales.com [Spec screenplay directory]
http://industrycentral.net/writers
[Includes Screenwriters Exchange section]
inktip.com [Free newsletter]
mandy.com [Worldwide production jobs directory]
mediaresourcecontacts.com/ukp3.htm
[Production companies in the UK]
screen-lab.co.uk
[Joint Screenwriters' Workshop/Euroscript initiative]
screenplayers.net
[A site created by writers; its Resources section is worth a look]
screenwritingexpo.com
[Annual L.A. event; see Taking it further: Industry organizations section; if you are serious about cracking the US, you need to visit]

scriptpimp.com                    [A handy free newsletter available]
shootingpeople.org                    [See paragraph above]
skillset.org
          [UK's respected support and training body for the creative
                                                        media]
startintv.com                              [Free newsletter]
theknowledgeonline.com
              [Benchmark database of UK production talent]
wftv.org.uk          [Women in Film and Television organization]
wordplayer.com                              [Recommended]

## Reviews, interviews, articles

http://geocities.com/Hollywood/5555
                    [Reviews of films from the 1920s and 30s]
aintitcool.com
          [Harry Knowles' infamous reviews site; still influential?]
critics.com                [Film reviews – needs updating perhaps]
darkhorizons.com                  [Handy info on up-to-date films]
efilmcritic.com          [Australian database of movie reviews]
fwfr.com                      [Four-word film reviews – just that]
metacritic.com      [Meta-site coordinating lots of other reviews]
mrcranky.com          [Mr. Cranky – he hates everything. Fun]
mrqe.com    [Movie review query search engine: comprehensive]
reelgeezers.com
      [Another plug for Marcia Nasatir and Lorenzo Semple Jr.]
rinkworks.com/movies    [At-a-glance condensed film reviews]
rogerebert.suntimes.com          [Ebert's famous review columns]
rottentomatoes.com                [Infamous 'bad films' review site]
wunderland.com/WTS/Ginohn/poetry/HMRlist.html
                              [Reviews reduced to haikus]

## Miscellaneous

anecdotage.com      [Barbed and acid anecdotes about the stars]
awardsdaily.com                          [An interesting forum]
blinkbox.com
              [Movie trailers access site with some very good reviews;
                          initially UK only, rolling out worldwide]

comingsoon.net
[One of many movie news sites, but recommended]
creativity-portal.com/cca/jurgen-wolff
[That man gets everywhere! Explore]
entsweb.co.uk/cinema/studios
[Links to all major and indie film studios]
festival-cannes.fr [The official Cannes website]
filmfestivals.com
[Excellent film fest info – worldwide links, contact, deadlines]
filmpapers.com
[Academic critiques to custom reviews: less dry than it sounds]
hkwriterscircle.com [Hong Kong Writers Circle]
iesb.net [Movie news]
quickstopentertainment.com
[Movie Poop Shoot: entertaining, informative]
timelesstheater.com
[Classic movies from the 1920s onwards to buy on DVD]
upcomingmovies.net [Another movie news site, recommended]
whatireallywantodo.com [Mmm, think about it]

## Software packages

Screenwriting software packages abound: formatting, plotting, characterization – you name it, they've got a programme for it. Heated debates erupt over which is the best: Character Pro, Dramatica Pro, First Draft, PowerStructure, Power Writer, Scriptware, ScriptWright, Scrivener, Sophocles, Storybase, Story View 2, Summarizer, Write Brothers Hollywood Screenwriter, Story Weaver 3.0, WriteWay 1.5, Writers Screen Kit, the Writer's Software Companion etc. One thing they do share is price: they are painfully expensive.

I'm not going to recommend one against the other (until somebody comes along and wants to sponsor me), but by far the most popular package is Final Draft – some now consider it the accepted industry standard (finaldraft.com; also on myspace).

A couple of others that have been specifically recommended to me are: Movie Magic Screenwriter (endorsed by the Writers Guild of America), MovieOutline (movieoutline.com) and, programmed for the Mac OS X system, Montage (marinersoftware.com).

If you are really obsessed about this, you'll find a wealth of handy information at: http://creative-writing-software-review.toptenreviews.com/.

Most of the screenwriters' websites (see earlier sections) eager to sustain a crust will have links to buy these bits of kit, and some software packages will have their own myspace page; and there's always amazon.com. Failing that, you might try:

absolutewrite.com
screenwriting-software.net
http://mockingbird.creighton.edu/NCW/software.htm
MasterFreelancer.com                         [Writers Software Store]
moviesoft.co.uk
screenplay.com
storymind.com
TheScreenwritersStore.com                    [A good UK resource]
writersstore.com

Go back to the end of Chapter 02 for some formatting software (some free downloads).

## Writing collaboration software

I have written elsewhere in this book about the revolutionary developments in online collaborative screenwriting (see Chapter 18). The best thing about these bits of kit are: they are free (to download). So do visit, sign in and try them:

Celtx.com                          ScriptBuddy.com
PlotBot.com                        WordCircle.org
Scripped.com                       Zhura.com

To repeat, the software that excites me is Celtx, precisely because it is stand-alone open-sourced, because you don't have to go online to use it and because of the handy pre-production call-sheet applications it has. Do explore. Or just visit this site and download it (for PC, Mac or Linux) http://www.netribution.co.uk/content/view/1503/182/

## DVDs and CD-ROMs

A few selected titles:

*Brainstorming with the 36 Dramatic Situations*

*Film School in a Box* [nine-hour course from filmschoolinabox.net]

*Hard Scrambled* [two-DVD set: Includes *Film School in a Box*, 20 tutorials including screenwriting]

Michael Hauge and Christopher Vogler discuss *The Hero's 2 Journeys* [Three DVDs available from screenplaymastery.com]

*Hollywood Camera Work* [High-end blocking and staging of scripts, perhaps of more interest for Directors; from hollywoodcamerawork.us]

*Screenwriting Expo Seminar Series* [Various useful series of titles; check them out at writersstore.com]

*Syd Field's Screenwriting Workshop* [Distributed by Final Draft]

*The Dialogue: Learning from the Masters* [Interviews with screenwriters, DVD series]

*Web Film School*: Dov S-S Simens renowned two-day film school transferred to 16 DVDs. [Available from webfilmschool.com]

*Write Ambition: Plan and Prepare to make Better Movies* [A CD-Rom I presented; made in collaboration with The Media School of The Sorbonne in Paris. Dating from 2006, you might still find a few out there. Try the distributors: www.mindscape.co.uk or amazon.co.uk]

## Useful books

John Ralph: *The Internet For Writers* (Teach Yourself Books, Hodder Education)

Christopher Wehner: *Screenwriting On The Internet* (Michael Wiese productions, UK Heinneman) www.mwp.com

For many more titles on this subject try:

www.writersservices.com/wbs/net_index.htm

Every Hollywood studio is obsessed with the net (it is claimed there are over 17 million movies out there in the – mostly illegal – 'dark net' just waiting to be downloaded and file-shared free: how do they compete with that?) and with the delivering of their content to smaller and smaller devices. Fact: you *need* to be connected-up.

**taking it further**

## Further reading

Book-buying these days mostly takes place online. Inevitably you will probably go to amazon.com or its overseas sites, or bol.com, or similar; but for out of print books you will find these websites helpful:

abebooks.com
alibris.com
antiqbook.com
bookfinder.com
glynsbooks.co.uk
UKbookworld.com
usedbooksearch.co.uk

Also try Amazon's Used & New links; you might find the book – or script – there very cheaply.

## General reference

*Guardian Media Guide* – published annually, Guardian Books, guardian.co.uk

*Hollywood Creative Directory* – directories of US writers, producers, directors etc.; approximately $60+ per volume, also on CD-Rom; hcdonline.com

*PACT Directory* – Producers Alliance for Cinema and Television; published annually; lists UK indie production company details; pact.co.uk/pactdirectory

*The Writers' and Artists' Yearbook* by Kate Mosse – published every November in the UK, considered essential; writersandartists.co.uk

*The Writers' Handbook* by Barry Turner – published every November; considered of equal importance in the UK; panmacmillan.com

*Writer's Market* by Robert Brewer – Writer's Digest Books; published annually; equally essential for the US market; writersdigest.com

## Screenwriting books

The number of books on screenwriting has grown exponentially since this modest little tome first hit the bookstores in 1995 (even then I considered the market close to saturation!). But to appreciate just how many titles there are out there, you could try visiting this site: www.Oscars.org/nicholl/bibliography.html or the superb www.goasa.com/bookstore.shtml site or put the following words into your search engine: Weaving Mill Film Workshop Screenwriting Bibliography [it's a group in Cyprus]. Believe me, the numbers of available titles today are daunting.

Ironically, most of us teachers agree that the books we keep returning to (besides this volume!) are the ones that started it all. Namely those by: Syd Field, Michael Hauge, Lew Hunter, Viki King, Linda Seger, Dwight and Joye Swain and Jurgen Wolff. Later there came John Costello, Ken Dancynger and Jeff Rush, Robert McKee, the Raindance Writers Lab, David Trottier, Christopher Vogler and Michael Chase Walker; and, more recently, James Bonnet, David Freeman, Noah Lukeman, Blake Snyder, John Truby and Jennifer Van Sijll.

## Marketing screenplays – and yourself

Max Adams: *The Screenwriter's Survival Guide: or Guerrilla meeting tactics and other acts of war*

Linda Buzzell: *How to Make It in Hollywood*

K. Callan: *The Script is Finished: Now what do I do?*

Elane Feldman: *The Writer's Guide to Self-Promotion and Publicity* (Writer's Digest Books)

Syd Field: *Selling a Screenplay: the Screenwriter's Guide to Hollywood*

Michael Hauge: *Selling your Story in 60 Seconds* [His long-awaited second book]

James Russell: *Screen and Stage Marketing Secrets*

Carl Sautter: *How to Sell your Screenplay*

Cynthia Whitcomb: *The Writer's Guide to Selling Your Screenplay*

Kathie Fong Yoneda: *The Script-Selling Game*

## Background books

Geoff Andrew: *Stranger Than Paradise: Maverick filmmakers in recent American cinema*

Aristotle: *The Poetics* [The first to examine story structures; the fundamentals haven't changed]

Alan Ayckbourn: *The Crafty Art of Playmaking* [Wisdom for all writers]

Peter Biskind: anything by him is worth a look, especially *Down and Dirty Pictures* (about Miramax, Sundance and indie cinema) and *Easy Riders, Raging Bulls* (revolutionary film-makers in the 1970s)

Jon Boorstin: *Making Movies Work* and *The Hollywood Eye: What Makes Movies Work?* [Good on affecting your audience]

Joseph Campbell: *The Hero with a Thousand Faces* [The classic study of myth in storytelling; not the easiest read, but worth it]

Joseph Campbell and Bill Moyers: *The Power of Myth* [Interview transcripts with Campbell; perhaps his most accessible book]

Adam P. Davies and Nic Wistreich: *How to Fund Your Film – the Film Finance Handbook* [Netribution.com creator Wistreich's original is still the best on the subject] available from fundyourfilm.info and netribution.com. You can also download a free chapter about online finance, marketing and distribution from: www.fundyourfilm.info/story.php? NEWS_ID=73

John Gregory Dunne: *Monster: Living off the Big Screen* [The history of *Up Close And Personal* through eight years and 27 rewrites]

Lajos Egri: *The Art of Dramatic Writing* [Another accepted classic; about plays, a bit polemical, but full of ideas]

Joel Engel: *Oscar-winning Screenwriters on Screenwriting*

Robert Evans: *The Kid Stays in the Picture* [Hollywood producer memoirs; so good they made it into a movie]

Julian Friedmann: *How to Make Money Scriptwriting* [Insider tips from an agent]

William Froug: *The Screenwriter looks at the Screenwriter* (2 vols) and *Zen and the Art of Screenwriting* (2 vols) [Insightful interviews with writers]

William Goldman: Anything by Goldman about the Hollywood jungle is essential reading, especially *Adventures in the Screen Trade* and *Which Lie did I Tell?*

Tom Holden: *Teach Yourself Film Making* (Hodder Education)

Karl Inglesias: *The 101 Habits of Highly Successful Screenwriters* [Interviews]

Genevieve Joliffe and Chris Jones: *The Guerilla Film Makers Handbook* [Recommended]

Michael Lent: *Breakfast With Sharks* [Hollywood tales]

Rob Long: *Conversations with my Agent* [A former *Cheers* writer's hilarious life]

Linda Obst: *Hello, He Lied* [Guess what? It's about Hollywood]

Roger von Oeck: *A Whack on the Side of the Head* and *A Kick in the Seat of the Pants* [Both are great for freeing-up creativity and brainstorming]

Alistair Owen: *Story and Character* [Interviews with British Screenwriters]

Robert Rodriguez: *Rebel Without a Crew* [The inspiring ultimate guerilla filmmaker]

David O. Selznick: *Memo* [His classic memos – and history – were extraordinary]

Shooting People: *Get your Short film Funded, Made and Seen* [Available from shootingpeople.org/shortsbook/]

Dov S-S Simens: *From Reel to Deal* [his two-day film school courses are now legendary]

Stuart Voytilla: *Myth and the Movies* [The Hero's Journey paradigm applied to 50 movies]

Jurgen Wolff: *Your Writing Coach* [The inner and outer journeys of the writer]

Also try www.allworth.com and click on Film & TV for a selection of books on the industry.

## Screenwriting magazines

All these titles in the next two sections originate from the USA, unless noted. You can also access them from most of the screenwriters' sites in Chapter 22, or you might try ordering them from amazon.com, writersstore.com or (in the UK) thescreenwritersstore.com.

*Creative Screenwriting:* creativescreenwriting.com also try: cweb.ws/csw/index.cfm (also on myspace) [Very influential bi-monthly]

*Hollywood Scriptwriter:* hollywoodscriptwriter.com [Bi-monthly]

*InkTip Magazine:* InkTip.com/scriptlog_nolink.php [Jerrol LeBaron's initiative; also on Facebook groups]

*Inscriptions:* inscriptionsmagazine.com [Register, then submit your logline for circulation around the industry]

*Mystery Scene Magazine:* mysteryscenemag.com [Murder, crime, suspense]

*Scr(i)pt:* scriptmag.com [Long-running and respected bi-monthly magazine]

*Scenario:* scenario-mag.com [French screenwriting magazine]

*TwelvePoint.com:* twelvepoint.com [Formerly UK's Scriptwriter Magazine – scriptwritermagazine.com is still online – *Twelvepoint* is now an online subscription presence]

*The Writer Magazine:* writermag.com [Popular UK monthly]

*Written By:* wga.org/writtenby/writtenby.aspx [Regular magazine of the Writers Guild of America, West]

*Writers' Forum:* writers-forum.com [UK based monthly]

*Writers' Journal:* writersjournal.com [UK based bi-monthly]

*Writers' News:* writersnews.co.uk [Leading UK magazine, *Writers' News* & *Writing*]

## General media magazines

*Broadcast:* broadcastnow.co.uk [UK weekly TV trade paper]

*Empire Magazine:* empireonline.com [World's leading monthly movie mag]

*Fade In:* FadeInOnline.com; myspace.com/fadeinmagazine [General film mag]

*Filmmaker Magazine:* filmmakermagazine.com (also on myspace) [More indie movie focused, used to be called *ScreenTalk*]

*Film Review:* visimag.com/filmreview [UK's longest running general movie mag]

*Filmwaves:* filmwaves.co.uk [Somewhat serious UK indie film-makers' publication]

Hollywood Reporter: hollywoodreporter.com [Weekly, exactly what it says]

*Internet Video Mag:* internetvideomag.com [Reviews and shoot your own movie links]

*Movie Maker Magazine*: Moviemaker.com (also on myspace) ['The Art & Business of making movies', UK]

*movieScope Magazine*: movieScopeMag.com [UK bi-monthly 80-page hard copy; read the free online edition; sign up for the free newsletter]

*Moving Pictures:* movingpicturesmagazine.com (also on myspace) [US behind the scenes mag]

*Premiere*: premiere.com [The other big player in the general movie monthlies]

*Screen Daily*: screendaily.com [Free daily e-zine from Screen International]

*Screen International*: screeninternational.com [Weekly US magazine, see above]

*Sight & Sound*: bfi.org.uk/sightandsound [UK magazine, detailed movie reviews]

*The Stage*: thestage.co.uk [The acting profession's weekly 'Bible', but much more than that; see also thestage.co.uk/connect/howto/writefilm.php]

*Total Film*: totalfilm.com [UK monthly, good film reviews]

*Variety*: variety.com [Hollywood's premiere movie daily, an institution; very useful free e-mail newsletters to sign up to]

*Widescreen Review*: widescreenreview.com [UK Home Theatre; interesting reviews]

# Industry organizations

[Note: All UK-mentioned organizations are based in London]

American Film Institute: afi.com also oscars.com

American Screenwriters Association: asascreenwriters.com and goasa.com [A superb website: explore the drop-down menus and links; subscribe to their free newsletter]

Arvon Foundation: arvonfoundation.org [Long-established and well-regarded writers' residential courses and workshops in centres across the UK]

BAFTA (British Film and Television Academy): bafta.org

BFI (British Film Institute): bfi.org.uk [Impressive educational site; superb archive and library facilities for reference and research; also links to regional UK development agencies; own YouTube channel]

EuroScript: euroscript.co.uk [Courses, industry and networking events, consultancy, script competition – it grew out of London's Screenwriters' Workshop – and moved it forward?]

Film London: filmLondon.org.uk [Film and media agency; handy if filming in the capital; small grants programme; some events]

Focal: focal.ch/E/ [European Training courses across Europe; click on Services, leads you to Script Academy in Germany]

London Film Academy: londonfilmacademy.com [Film School; also home to ClubPanico@LFA, a networking set-up for graduates]

London International Film School: lifs.org.uk [Includes established screenwriting courses up to MA degree level]

Met Film School: metfimschool.co.uk [Short courses, including screenwriting; the NFTS are course advisory partners]

National Film and Television School: nftsfilm-tv.ac.uk [Long-running institution; the first of its type in the UK and still going strong]

NPA (New Producers' Alliance): npa.org.uk [New filmmaker eager to break in? Here's a good place to start; £85 annual subscription]

PACT (Producers Alliance for Cinema and Television): pact.co.uk [Industry body for – more established? – UK indie production companies]

Player-Playwrights: groups.msn.com/PlayerPlaywrights [Still active, strong on performed readings of new writers' works; good pedigree]

The Raindance Institute: raindance.co.uk [London based; annual Indie Film Festival and awards, Raindance.tv, courses, seminars; check out their Writers Lab]

RTS (Royal Television Society): rts.org.uk [Not as crusty as it sounds; regular industry seminars and good for networking]

ScreenLab: screen-lab.co.uk [First created by Screenwriters' Workshop, continued with Euroscript; script development, assessment/one-to-one consultations; you can also download a free script template]

Screenwriting Expo: screenwritingexpo.com [Annual November L.A. pow-wow of talks, networking, tutors, guests, pitching and so much more; if you are serious about cracking the US, you need to be here]

The Script Factory: scriptfactory.co.uk [Film Council-funded script development initiative; events, training, performed readings, they also offer a Diploma in Script Development – get involved]

The Script Vault: thescriptvault.com [Script Registration and Deposit store; offer script reading and appraisal; linked to Writers Guild of GB]

Skillset:skillset.org [Government skills training initiative (but indie in feel) for all types of creative media. Don't be put off, worth exploring]

The Society of Authors: societyofauthors.org [UK-based authors' body. £90 per annum, they also offer independent contract appraisals]

The Sundance Institute: Sundance.org and Sundancechannel.com [Robert Redford's pioneering and important indie new talent juggernaut, including its Screenwriters Lab and script readings]

T.A.P.S. (Television Arts Performance Showcase): tapsnet.org [Develops scriptwriters: courses, master classes, reading-in-performance; good UK TV industry links]

UK Film Council: ukfilmcouncil.co.uk [The umbrella organization for UK film: explore the links to Short Films, Publications and Apply For Funding sections; branch office in Los Angeles]

UK Media Team: mediadesk.co.uk [Promotes/administers the EU's MEDIA programme for the UK: funds, training, networking]

Women in Film and Television: wftv.org.uk and wifti.org [For the international spread of this organization; serious networking here]

Writernet: writewords.org.uk [Formerly the New Playwrights Trust, their website has much broader links and information for all forms of writing; try the tab Writing Jobs]

Writer's Digest Books: writersdigest.com [Huge selection of books and resources of interest to the writer; explore the tabs and surf away]

Writers Guild of America (east): wgaeast.org [New York; a wealth of links to explore for the screenwriter]

Writers Guild of America (west): wga.org [Los Angeles: more a members/ industry-focused page design, but links still worth exploring]

Writers' Guild of Great Britain: writersguild.org.uk [UK's 'union'; not just for general writers, good facilities for screenwriters. Recommended]

## Online screenwriting courses

(See also the screenwriting-specific websites mentioned in Chapter 22.)

absolutewrite.com

http://www.filmprograms.ucla.edu/online.htm [California's renown UCLA film school]

filmschoolonline.com

globalfilmschool.com [UK–US-Australian film schools joint venture; but seems currently dormant]

learner.org/interactive/cinema/screenwriting.html

singlelane.com/escript

wizardacademy.com [US screenwriting academy]

writingclasses.com [Gotham Writers' Workshop; click on 'online classes']

xerif.com [Virtual Script Network – recommended and successful courses, linked to London University's Birkbeck College]

Also put the words University Miami Online Screenwriting Course into your search engine and explore (the URL is far too long to print here).

## Coverage: script reading and assessment services

There are many out there offering these services (including me!) – it's now a hugely expanding market. Each, for a fee (check the rates first), will give you a detailed written assessment or a one-to-one personal seminar. Look for users' endorsements and praise.

You will also find many writers groups and most industry organizations (above) offering this service, including: EuroScript, Writernet, the Raindance Institute and various institutions with myspace pages. Also try:

myspace.com/tyscreenwriting [Inevitably!]

absolutewrite.com

alphamedia.tv/scripts

coverscript.com

daramarks.com

deepfeedback.com

goasa.com/critiqueservice.shtml [American Screenwriters Association]

hollywoodlitsales.com [$75 introductory offer]

hollywoodscript.com

screen-lab.co.uk [Euroscript]

screenplayservices.com
scriptapalooza.com
scriptconsultancy.com [Free script advice, it says]
scriptdoctor911.com
scriptpimp.com
scriptservices.com
scriptshark.com
scriptshop.co.uk
scriptXray.com
studionotes.com
theoxfordeditors.co.uk
thescriptvault.com
thesource.com.au [Australian site]
ukscriptdoctor.com
writernet.co.uk
writersworkshop.co.uk [Run by writers, for writers]

Finally, bearing in mind the number of scripts I see these days that are badly spelt and with appalling grammar, I reckon this is a much-needed new service: script proofreading from www.scriptsavvy.com.

## Agent-related sites

agentsassoc.co.uk [London based, might at least send you a list of agents]

goasa.com [American Screenwriters Association, excellent site; click on Writer Resources tab and then on Agents; then click on their Bookstore tab for a Guide to Literary Agents]

screenplaywritersagency.com [A growing company]

scriptreferrals.com [Agent Maggie Field's helpful site]

wgaeast.org [Writers Guild of America, click on Resources tab, then Agents and Agencies]

wlwritersagency.com [Writers Literary Agency]

wlscreenplayagency.com [ditto]

writersservices.com/agent/index.htm [link to UK agents list]

# Answers

## Chapter 01:

You only need steps 1 and 10 – the rest can be deduced by the audience.

## Chapter 04:

(Taglines)

1 *The Usual Suspects*
2 *The Truman Show*
3 *Road To Perdition*
4 *The Shawshank Redemption*
5 *Gangs Of New York*
6 *The Talented Mr. Ripley*

(Theme)

1 *Field Of Dreams*: It is important for us to have dreams – even if those dreams are not ultimately fulfilled, it is important for us to have them.
2 *Spider-Man*: 'With great power comes great responsibility'. The movie is essentially a coming-of-age story, of learning to accept the responsibility for the decisions/choices we make – even if they prove to be the wrong ones (especially so); and only after that do we begin to mature. It's also about identity ('Who am I?'/'Who is that?'), atypical for the genre.
3 *Erin Brockovich*: It's to do with self-esteem and self-worth; of not being dismissed or laughed at, but being recognized for one's own abilities and talents; and that self-respect (and self love) comes from selflessness.
4 *The Legend Of Bagger Vance*: We can only achieve our true potential (both public and private success) in life once we are at peace with ourself (have confronted, come to terms with and conquered our inner demons/fears). (Note the similarities of theme with *Good Will Hunting*).
5 *A.I. (Artificial Intelligence)*: Our humanity – and being human – is defined by our capacity to love and be loved.

# Chapter 07:

(Key-lines)

1 *Spider-Man*: 'Don't ever be afraid of who you are' (spoken by Dr. Osborn to his son Harry in the back of the car).

2 *Erin Brockovich*: 'I just wanna be a good Mom, a nice person, a decent citizen' (this also actually states Erin's goal – even though she doesn't realize this at the time it is said).

3 *Chinatown*: 'You gotta be rich to kill somebody, anybody, and get away with it'.

(Inciting Incident)

1 *My Big Fat Greek Wedding*: When Ian enters the restaurant for the first time and Toula, having just said 'It's useless to dream 'cos nothing ever happens', sees him. (Again, note the similarity of Theme with *Field of Dreams*.)

2 *The Truman Show*: Truman sees his 'dead' father on the street as a tramp.

3 *Erin Brockovich*: Ed Masry asks Erin to open a new case file on 'a real estate thing, pro bono'.

4 *Spider-Man*: This is an interesting one. Although the bite from the genetically-modified spider occurs quite early on (nine minutes), Peter's actual transformation – the consequences of the bite – happens at 16–18 minutes. You decide – both are equally valid (and it is a fast-paced movie).

5 *Field Of Dreams*: When Ray, having built the baseball diamond and the story seemingly over, hears the voice 'Go the distance'.

6 *Cruel Intentions*: The wager is struck between Sebastian and Kathryn over Annette Hargrove. (This also sets up Sebastian's long-term goal, as he sees it at the time.)

(TP1/First Turning Point)

1 *My Big Fat Greek Wedding*: Toula's father decides that she should work at the travel agency; she starts immediately.

2 *The Truman Show*: The beach scene when Sylvia/Lauren tries to tell him 'Everybody's pretending ... it's all a fake ... Get out of here' and she is taken away.

3 *Erin Brockovich*: The first mention of chromium during the initial interview with Donna Jensen – 'That's what kicked this whole thing off'.

4 *Spider-Man*: The rooftop 'Go, web' scene when Peter swings on the web for the first time.

5 *Field Of Dreams*: Following his first encounter with 'Shoeless' Joe Jackson ('I built this for you'), Ray declares 'We're keeping the field'.

6 *Cruel Intentions*: When Sebastian and Annette swim together and he starts to regard her as perhaps more than just another conquest.

(Half-way point/Point of No Return)

1 *My Big Fat Greek Wedding*: When Ian asks Toula 'Will you marry me?'

2 *The Truman Show*: Truman drives across the bridge (conquering his phobia of water) and 'escapes' Sea Haven Island for the first time.

3 *Erin Brockovich*: When Ed finally agrees to take on the case (if Erin will provide the supporting evidence).

4 *Spider-Man*: Peter (in his new Spider-Man costume for the first time) decides, as a consequence of Uncle Ben's death (and his own part in it), to dedicate himself and his powers to good for others, and not for any selfish motives; and, over the film-footage crime-fighting montage comes the voice-over 'With great power comes great responsibility'.

5 *Field Of Dreams*: At the baseball game with Terence Mann, when Ray sees the sign about Archibald 'Doc' Graham and again hears the voice saying 'Go the distance'.

6 *Cruel Intentions*: Sebastian sleeps with Cecile (it has major dire consequences for his future relationship with Annette).

(TP2/Moment of Truth)

1 *My Big Fat Greek Wedding*: The poignant scene in which Toula asks 'Is my marriage killing Dad?' and her mother responds 'I gave you life so that you could live it'.

2 *The Truman Show*: When the production team discover that Truman has escaped from his house.

3 *Erin Brockovich*: The meeting with new partner Kurt Potter (and his assistant Theresa) when Erin realizes that the case has effectively been taken out of her hands, it is no longer her responsibility.

4 *Spider-Man*: During Aunt May's Thanksgiving dinner, Dr. Osborn sees the gash on Peter's arm and realizes he is Spider-Man. (Shortly after, in the hospital scene, Peter realizes this: 'He knows who I am'.)

5 *Field Of Dreams*: Ray's expositionary speech while driving the van home, having just picked up the young Archie Graham.

6 *Cruel Intentions*: When Sebastian splits up with Annette ('You don't know me ... You mean nothing to me'.)

Act I **113–125**
Act II **125–135**
Act III **135–140**
actor direction **28**
adapted screenplays **4, 256–57**
Agents **250–254**
audience identification (with character)
     **90–93**

backstory **80–81, 119, 185**

camera angles **25**
cast design **83–88**
cast design (hero's journey) **85–88**
character arc **95–97**
character biography checklist **77–80**
character – creating 3D characters **74–76**
character decisions **75**
character flaws **88–90**
character functions **76**
character growth *see* character arc
character motivation **98–101, 104, 108,
     183–186**
climaxes **124, 133, 135–140**
collaboration (collaborative process) **5,
     262–63**
conflict **101–103, 105–106**
copyright **244–249**
cost **68–69**
counter-character chart **88–89**
Coverage **14–16**
covering letter **234, 236, 240**

development (in development) **272–73**
dialogue **28, 173–176**

emotion *see* passion
endings **140–141**
entry point **117, 177**
exploratory (first) draft **33, 210–211**

feedback **232**
film v television (similarities/differences)
     **8–9**
first ten pages **115–116**

flashbacks **172**
focus point 1 **127**
focus point 2 **131–132**
format (film script – sample) **20**
format (general) **17–31**
format (television script – sample) **21**
four- and five-act structure *see* structure

genre **48–53**
goals (character) *see* character motivation
goals (screenwriter's) **35**

half-way point (point of no
     return/midpoint) **128–131**
hero/ine (protagonist), **76–77, 83**
hero's journey (structure) **145–150**
hook **116–117**

ideas
     developing **42–70**
     filtering and testing **40–1**
     generating **38–40**
image systems **200–201**
inciting incident **121–123**
industry
     breaking in **265–266**
     your place in it **266–267**
information (revealing and concealing)
     **196–198**
interleafing (interleaving) **155**
Internet
     communities/forums/bulletin boards
          **300–302**
     e-zines/newsletters **300–302**
     filmmakers' databases **292–94**
     homepages **294–296**
     miscellaneous **308–309**
     networking/openings/opportunities **307**
     reference databases **289**
     reviews/interviews/articles **308**
     screenplays (free/to buy) **296–298**
     screenwriters' databases **290–292**
     script competitions **306**
     search engines **288**
     software packages **309–310**

journey movies **141–142**

keyline **117–118**

marketing **275–76**
medium **69–70**
midpoint *see* half-way point
minor characters **81–83**
mirror (reflection/support) character **84**
momentum *see also* tension **186–190**
montages **26**
multi-plotting **152–156**

names **73**
networking **265, 278**

obstacles **95, 103–104**
one-liner **55–56**
opposition (antagonist/nemesis) character **83**
original screenplays **4**
overstructure **110**

pacing **192–195**
passion (burning passion factor) **35–6, 106–7, 228–29**
pitch and pitching **270–272**
plants and pay-offs **198–99**
plot (definition) **43**
plot (variations) **155–156**
Points of No Return *see* half-way point
Portmanteau films **157**
P.O.V. (point of view) **54, 155, 177**
presentation **18, 233**
pre-writing **33**
producers **268–270, 281**
proposal *see* synopsis
protagonist *see* hero/ine

raising the stakes **191–192**
Readers **14–16, 281–283**
rejection **277–278**
reputation **276–277**
research **69**
resolution (denouement) **139**
rewriting **33, 212–230**
romance character **84**
rule of three **201**

scene
    'the business' **23–6**
    construction **164–172**
    direction **23–5**
    headings **22–3**
    entrances and exits **27**
screenplays (free and to buy) **296–298**
Screenwriters' Workshop **2, 318**

script format *see* format
script readers *see* Readers
secondary characters **81**
self-discipline **12**
sequences **159–163**
series **259–260**
setting **61–63**
short films **257–259**
sitcoms **261–262**
soaps **259–260**
sound **30–1**
stakes (see raising the stakes)
starting out **10**
step outline **204–206**
story concept **43**
story
    definition **43**
    choosing main story **44**
    only eight basic stories **45–6**
structure
    two-Act **156–157**
    three-Act (linear) **109–143**
    four- and five-Act **157**
    hero's journey **145–150**
    variations **155–156**
subplots **64–68**
subtext **179–181, 191–192**
suspense **187–190**
synopsis (as writer's tool) **203**
synopsis (as selling document/proposal) **240–42**

taglines **56–58, 201, 240**
targeting the market **267–268**
teasers/teaser scene **118, 156**
tension **186–188**
theme **58–60**
thinking creatively **37**
three (rule of) **201**
time-lock **104, 115, 122–123**
title **60–61, 232–233**
title page **233–235**
transformational arc (see character arc)
transitions **193–194**
treatment (as writer's tool) **206–208**
treatment (as selling document) **243**
turning point 1 (TP1) **124–125**
turning point 2 (TP2) **133–135**
turning points (role of) **123–124**

understructure **110, 217**
upping the ante **195–196**

voice-overs **24, 176–179**

writing backwards **45**
writing courses and seminars **278–279**